THE PRICE OF LIFE

The Future of American Health Care

THE PRICE OF LIFE

The Future of American Health Care

ROBERT H. BLANK

Columbia University Press • NEW YORK

Columbia University Press
Publishers Since 1893
New York   Chichester, West Sussex

Library of Congress Cataloging-in-Publication Data
Blank, Robert H.
    The price of life : the future of American health care / Robert H.
Blank.
        p.   cm.
    Includes bibliographical references and index.
    ISBN 0–231–10294–1 cl   0–231–10295–x pa
    1. Medical policy—United States.   2. Health services
accessibility—United States.   I. Title.
RA395.A3B5443   1997
362.1'0973—dc20   96–34653
                                                   CIP

⊗

Casebound editions of Columbia University Press books are printed on
permanent and durable acid-free paper.

Printed in the United States of America
c   10 9 8 7 6 5 4 3 2 1
p   10 9 8 7 6 5 4 3 2 1

CONTENTS

PREFACE

This is not another book on how to restructure the American health care system nor does it purport to detail a new means to finance health care. Rather, it is an examination of the public and its perceptions of health care, of life, and the value we place upon it. It argues that the core problems of American health care are not solely economic or even political but instead emerge from a set of uniquely American illusions about health, health care, and the role of government. Before we can hope to build a sustainable and workable system and ensure a healthy population at reasonable cost these illusions must be shattered.

This book is designed to explain what went wrong. Why does the United States stand virtually alone among Western democracies with uncontrolled costs, lack of universal access, and health outcomes that fail to reflect the massive investment in high technology medical care. A spoiled American public, a distorted incentive structure, and continuing social and economic inequities make real reform unlikely.

This book argues for a shift from medical care to health promotion, from individualized medicine to collective health, and from individual rights to individual responsibility. It concludes that we must make major value shifts and moderate considerably our expectations of what medical technology can actually contribute to health. Ultimately this requires setting limits, constraining the development and diffusion of medical innovations, rationing scarce medical resources, and reevaluating the price of life. We must overcome our reluctance to say enough is enough and put the entire system back into balance if we are to work toward the primary goal of maximizing the health of the population.

INTRODUCTION

By almost every measure, the U.S. health care system is failing. Despite almost two decades of cost containment initiatives, health care costs are out of control. Currently, we spend over 15 percent of our gross national product on health care, almost double that of most other industrialized nations. Moreover, in spite of these massive expenditures on health care at least 35 million citizens have been left outside the insurance system and have no assurances of access to health care resources. Again, this is at odds with other Western countries which have universal coverage under some form of national health system. Although there is no doubt that Americans have the most extensive range of sophisticated medical technology in the world, we fall well short of most other nations in health promotion, preventive medicine, and access to primary care. Health outcomes as measured by morbidity and mortality rates fail to reflect the vast expenditure differential with other nations. Something, therefore, is dreadfully wrong.

President Clinton made health care reform the highest priority of his administration and initiated an overdue national debate triggering a broad array of alternative reform plans. Unfortunately the resulting debate over health care reform has largely missed addressing the core problems. Both the Clinton plan and the congressional and professional responses focused on the means rather than the ends of modern medicine and health care. The result is that Americans are not asking themselves the hardest questions as to what type of society they wish to be part of, what the goals of health care ought to be, and how much they are willing to sacrifice in order to achieve those goals.

Although public opinion polls consistently show that about 90 percent of the public feels we have a health care crisis, the recent responses of interest groups, policy makers, and the public to the President's reform proposals demonstrate that there is little resolve to make the hard decisions and pay the cost of our actions. Every group wants reform but only if someone else ends up paying for it. At the base of this public ambivalence is a set of illusions that continue to frame our conceptions of health, health care, and medicine. This book is an effort to explicate these underlying misconceptions and illustrate how they function to preclude genuine health care reform. Its primary objectives are to expose these myths and present a less obstructed view of what actions are necessary to redress the continuing deterioration of the American health care system.

THE ILLUSIONS

One illusion is that medical care is synonymous with health care and that, as a result, medicine alone can lead to better health. Health care in reality is a much broader concept which includes all aspects of life but which at some level centers on health promotion and disease prevention. Due to a combination of the abdication of social responsibilities and the strong interests of the medical community, we have come to believe that the medical care system can resolve, and is the correct mechanism for doing so, a whole range of social problems. Our "health" care system has been defined largely as a "disease" care system. A significant proportion of medical costs are directed toward dealing with the products of poverty, crime, drug and alcohol abuse. There is, however, substantial evidence that health outcomes of populations are more highly correlated with the economic and social environment than on how much is spent on medical care.

Moreover, there is evidence that core social problems cannot be resolved by medicine. The asumption that there is a medical solution to every misfortune, that there is some technological fix to longstanding social problems, therefore, is misleading at best and dangerous when it shapes policy. Instead of spending more on medicine, we must seriously consider shifting policy emphasis and resources from medical care to programs designed to reduce illiteracy, poverty, unemployment, crime and other social ills that are linked to health and to guarantee a safe and secure environment for all citizens. In the end, these measures are more likely to improve the health of the population than expanded use of ever more sophisticated medical technologies.

A second and related illusion is that higher levels of spending for medicine and medical technology will automatically result in better health care and health outcomes. Again, there is strong evidence that the very large increases in spending over the last two decades have not led to corresponding improvements in mortality rates. Furthermore, the United States does not fare well on a wide array of health status indicators when compared to other Western nations, all of which spend considerably less per capita on medical care. Although the health systems of these nations vary, by and large they place considerably more emphasis than we do on health promotion, health education, and the provision of broader welfare-oriented services. Although it is true that the United States has the best *medical* system money can buy, the view that this naturally leads to the best *health* care system is illusory. Preventive programs, designed to reduce the need for medical care, although not necessarily always cost-effective, ultimately are more likely to achieve the goal of a healthy population.

Another set of illusions is that (1) we do not ration medical care, and that (2) we should not entertain doing so. In the United States, " 'Ration' is a six-letter four-letter word. Those who use the term typically do so to condemn, to shock, or to scandalize" (Baker 1995:57). We could not be more mistaken on either count. We have finite resources and potentially infinite demands as technologies exponentially extend our capacities to intervene. Unlike other industrialized nations that depend on supply-side, nonprice rationing imposed by government intervention, we depend on a haphazard and patently unfair mix of demand-side, price rationing where rationing centers on ability to pay or to obtain insurance coverage. We also ration expensive medical care through physician discretion, litigation, public relations campaigns, corporate benefits managers and an array of other mechanisms that put persons into categories that compete for the resources. Although we do not ration in the sense that national health systems do (by limiting supply or by waiting lists), it can be argued that our rationing is more insidious. The question then is not whether we should ration medical care but how we can best assure a fair and equitable system of rationing. Although in an ideal world with unlimited resources rationing would be unnecessary, because of aging populations, the proliferation of medical technologies, and heightened public expectations, rationing is essential in all health systems and can no longer be denied in the United States.

One of the central tenets of a liberal society is that there is no one conception of the good life; in other words, individuals have a right to live their lives as they desire as long as they do not harm others. This value when taken to its extreme leads to the illusion that society cannot legitimately tell people how they ought to live. If people want to engage in behavior that might be dangerous to their health that is their business according to this view. One extension of this position is that society should not deny health care resources to persons who contribute to or even cause their own ill health and that any such policy represents victim blaming. Again, however, substantial evidence demonstrates that individual behavior is highly correlated with health status and with health care costs. Diseases of this era increasingly are those which are the result of individual lifestyle choices. Persons who engage in high-risk behaviors such as smoking, drug and alcohol abuse, poor diet, lack of exercise, violence, sexual promiscuity, and so forth, contribute inequitably to escalating health care costs, and along with the very elderly constitute the high users of medical care. More importantly, any efforts to prevent disease, improve population health, and constrain health costs require intervention in individual lifestyles and a renewed emphasis on individual responsibility for health. To argue otherwise in light of current disease patterns and medical evidence is to ignore reality.

Another illusion is that we can effect needed changes in health care without feeling any pain. This illusion of a painless solution is reflected in the notion that we can resolve the health care crisis through restructuring medical care, managing competition, eliminating waste and fraud, or shifting costs. Much of the public debate over the Clinton plan degenerated into questions of how many Americans would pay more and how many less and whether benefits of those currently covered would increase or decrease, not on whether it in fact would improve health care and health status of Americans. This lack of a collective social conscience is not surprising given our individualistic culture, but the notion that we can improve the overall system without personal sacrifice (either fewer benefits or increased costs) is illusory. We will never really reform health care if we cannot agree that the overall goals are more critical than the marginal impact on particular individuals or groups. Moreover, both the Administration and especially Congress have catered to this illusion that the problem can be fixed with relatively painless adjustments and without explicit rationing.

Finally, there is a uniquely American illusion that we can control health care costs without setting global prospective budgets and adopting national fee structures. It is no coincidence that those countries that have been most successful in constraining costs are those with tight budgetary controls over medical costs, whether they are primarily private- or public-funded systems. Japan, for instance, which has a largely private health care system like the United States, has been very successful in providing universal access and keeping per capita costs at less than half of that of the United States. But it has done so only by instituting a national fee structure with central billing and payment and no allowable excess billing, and fostering a philosophy of individual responsibility. In contrast, proposals for reform in the United States continue to be at best half-way measures that fail to institute meaningful debate over health goals or debunk the illusions of American health care.

I argue here that these illusions have been powerful forces in shaping a failing U.S. health care system. Until we face these myths head on and thoroughly reevaluate our policy priorities, no simple restructuring of the system can succeed in resolving the intensifying crisis. We must clarify our goals and set new health care priorities that fit reality rather than the illusions. This requires addressing fundamental questions including: What do we think we have? What do we really have? and, Assuming that our goal is to maximize the health of the American population, in what direction ought we to be moving? Unless we have the resolve to surmount these comforting illusions and address the core problems they obscure, attempts to reform the system through restructuring, cost-shifting, or other means are bound to be short-term and deceptive solutions at best and will serve only to postpone the difficult decisions to the next generation.

HEALTH POLICY AND GOVERNMENTAL ACTION

Although there are many specific goals to which health policy can relate, generally there are three principle purposes of government within which health policy must be defined. Much of the controversy in politics and public policy centers on how vigorously a government ought to perform each of these functions and which one should take precedence when they conflict. Together, then, they define the breadth of acceptable public action.

The first purpose of government is to maintain order. Although non-governmental agents might have policies designed to maintain order in their respective spheres, only the government can make rules that are binding on the whole of society. In Western nations the function of maintaining order has largely been framed as protecting the security, property, and lives of its citizens. This function is most clear in any public health measures designed to contribute to social order such as laws requiring immunization, use of seat belts, and quarantining. One controversy in all societies is the extent to which the government can regulate the private sector and constrain individual freedoms in order to maintain order. With rare exceptions these functions are performed through regulatory-type policies.

A second purpose of all governments is the provision of public goods, which are normally defined as those goods and services that will benefit all individuals but which are unlikely to be produced by voluntary acts of individuals in part because they lack the resources. In other words, societal-wide effort is needed to effectuate these collective goods for the population. Public goods are defined by each society differently depending upon how broadly government responsibility is interpreted. The provision of public goods represents distributive-type policy and is generally accomplished through the collection of general revenues or fees which are then distributed widely in society. Clean water and air, sanitation systems, education, parks and public health are usually included under this purpose. Moreover, in those countries with national health services, health care of citizens has been incorporated as a public good, i.e., guaranteed by government entitlement. The United States stands out as an exception to inclusion of health care as a public good; except for the elderly and the poor it is left to the private sector. The resulting inequality would not be tolerated in a society that accepted health care as a public good. In all societies, however, there is constant disagreement as to how broadly to define the welfare state and the collective goods that go with it.

The third purpose of government is to promote equality: political equality, equality of opportunity, and equality of outcome. Although all Western democracies have achieved relatively high degrees of political equality, actual political influence remains far from equal. Similarly, while equality of opportunity has been on the political agenda of Western nations for several decades and some of the most overt forms of discrimination have been outlawed, the degree to which this is a matter of government policy is still an unsettled question in many countries. By far the most controversial form of equality is equality of outcome. To be successful, this requires considerably more governmental intervention in the lives of its citizens. Because individuals have widely varied needs for health care, the goal of equality requires a heavy redistribution of resources from the largely healthy population to the high users of health care, often the elderly and the poor. The variation of needs for health care across racial, ethnic, and cultural cleavages also raises difficult questions for pursuing the purpose of equality.

As noted above, many of the most challenging dilemmas in democracies emerge as governments struggle with finding the proper mixture of these often conflicting purposes. In addition, conflict over the role of government often pits various notions of individual rights against those of societal good. The negative right to be left alone and to use one's resources as one sees fit is violated by all types of government activity but especially redistributive social policies which to some degree deny full autonomy in use of resources. Positive rights impose obligations on others in society to provide those goods and services necessary for individuals to exercise those rights, and imply freedom from deprivation - an entitlement to at least a decent level of human existence. One central question for health policy is whether all citizens have an entitlement to health care and, if so, what it should entail. Conversely, what limits can be set on entitlements to health care?

Societal or collective good goals always require limits on negative rights and usually necessitate some constraints on the scope of positive rights. While social good theories do not necessarily ignore rights, when the rights of individuals conflict with the collective good of society or the community, the benefit of doubt goes to the collective good. Societies that emphasize the community have less difficulty justifying limitations on individual claims for societal resources or even for individual freedom from interference in organizing one's life. Such societies, therefore, have an easier time setting societal-wide priorities because at some level they assume there is a high-order social good to be pursued.

SOCIETAL GOALS AND HEALTH CARE

The crisis in health care in the United States cannot be separated from a broader crisis in American society that has its roots in a deep-seated confusion as to what type of society we want. Although both freedom and equality are both highly valued, the role of government in promoting equality and in expanding positive rights remains a contentious issue. Furthermore, our heavy emphasis on individualism and our ambivalence concerning societal authority diminishes the possibility of developing consensual social goals and priorities to guide governmental action.

Likewise, public goods have been more narrowly defined in the United States than in other Western nations. For instance, while health care is considered a collective activity in European nations despite variations in health systems, in the United States individualism and the belief in the private sector negates a similar view. As a result the trade-off between the public good and private benefit is generally resolved in favor of the latter. Although the preoccupation with individual rights and liberties has many strengths, in health care this value bias has favored maximization of the care of identifiable individuals over the maximization of health for the community as a whole. Although it is not likely given the strength of this bias that the United States will ever place societal good over the perceived good of individuals, if we are to resolve the health care crisis it is essential that we move toward a balance between these competing goals. The question is one of resolve:

> To what extent are we willing to suffer the consequences of maximizing individual use of health care resources and the threat this poses for society as a whole—from rising costs to limits in coverage—and, ultimately, to all individuals? *(HCTI 1994:8).*

The major problem with U.S. health care is that we have never clearly defined our goals. Without clarity of purpose reforms are pointless because it is impossible to measure success or failure (Churchill 1994:12). As noted by Callahan if we are not able to relate health to broader social goals then health becomes an end in itself:

> Lacking a sense of the proper ends of society, a sense of overall societal purpose and rationale, the pursuit of health becomes its own goal, one that focus exclusively on individual health, one that feeds on itself, and one that knows no direction and no possible limits.   *(Callahan 1990:113)*

In part this failure to clarify goals is a result of the ambiguity over the relationship of the individual and the collectivity and in part it reflects the lack of a national health policy. What we have instead is a "creature of incremental growth" (Churchill 1994:2) that has evolved without any debate over what its purpose or ends should be. Barer et al.'s description of health systems is most appropriate to the unplanned and impulsive U.S. system: "Like a neoplasm, they are quite content to feed on their hosts, oblivious to the fact that the more they gorge themselves, the less able the 'organisms' are to support them" (1994:89).

Other nations have understood this and have done considerably better jobs in shaping and controlling the health care neoplasms. What is necessary in the United States is even greater commitment to this end because the individualistic value system works so heavily against societal-wide goals and obfuscates any attempts to implement them.

Because of the lack of a clear societal goal for health care and the failure to address the core question of what we expect from medical care we have suffered from what might be described as a "theme of the decade" approach. In the 1950s "quality"—as largely defined by medical progress—was the watchword. In the 1960s the theme of quality was eclipsed by the theme of "access," particularly for the elderly and the poor—access to the full range of medical science. The 1970s theme represented a transition from expansion of technological medicine and access toward cost containment, which became the centerpiece in the 1980s. In the 1990s this theme of cost containment has been merged again with access, this time packaged as universal access within the context of managed competition.

Throughout these decades other themes have included patient choice, protection of the medical profession, meeting health care needs, and protection of the medical market place. Lacking an over-all guiding set of priorities and a clearly articulated goal, it is not surprising that U.S. health policy over the last four decades has appeared to be treading water.

I argue here that the primary goal of the health care system should be to maximize the collective health of society, not individual medical benefit. We need to foster a collective responsibility for the common good. Churchill terms this goal solidarity "grounded in understanding the value of sharing common resources, resources that are universally needed, acknowledged to be scarce, and supported by public revenues and energies" (1994:30). In other words, we need to expand and clarify the goal of public good as applied to health. Unlike the United States this sense of community is a central feature of the health services of most other Western democracies, thus to some extent undercutting the argument that it is undemocratic.

This shift to the goal of societal health requires creation of policies that produce healthier living conditions and protect the health of the population. Moreover, health must be measured in the broadest sense including physical, mental, and social well-being. To this end it is argued, the medical system is but one element, and not necessarily the most important one. While the dominant medical model promises much, evidence suggests that in terms of collective health its actual contribution pales in comparison to social and economic determinants of health. The shift to a collective health goal will, therefore, require a thorough reassessment of our investment in medical care as compared to other components of the common good.

The shift toward collective good will also require a balancing of individual rights to health with an individual responsibility for health. Individual-oriented medicine that fails to set boundaries on the amount of resources devoted to individual patients ultimately will fail to serve both the collective good and the good of the individual members: "When individual choice results in an imbalance of social welfare, as it does when individuals elect expensive treatments that deny basic minimum benefits to others, government may step in and readjust the balance to enhance the public good" (Patrick and Erickson 1993:362).

Although a decent society will not abandon those members in need and will provide basic levels of health care, the primary goal of collective health should not be sacrificed. The price of individual life at times, therefore, may be too high a price for the life and health of society at large.

A Summary Note

The tone and thrust of this book will often come across as being antitechnology. Rather than being antitechnology, I am arguing for a balanced health care model that will however require a significant reduction in our dependence on technological medicine. Although I do not fully agree with Illich (1976) and other vitriolic critics of the medical profession, I wholeheartedly agree with Callahan (1990), Mechanic (1994), and many others that the individual-oriented technological medical model must be drastically modified if we are to regain control of the health care system and ensure the collective health of society.

This book reiterates the centrality of nonmedical determinants of health and the need to shift resources from individual medical care toward a reduction of social and economic inequities and the health problems that accompany them. We do no service to the medical profession in the long run by assigning to it unrealistic tasks. Although it has become easy under our current economic incentive structure to medicalize all of society's problems, this strategy is bound to fail us in the end.

THE PRICE OF LIFE

The Future of American Health Care

Chapter 1

Realities

The Growing Health Care Crises

Although all countries are experiencing problems with health care, none approaches the scope of problems apparent in the U.S. The U.S. is experiencing severe problems in access, cost and to a lesser extent health outcomes. Although the problems are many and the solutions elusive, two major issues have dominated recent debate: the costs of U.S. health care and the failure to provide universal access. While the latter issue has received greatest attention recently in large part due to its predominance in the Health Security Act debates, the spending issue represents the core problem because other goals will be unachievable without control of the escalating costs of health care. Moreover the costs of health care cannot be stabilized without imposing constraints on very powerful economic interests.

A less obvious but equally important policy issue is that the distribution of health care is skewed heavily toward a small proportion of the population. This is a critical problem for several reasons. First, any attempts to constrain health care costs through reallocation or rationing will impact most directly the high users of health care. Second, this maldistribution raises ethical questions of fairness and political questions concerning the scope of redistribution. And third, demographic trends clearly demonstrate that the elderly component of society will increase significantly in the coming decades. Because the heaviest users of health care are the elderly, this trend will exacerbate political conflict over increasingly scarce health care resources and heighten pressures for escalation of health care spending. This chapter examines these problems that are central to understanding the U.S. health care crisis.

UNBRIDLED HEALTH CARE SPENDING

The United States continues to lead the western world in spending for health care by a wide margin. The cost of health care in 1995 is estimated to be $1.1 trillion or approximately 15 percent of the Gross Domestic Product (GDP). This represents a cost of about $4050 for each man, woman and child. Without a radical change these figures will be $1.7 trillion or 18 percent of the GDP in 2000 and $16 trillion or 32 percent of the GDP in 2030. Reinhardt (1990:25) has calculated that if health care costs continue to outstrip GDP growth at the same rate they have since 1980, by 2065 all of America's GDP would be devoted to health care. Obviously, something must change, and the change required must be radical and rapid.

Although some observers argue that America should be able to spend more of its GDP on health care than other less affluent countries, this ignores the impact such spending has on other societal objectives. For instance while we spent $3150 per person on health care in 1992 we spent only $1480 per person on education - public and private, kindergarten through graduate school (Fuchs 1993:157). Similarly, it is estimated that in 1995 Americans will spend more on health care than on food and housing combined (Center for Health Economics Research 1993:92). At the current rate of growth, a family of four could be spending $30,000 a year on medical care by the late 1990s; more than they would be paying for food, clothing, transportation, and housing combined (Kassler 1994:5). While America might be affluent, it is unlikely we can afford to continue to divert resources from all other aspects of life to health care.

The disproportionate share of the GDP spent on health care also adversely affects the U.S. competitiveness internationally. Much of the money spent on health care because it is not productive reduces

American productivity as compared to nations like Japan and Germany which spend about half of what we spend. Also, when United States automakers spend an average of $700 or $800 per car just to pay the costs of employee health care, competitive advantage dissipates. Moreover, the fiscal burden to the state and federal governments is severe and worsening. In 1993 governments combined spent nearly $400 billion on health care. In many states health care is diverting badly needed funding from education, welfare, and infrastructure. In 1992 alone Medicaid costs increased by 29 percent (Mechanic 1994:237). Medicare promises to blow out the federal budget unless major cuts are forthcoming.

Importantly, the inflation of health care costs has continued despite major efforts at cost containment over the past decade. From 1981 to 1991 health care registered a 62 percent increase even after adjusting for economy-wide inflation. Ironically also during the 1980s the percent of Americans who lacked health insurance of any kind grew from 12.5 to 15 percent, an additional 8 million people (Center for Health Economics Research 1993:7).

The cost of health care, then, is a problem that until now has shown little responsiveness to all efforts at constraint. Following chapters will analyze what is driving cost escalation and what must be done to control it. Whether one agrees or disagrees that disproportionate spending for health care, in itself, represents a crisis, it is not possible to ignore the implications for other areas of social spending and thus for our priorities. As cogently stated by Beauchamp, the issue is not the growth in per capita spending per se, the issue is whether the rate of growth in medical expenditures is wise, given the condition of our economy, the resources of taxation, and other needs of society, including housing, nutrition, and employment. In other words, what should we spend on medicine, given the health of the republic as a whole? (1988:240)

MALDISTRIBUTION OF HEALTH CARE

The problem of the high rate of growth in expenditures on medical care in the United States is confounded by the patterns of distribution of expected costs and benefits across society. Health care is a prime example of what Wilson (1980) terms client politics, where benefits are concentrated and costs dispersed. The benefits of health care spending in the United States generally fall to the providers and producers of medical care, the private insurers, and a small proportion of the population that are high users of these resources. In contrast, the costs are spread across the population by government and third-party reimbursement. Client politics gives those groups that potentially benefit from a policy a powerful incentive to mobilize support. In contrast, the broader public has little incentive to organize against the policy as long as its costs are reasonable and there is a perception that the benefits will be available should they ever be needed. There are powerful incentives, therefore, to undermine any threats to the continued flow of money into health care. For Reinhardt:

> Unfortunately, at this time there is no political force in the United States strong enough to reform the American health system toward greater social equity and economic efficiency, whereas there are numerous groups powerful enough to block whatever reform might harm their own narrow economic interests.
>
> *(1992:637)*

Once the costs for individuals are perceived as too high relative to any potential benefits that might accrue, however, public support is likely to deteriorate. Concurrently, if the powerful interests see their benefits decreasing, they will take action to alter the situation.

Only recently have insurance companies and corporations exhibited concern over the long-term dangers of unbridled escalation of health care costs. Historically, they have, by and large, simply paid the costs and then passed them on to policy holders in the form of higher premiums. Because of tax incentives, themselves the products of successful lobbying by health care providers, unions and employers, health insurance continues to be heavily subsidized by the taxpayers. Although this policy has proved attractive to all parties including consumers, it continues to fuel cost escalation and institutionalize inequities between the middle class professionals and union workers who enjoy comprehensive coverage as an untaxed fringe benefit and those groups without comparable coverage.

Soaring insurance premiums, however, are causing a reevaluation on the part of all parties. Employers can no longer afford to provide comprehensive coverage to their employees. For instance, while health spending by business equalled 14 percent of corporate after-tax profits in 1965, businesses spent more (107.9 percent) on health care in 1990 than they earned in after-tax profits (Graig 1993:24). Employees, too have become dissatisfied with the growing share of premiums they must pay and with the less complete coverage they enjoy. Finally, insurance companies are beginning to realize that costs can no longer simply be shifted to policy holders without grave long-term consequences.

The allocation of health care resources is complicated because the distribution of these resources is skewed toward a small proportion of the population. One 16-year longitudinal study found that over their lifetime approximately half of the population has few health care needs other than routine measures, 45 percent will incur substantial lifetime health care costs, and 5 percent will experience extraordinary health needs and expenses throughout their lives (Roos, Shapiro, and Tate 1989). Moreover, as priorities in health care spending have shifted toward sophisticated curative care, health spending has become concentrated in a relatively small number of patients in acute care settings. As a result, each year a small proportion accounts for a majority of the costs. Zook and Moore (1980:997), for instance, in their extensive longitudinal study found that 13 percent of the patients accounted for as much hospital billing as the other 87 percent and that the most costly 10 percent of the patients consumed between 42 and 47 percent of hospital billings. Since only about one person in ten enters the hospital in any given year in the U.S., these figures suggest that as few as 1.3 percent of the population consumes over half of the hospital resources used in a given year.

Table 1.1 demonstrates the extent of this increasing concentration of health resources. In 1987 the top 1 percent of users in the United States accounted for 30 percent of all health care expenditures; the top 5 percent used 58 percent; and the top 30 percent used 91 percent. In 1980 per capita outlays were 29 times the national average on the top 1 percent and 11 times for the top 5 percent making the greatest use of health care. "Given per capita health spending in 1990 of approximately $2,500, per capita outlays in health care for the most costly 1 percent and 5 percent of the population averaged $72,500 and $27,500 respectively" (Aaron 1991:52).

It is possible that these figures could simply reflect the fact that only a small proportion of the population becomes ill each year even though everyone uses medical care identically in the long run. Mechanic (1992:1723), for instance, argues that this pattern should

TABLE 1.1

Distribution of Health Expenditures for the U.S. Population by Magnitude of Expenditures for Selected Years Between 1963–1987

% of U.S. Population Ranked by Expenditure	1963	1970	1977	1980	1987
Top 1%	17%	26%	27%	29%	30%
Top 5%	41%	50%	55%	55%	58%
Top 30%	—	88%	90%	90%	91%
Bottom 50%	5%	4%	3%	4%	3%

SOURCE: Berk and Monheit 1992.

not be surprising since each year only a small proportion of the population suffers critical illness. However, that small proportion is not necessarily the same people who are using expensive resources in other years. Although this explanation has merit and likely reduces the proportion of medical care going to high users over time, as found by Roos et al. (1989) even over a period as long as 16 years, a minority of the population uses most medical care and the majority uses little. No matter how the data are spread, there is considerable evidence that high-users of medical care constitute a minority of the population.

It is also important for public policy that the high users of medical care predominantly are identified as individuals who have unhealthy lifestyles or as noted earlier, the very elderly. Alcohol abuse, heavy smoking, and obesity are particularly prominent among high users of medical care (Zook and Moore 1980:1001). Patients in whom these habits were indicated required greater repeated hospitalization for an illness, thus increasing the "limit cost" of the illness. This small proportion of patients exerts disproportionate leverage on medical resources by repeated use of hospital facilities. The authors suggest: "preventive incentives through insurance or health taxes on selected hazardous habits (or the commodities that they consume) may deserve careful attention in any debate on national health insurance" (1980:1001).

In a longitudinal study of 7,000 people in Alameda County, California, begun in 1965, researchers found that lifestyle choices are significantly associated with better health and lower death rates when adjusted for age. They found that the healthiest people usually were those who followed all or most of seven personal habits: (1) sleeping at least seven or eight hours per night; (2) eating breakfast; (3) rarely snacking between meals; (4) maintaining a reasonable diet; (5) not smoking; (6) drinking alcohol in moderation or not at all; and (7) often taking part in physical activity. A preliminary report of this research (Belloc and Breslow 1972:419) concluded that while each practice taken alone contributed to better health, those persons who followed all seven practices enjoyed health comparable to that of persons 30 years younger who followed few or none. Moreover, the death rate among men who followed all seven good health practices was only 28 percent that of men who followed three or fewer. These earlier findings, except for the contribution of breakfast and eating between meals, were reconfirmed in the final report (Berkman and Breslow 1983).

In addition, Anderson and Steinberg (1984:1349) cite findings that users of high-cost medical care are more likely to be persons with chronic medical problems who are repeatedly admitted to the hospital than persons with single cost-intensive stays. According to Zook and Moore (1980), persons over 65 years of age are disproportionately represented in this high-cost group. Of the 30 million people who in 1976 had a debilitating illness that lasted three months or more, the rates per 1,000 population varied considerably by age: for those under 45 it was 67; for those 45–65 it was 242; and for those 65 and over it was 453 (Lawrence and Gaus 1983:366). Furthermore, Medicare expenditures are highly concentrated on a small percentage of elderly beneficiaries who are repeatedly admitted to the hospital. Almost 60 percent of Medicare's inpatient hospital expenditures between 1974 and 1977 were attributable to the 12.5 percent of the patients who were discharged three or more times during that period, and 20.3 percent of inpatient expenditures were attributable to 2.6 percent of beneficiaries discharged more than five times (Anderson and Steinberg 1984:1351).

These data have serious implications for the financing of health services on several grounds. First, they suggest that any efforts to reduce health care costs must be directed at the high users simply because they collectively consume such a large proportion of the funds. Second, the data demonstrate that considerable redistribution of societal resources is necessary if these individuals, many of whom are poor and/or beneficiaries, are able to obtain the health services they need. Third, they raise serious questions concerning the extent to which society can afford to support individuals who knowingly engage in high risk behavior. (For details on external costs of smoking, heavy drinking and sedentary lifestyles see Manning et al, 1991). This is a particularly salient issue when these needed services include extensive and expensive interventions such as liver, heart and lung transplantation. The final issue centers on the fact that with this knowledge, private insurers are able to selectively exclude from coverage groups and individuals who are likely to be in high risk categories. Without government regulations prohibiting this pattern, the low-risk, healthy groups are concentrated in the private sector while increasingly actual and potential high users must turn to the public sector.

AGING POPULATION

The maldistribution of health care will continue to heighten in part because more intensive technologies will increase the potential interventions and thus the costs of high users. More important, however, is the aging of the population. It is a fact of life that the older people become, the more health resources they consume. Individuals over age 65 enter the hospital twice as often as younger persons and they stay longer. Average per capita expenditure is approximately four times higher for the elderly than the non-elderly and more importantly the rate of increase in such spending for the elderly is nearly three times that of the non-elderly. In 1987, for instance, per capita health spending in the United States averaged $745 for persons under 19, $1535 for those aged 19 to 64, $5360 for those aged 65 and older, and $9178 for those aged 85 and over (Waldo et al. 1989:116–18).

Ironically, because of medical improvements and technologies that prolong life, chronic disease requiring frequent medical care has become an increasing drain on scarce medical resources. Persons who in earlier times would have died of one illness are often kept alive to suffer long-term decline in quality of life. However, the demand for such intervention will continue to increase in an aging population. Furthermore, because of the concurrence of multiple and often chronic conditions, the cost of prolonging life at older ages is higher than at younger ones, increasingly so since the introduction of antibiotics in the 1940s reduced the incidence of death from illnesses such as pneumonia (Ricardo-Campbell 1982:7).

At present, 40 percent of U.S. health care resources go to the approximately 12.5 percent of the population that is 65 years of age or older. Americans who turned 65 in 1994 can expect to receive on average about $200,000 worth of health care before they die, with approximately one-third of that spent in the last year of life (Fuchs 1994:113). Given these spending figures, the trends in the aging of the U.S. population are most troubling.

As indicated in table 1.2, the demographic trends and projections of the percentage of the population 65 and over suggest a significant expansion in that age cohort over the next 30 years in most Western nations. Although the growth in the United States is less than some European nations, by 2030 approximately one in five Americans will be over 65. This aging of western populations is a product of two major factors: a decline in fertility rates after the baby boom generation and increased life expectancies.

The primary cause of the aging is the precipitous decline in fertility rates which has naturally increased the proportion of elderly. Furthermore, this trend is exaggerated because of the sharp upturn in birth rates after World War II produced a bloated age cohort in the baby boom generation which is aging. Even if life expectancy is unal-

TABLE 1.2

Percentage of Population Aged 65 and Over, 1970–2040

	1970	1980	1990	2000	2010	2020	2030	2040
Australia	8.3	9.6	11.1	11.7	12.6	15.4	18.2	19.7
Austria	13.0	15.5	14.6	14.9	17.5	19.4	22.8	23.9
Belgium	12.6	14.4	14.2	14.7	15.9	17.7	20.8	21.9
Canada	7.9	9.5	11.4	12.8	14.6	18.6	22.4	22.5
Denmark	12.8	14.4	15.3	14.9	16.7	20.1	22.6	24.7
Finland	11.1	12.0	13.1	14.4	16.8	21.7	23.8	23.1
France	12.9	14.0	13.8	15.3	16.3	19.5	21.8	22.7
Germany	13.2	15.5	15.5	17.1	20.4	21.7	25.8	27.6
Ireland	11.2	10.7	11.3	11.1	11.1	12.6	14.7	16.9
Italy	10.9	13.5	13.8	15.3	17.3	19.4	21.9	24.2
Japan	7.1	9.1	11.4	15.2	18.6	20.9	20.0	22.7
Netherlands	10.2	11.5	12.7	13.5	15.1	18.9	23.0	24.8
New Zealand	8.5	9.7	10.8	11.1	12.0	15.3	19.4	21.9
Norway	12.9	14.8	16.2	15.2	15.1	18.2	20.7	22.8
Spain	9.8	10.9	12.7	14.4	15.5	17.0	19.6	22.7
Sweden	13.7	16.3	17.7	16.6	17.5	20.8	21.7	22.5
Switzerland	11.3	13.8	14.8	16.7	20.5	24.4	27.3	28.3
U.K.	12.9	14.9	15.1	14.5	14.6	16.3	19.2	20.4
U.S.	9.8	11.3	12.2	12.2	12.8	16.2	19.5	19.8
OECD Average	10.6	12.2	13.0	13.9	15.3	17.9	20.5	21.9

SOURCE: OECD 1988.

tered, this wave of aging baby boomers along with declining fertility rates guarantees an increasing proportion of elderly.

The second factor contributing to the aging of the population is the increase in life expectancies. In the thirty years between 1950 and 1980, life expectancy at birth increased by 8.5 years for females and 6.0 years for males. At age 60, expectancy increased 3.5 years for females and 1.1 years for males. These significant gains result from improved social factors, health habits, and the new capacities of medicine to reduce infant mortality and extend the life span (see Lonergan 1991). It is important to note that in the past gains in life expectancy have been underestimated, meaning that there could be even more significant increases in average life span in the coming decades. Moreover, substantial differences in average life expectancy across countries at present strongly suggest that further gains could be made in a number of countries (OECD 1988:17). Many of these gains might follow adoption of healthier lifestyles and other health promotion activities. Along with low fertility rates these trends could add considerably to population aging.

These aging trends are accompanied by two critical changes in the population structure. First, within the overall trends toward older populations is the aging of these elderly populations themselves. At present the most rapidly growing segment of the elderly population is the cohort aged 80 and over whose weight in the population aged 65 and over in OECD countries increased from an average 18.2 percent in 1980 to 21.7 percent in 1990. In the United States between 1960 and 1990 those aged 85 and over increased by 232 percent; compared to an increase of 39 percent in the total population.

> Although this age group made up just 1 percent of the total population and 10 percent of the elderly population in 1990, demographers are watching it carefully. The higher rates of disability and poverty among these people are likely to have a growing impact on the nation's families and health and social service systems   *(Randall 1993:2332).*

Figure 1.1 illustrates the dramatic growth projected in persons 80 years or older and suggests that they could exceed 15 million by 2050, five times the present number. Moreover, some demographers put the number substantially higher at 20 to 40 million.

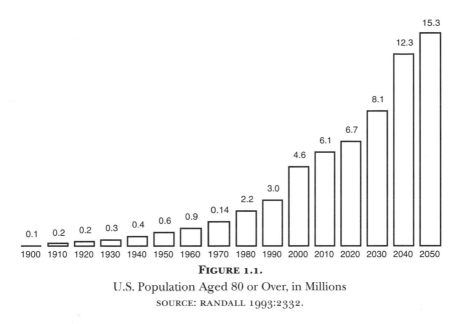

FIGURE 1.1.
U.S. Population Aged 80 or Over, in Millions
SOURCE: RANDALL 1993:2332.

The second trend within a trend relates to the sex composition of the elderly population. As a result of their longer life expectancy, women outnumber men significantly in the elderly age cohorts. Furthermore, the sex imbalance increases with age, meaning that as the very elderly cohort expands the proportion of women elderly will heighten. Table 1.3 demonstrates the extent of this imbalance particularly in the 80 and over group where women outnumber men by an almost 2 to 1 margin. Even though this imbalance is projected to narrow over time especially at the younger end of the elderly age group, women will continue to constitute a substantial majority of

TABLE 1.3
Projected Sex Composition of Population Aged 65 and Over in OECD Countries

	1980	2000	2030	2040	2050
Number of men per 100 women aged					
65–69	81.9	87.5	89.7	90.7	90.6
70–79	71.2	71.3	76.3	78.2	78.4
80 and over	51.2	47.2	53.0	53.2	53.9

SOURCE: OECD 1988:23.

the elderly and will remain particularly marked among the most elderly (OECD 1988:24). As with the other trends this will have considerable impact on health care needs of the population.

SOCIAL POLICY IMPLICATIONS OF AGING POPULATIONS

These trends toward aging populations have clear ramifications for the distribution of societal resources and for determining social priorities. Resources now devoted to children and young families, particularly education and family benefits, will be shifted toward health care, pensions, and other support services directed toward the elderly. Table 1.4 illustrates shifts in expenditures by spending category and age cohort. Expenditures for education are expected to decline from 32 percent in 1980 to 20 percent in 2040 while pensions and health show a large and a moderate increase, respectively. Similarly, while expenditures on those under 65 will by necessity decrease, spending on the elderly shows an increase from 39 to 56 percent.

Although the proportion of social budgets dedicated to health care shows only modest aggregate gains as compared to pensions, these growth rates represent a sizable cumulative increase in resources necessary to finance health care purely because of the aging factor. Setting aside differences among countries it appears likely that by the year 2030 OECD countries will be faced on average with total health expenditures some 30 percent higher and per capita expenditures some 20 percent higher solely as a result of population aging. "At current levels of expenditure, this represents an additional burden of 2

TABLE 1.4
Shifts in Expenditures by Major Program and Age Cohort, 1980 and 2040

	1980	2040
Education	32	20
Health	22	24
Pensions	40	52
Ages 0–14	21	14
Ages 15–64	40	30
Ages 65>	39	56

SOURCE: OECD 1988:37.

to 3 percent of GDP," assuming all other cost-inducing factors are held constant (OECD 1987:91). Any increase in utilization and intensity of care per person that leads to an increase in real benefits per capita and any increase in health care prices over the general rate of inflation would add to this financial burden. According to OECD,

> Given adequate growth in productivity and employment, the aggregate economic burden need not prove insuperable. But it would require significant reallocations of resources from other competing goals and a political willingness to provide the mechanisms which will accommodate such a shift in priorities *(1987:91)*.

Table 1.5 illustrates comparative data on the estimated increases in health expenditures going to the elderly. Although there is significant variation by country, the trend toward a heightened concentration of health care resources in the elderly is universal with most countries registering over 50 percent by 2040.

The aging population not only increases health care spending and shifts it toward the elderly, it also has considerable potential impact on the type of health care provided. The growing number of old people will generate a greater demand for geriatric care and thus a proportionate increase in geriatric facilities and personnel.

TABLE 1.5

Projected Changes in the Proportion of Public Health Expenditure Going to Population Aged 65 and Over*

	1980	2000	2020	2040
Australia	34.5	40.2	46.4	56.0
Belgium	21.8	21.8	25.0	30.4
Canada	32.4	39.4	48.9	57.1
Denmark	40.5	41.1	49.3	57.3
France	28.4	30.0	35.8	41.1
Germany	32.7	34.1	40.0	49.4
Italy	33.2	34.3	38.9	46.8
Japan	31.3	42.4	52.5	55.9
Netherlands	37.0	41.2	49.6	60.1
Sweden	51.5	54.2	59.6	63.3
U.K.	42.5	43.0	45.6	54.1
U.S.	47.0	48.8	56.9	62.9

SOURCE: OECD Secretariat estimates.
* Assuming constant per capita expenditure by age.

Because of the higher incidence of illness among the elderly than in other age cohorts, the aging population will result in increased incidence of illness per head of population, particularly of long-term chronic diseases. Okolski (1986:151), for instance, notes that in those countries where the aging process has advanced the furthest, a rapid rise in the number of disabled persons has been observed. For those over 60 years of age, 25 percent of males and 20 percent of females are permanently disabled to some degree, according to Okolski (1986:151).

The recent emphasis on the AIDS 'epidemic' has overshadowed a disease category that will have increasing policy ramifications and create even greater economic costs: dementia, or senility. The most common form of dementia is Alzheimer's disease, which accounts for about two-thirds of all cases, although over 70 other disorders can cause dementia. Alzheimer's disease causes progressive deterioration of memory, intellect, language, emotional control, and perception. The disease is insidious, gradually progressing from subtle symptoms to almost complete mental deterioration. Victims in the advanced stages may be completely dependent on others for years or even decades, causing serious disruptions to the family and a huge financial burden. The number of persons affected by Alzheimer's disease is expected to double in the next decade, primarily because more and more people are living into their seventies or eighties, the ages at which dementia usually strikes. The likelihood of developing dementia of some type is estimated at 20 to 30 percent for persons age 85 and over, as compared to only 1 percent for those between 65 and 74 and 7 percent for those aged 75 to 84 (Cross and Gurland, 1987).

It is likely that advances in medical treatment are allowing elderly persons who are frail and who suffer from fatal degenerative diseases to survive longer after the onset of the disease than in the past. The result is that age-specific morbidity and disability rates and their duration will substantially increase. Unfortunately, "even if rates of morbidity and disability remain constant, the number of people surviving with conditions of frailty will definitely increase because of the rapid growth in the size of the elderly population resulting from population aging and declining old-age mortality" (Olshansky et al, 1990:639). Even if improved lifestyles and medical technologies are successful in reducing the major causes of premature death, we will be left with a rapidly growing elderly population whose additional years of life may be dominated by nonfatal but highly debilitating conditions such as arthritis, osteoporosis, and Alzheimer's disease. The result could be longer life, but worsening health, thus an actual decline in active life expectancy. Olshansky et al (1990:639) suggest a major shift in research efforts from prolonging life to a strategy aimed at postponing morbidity and lessening the adverse effects of nonfatal but highly debilitating conditions to reduce the duration of frailty for that part of the population that has already approached its biological limits.

Several additional aspects of the aging of populations are critical in order to understand the full range of implications in health policy. Although attention here has focused on the increased expenditures generated by the growing proportion of elderly, the other side is that as populations age the size of the productive sector decreases, thus raising concern over the capacity of society to support the new demands. The ability of any country to finance increased costs associated with the aging population depends upon the relative size of the productive population (usually measured by dependency ratios of some type), as well as unemployment rates and productivity. As the workforce, and tax base, is reduced through aging and continued low levels of fertility the pressures on the remaining working age population will intensify. Figure 1.2 illustrates the sharp decline in work-

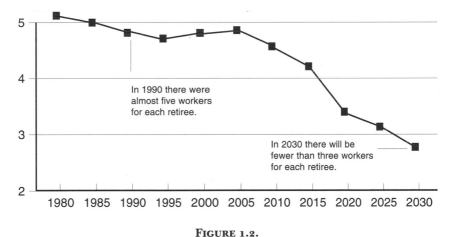

FIGURE 1.2.
Ratio of Persons Aged 20 to 64 to Persons 65 and Older
SOURCE: BIPARTISAN COMMISSION 1995:16.

ers per retiree after 2005. As illustrated, by 2030 there will be fewer than three workers for each retiree.

Finally, just at the time where there is an increased need for long-term caregiving, social changes have undermined traditional, largely informal care mechanisms for the elderly. The decline in the extended family, increased mobility, and trends toward more working women and fewer children have reduced the willingness and ability of families to care for the elderly. As a result, the demands for formal long-term care services will intensify, services that will depend increasingly on public funds. Those countries without adequate funding infrastructures for long-term care such as the United States are most vulnerable to severe problems in this regard.

AGING POPULATION AND U.S. HEALTH POLICY

The aging population in itself, however, is not the major threat. As illustrated above many European countries have demonstrated capacity to serve considerably older populations than the United States while expending considerably less of their GDP on health care and providing universal coverage. What is likely to be disastrous is the combination of an aging population and a health care system where a significant proportion of resources are devoted to high technology interventions on the elderly. As noted by Callahan (1993:12), although we are likely to muddle along for several decades until the problem becomes unendurable, the trend in spending for the elderly must be moderated well before that time.

It is a doubling in the size of the over 65 age cohort in combination with the expectation by the elderly that high technology interventions will be provided that will exacerbate the problem in the United States. For Illich: "They [the aged] have been trained to experience urgent needs that no level of *relative* privilege can possibly satisfy. The more tax money that is spent to bolster their frailty, the keener is their awareness of decay. At the same time, their ability to take care of themselves has withered, as social arrangements allowing them to exercise autonomy have practically disappeared" (1976:222).

Because there is nothing that can be done to stem the aging population, the only feasible option is to drastically scale down our expectations and delimit technological interventions beyond a reasonable point: "As financial and ethical pressures mount, we probably will see the right to death with dignity transformed into an expectation and eventually into an obligation. This development will create enormous stress for patients and their families, health professionals, and government" (Fuchs 1994:113).

Although such a scenario is alien to American values, evidence suggests that it is inevitable that at some point even insured elderly can no longer demand and receive all of the care that might do them some good.

Nowhere is the problem of the aging population more vivid than in regard to Medicare. In 1994 approximately 32.1 million elderly were covered by Medicare Part A with approximately 7.0 million receiving reimbursed services. Of these approximately 31.4 million opted for Part B coverage and of those 26.7 million received benefits. The combined spending on Medicare A and B exceeded $181.5 billion in fiscal year 1995. This constituted about 12 percent of the entire federal budget. With the increase in life expectancy at age 65 expected to increase from current 17.5 years to 18.8 in 2025 and the increasing elderly recipients and decreasing contributors, Medicare faces a "continued and deepening financial crisis" (King 1994:39).

The Hospital Insurance Trust Fund which finances Medicare Part A hospital insurance for the elderly and disabled is projected to be bankrupt by 2002 (see figure 1.3). Part B which pays for physician services, diagnostic tests, and other outpatient services is funded through general revenues and premiums and therefore will not go bankrupt. "However its rapidly escalating costs will add more than $100 billion per year to the federal deficit by the year 2000" (Bandow and Tanner 1995:1). Table 1.6 shows how dramatically Part B, supplementary Medical Insurance, is increasing its share of the GDP. Certainly Bandow and Tanner are correct in stating that "Clearly, no serious attempt to balance the budget can take place without reform of the Medicare system" (1995:8).

It must be reiterated that the crisis in Medicare is preceding the coming boom in the size of the elderly cohort. Part A is projected to go bankrupt at a time when there are still about five workers for each enrollee. Part B costs are skyrocketing even before the boom. Already the intergenerational transfers from the young to the old means that the average person retiring at age 65 in 1994 will get $5.19 in benefits for every dollar contributed (King, 1994:42). Obviously unless draconian limits are forthcoming massive generational inequities will be necessary to meet the "staggering future needs" (Wolfe 1993:1).

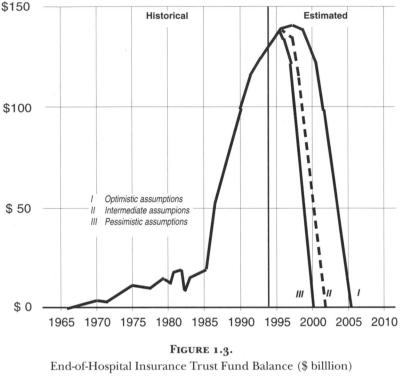

FIGURE 1.3.
End-of-Hospital Insurance Trust Fund Balance ($ billlion)
SOURCE: BIPARTISAN COMMISSION 1995:17.

The compact between generations assumes that the working generation will support benefits for the retired generation. In turn future
generations will pay taxes that will support the same benefits for
them and so on. Such a system depends on an expanding population
base and a consistent ratio between the generations, an assumption
no longer operative. As a result, young workers are now paying taxes
for benefits they are unlikely to receive. Moreover, they are inheriting
debts accrued by the current generation.

According to Lamm (1990:130), our children are going to wake
up some day and see how badly we screwed things up. He argues that
because age is not a static group but rather a status which we all go
through, shifting limited resources from the elderly to the young is
essential. Furthermore, "such a policy is not age discrimination; it's a

TABLE 1.6

Projected Medicare Spending as Proportion of GDP, 1993–2040

Calendar Year	Part A (hospital insurance)	Part B (supplementary medical insurance)	Total
1993	1.52%	0.88%	2.40%
1994	1.60	0.93	2.53
1995	1.66	0.99	2.65
1996	1.95	1.31	3.26
2005	2.24	1.77	4.01
2010	2.48	2.37	4.85
2015	2.84	2.91	5.75
2020	3.22	3.27	6.49
2025	3.64	3.67	7.31
2030	4.04	4.01	8.05
2035	4.33	4.17	8.50
2040	4.47	4.16	8.63

SOURCE: King 1994:41.

common sense answer to the question of who should get any limited resources" (1990:130). As Menzel states:

> What is clear is that people of integrity, appreciating all the ages they might live into, will not hide their heads in the sand about what the real costs of life-saving are, including later health-care expenses and added years of pension benefits. There's seldom a free lunch, and life-saving care in old age is certainly not one of them   *(1993:147)*.

Traditional remedies for reforming Medicare, including increasing the payroll tax or Medicare premiums, and use of managed care and restricting reimbursements, however, have failed to resolve long-term budget problems. Moreover, despite the blowout in Medicare expenditures, older Americans are spending increasing sums out-of-pocket on health care. Not counting nursing home care, such costs averaged $2,803 per person in 1994 up from $1,323 in 1987. In addition to a Part B premium ($458 in 1994), limits in Medicare coverage, hospital deductibles and co-insurance requirements mean that many elderly feel that they are being short changed on health care (AARP 1994). Although some observers disagree and argue that front-end coverage and low deductibles give Medicare recipients little incentive to avoid unnecessary expenses and thus represent primary causes of the rapid growth in expenditure (Bandow and Tanner 1995:4), out-of-pocket costs for the elderly rose 112 percent between 1987 and 1994 while household income increased by only 28 percent (AARP 1994:5).

Whatever one's view on whether the elderly are getting their fair share of the health budget, there is no denying that the aging population is a major problem for the distribution of health care resources and in fact in the redistribution of all societal resources. It is also clear that the problem is getting progressively worse and that existing patterns in health policy are not only inadequate but counterproductive. Any debate over setting limits to medical technologies, shifting resources to preventive care, or rationing health care must address the intergenerational redistribution of resources and the implications of any policy changes for the elderly. It is likely that as the issues raised here become understood by the current younger generations (those persons now under 30) that a form of intergenerational warfare will ensue. Unfortunately the battle lines are becoming increasingly intransigent as the crisis looms and the stakes heighten. I agree with MacManus that "Intergenerational conflicts in health care policy will intensify in situations in which health care rationing becomes necessary" (1996:196).

Chapter 2

Great Expectations

The American Public

Health care in the United States, as in any country, is the product of many cultural, social, and political factors. It is impossible to explain the reaction of a citizenry or its leaders to health issues without an understanding of these factors. Although it is not feasible here to examine all of the complex historical and cultural determinants, there are several critical factors which largely define the unique context of medical decision making in the United States.

Central to this framework are the political structures, institutions, and processes that define the boundaries of policymaking. Full understanding of this political context is essential if we are to comprehend the particular priorities and the apparent inconsistencies found in the health care system. In the United States, this context includes the basic institutions of federalism, separation of powers, and popular consent, as well as the actual procedures of policymaking. It is difficult to envision a national health policy in a country where each of fifty states is responsible for public health and there is no single locus of power at any level. Moreover, one need understand what rules of the game must be followed to achieve a particular goal, and what constraints are there on the government in bringing about these ends. Attention here is focused on the value system which both reflects and shapes the political framework.

Political culture is the complex of beliefs, values, and attitudes concerning government held by the population. To focus on those elements of political culture which influence health policy, one must look at beliefs concerning definitions of health, the role of the government in the health arena, and the extent to which health care represents an individual right or a privilege granted by society. Although it is always dangerous to generalize to entire populations, cultural orientations that largely define the framework for health care policy in the United States are deep and consistent across much of the citizenry.

INDIVIDUAL RIGHTS TO HEALTH CARE

Although individual rights are emphasized in all Western nations, in the United States they have been elevated to a status where they are absolutely dominant over collective interests (Lemco 1994:6). Americans believe in exalting the individual and as a result are hesitant to sacrifice the individual's needs for the common good. While in many ways this is a major strength of U.S. society, when applied to health care it has a distorting influence because it leads to the assumption that health care is a basic necessity of life to which all Americans are entitled not as members of a collective whole but rather as individuals with rights (see Wallner 1993; Jacobs and Shapiro 1994:290). As described by David: "Americans view health care as an unmitigated, unqualified good. And surveys also show that if given a choice, they will virtually always choose to consume more health care rather than less" (1993:30).

As a society, the United States has been hesitant to institute policies that place limits on the amount of medical resources that are committed to an individual. Cost containment measures that attempt to set limits on individual care are widely attacked as counter to the goals of health care. Moreover, the right to health care is proselytized in the press and fought over in the courts. The solution of choice has been to depend on a competitive marketplace to allow individuals to choose providers and exercise their rights. Although market solutions are most compatible with the rights conflict, they are bound to fail, however, because they serve to reaffirm individuals' claims to unlimited resources and favor acute care for individuals, regardless of prognosis, over those measures which would improve the health status of the community as a whole. Furthermore, markets exist not only to meet demands, but by their nature they also create demands: "In health care, demands are transformed by their cultural significance into needs, that is, into something more profound than consumer desire. Moreover, in health care, our needs seem to be insatiable" (Churchill 1994:8).

Although the government has the authority to assert the collective best interest over individual self-interest, within the liberal tradition democratic institutions seem to face paralysis when the constraint of perceived individual rights is imminent. Although I argue we must be willing to use our democratic institutions to stem the tide and restrain our overindulgence of medical care for the individual, there is little evidence that U.S. institutions are either willing or capable of executing such a change from above. Moreover, a series of court rulings have interpreted the right to life to include an inherent claim of citizens to health care and to considerable choice in making health decisions. When rights and the common good conflict, the individual's claims to health care are given preference. As stated by Kassler: "Our premium on individual rights and our emphasis on the differences between us is a far cry from the social beliefs that back the health systems of Europe, Canada, and Japan, in which more homogenous societies band together for the common good" (1994:130). In addition, promoting the general welfare is difficult in the United States because progress is measured incrementally due to the wide diversity of individually oriented interests (Achenbaum 1994:23).

THE TECHNOLOGICAL IMPERATIVE

American culture is also predisposed toward progress through technological means. This desire for control is crucial to understanding characteristic health care decisions. Presumably, equating the reduction of uncertainty with progress facilitates acceptance of a wide range of technologies. The result, unfortunately, has been an unrealistic dependence on technology to fix health problems at the expense of nontechnological solutions. It is far easier to look for the quick technological fix than to alter individual behavior to prevent the disease, or at least reduce the risk, in the first place.

Americans identify high quality medicine with high technology medicine and feel that the best health care is that which uses the most sophisticated new techniques. In turn, new technologies and medical breakthroughs accelerate and widen public demands. Although all Western nations share this demand for medical technology, it is exaggerated in the United States by the dominance of medicine by specialists and subspecialists who often shape innovations by broadening the indications of use. For Mechanic the "incentive structure that affects adoption and use of new technology encourages utilization when little benefit is expected" (1994:8) thus driving up costs. Medical technologies that did not exist two or three decades ago account for the bulk of medical expenditures and explain most of the rise of health care spending (Aaron 1991:26).

This heavy dependence of technological fixes leads to a very aggressive form of medicine in the United States. The United States does four surgeries for every one performed in Japan (per 1000 population) and the average outpatient cost in the United States is 6.5 times higher largely because American physicians practice a style of medicine that is much more high technology and specialist dominated (Drake 1994:138). As a result, the average annual cost of a U.S. hospital bed ($170,199) is 62 percent higher than in Canada.

> No other Western industrial countries have invested as much in medical technology as the United States. There is little indication we are prepared to slow down its diffusion. New technologies are constantly being introduced and funded by government. New technologies are justified by the claim that they will save lives of young people, but inevitably they are extended to elderly patients whose benefit is increasingly marginal.
>
> *(Rhodes 1992:188)*

This fascination with technology has led to an unending stream of innovations fueled by an expansion of the National Institutes of Health budget from $26 million dollars in 1945 to $7 billion dollars in 1990. Combined with approximately $12 billion invested by industry in 1991, there are strong incentives to keep the technological imperative alive. In many ways the medical research establishment has not disappointed the American need for more technology. Vast improvements in surgical procedures, tissue matching, and immuno-suppressant drugs such as cyclosporine are making repair and re-placement of organs increasingly routine. Whereas in the recent past we were dependent on cadaver organs and low patient survival rates, now transplants from brain dead individuals, other species such as baboons and pigs, and artificial organs are revolutionizing organ substitution possibilities. Furthermore, improvements in diagnostic machinery are continuing to accelerate. Computerized axial tomog-raphy (CAT) scanners and magnetic resonance imagers (MRIs) have been quickly followed by positron emission tomography but at high cost. Proton-beam accelerators are being developed to increase radi-ation dosage to cancers with reduced damage to surrounding tissues at a total facility cost of $60 million (Aaron 1991:49).

Likewise, human genetic technology offers an expanding array of diagnostic and therapeutic applications that are giving us consider-ably more control over determining the health and the characteris-tics of future generations. Biotechnology is giving us among many other products unlimited supplies of pure human insulin, inter-feron, and human growth hormone as well as monoclonal antibod-ies that promise widespread benefits to society and its members. Furthermore, advances in cosmetic surgery, computerized prosthet-ics, and the development of artificial skin (Fisher 1990) extend our capabilities to improve upon nature or restore individuals to a full life. Finally, the development of more effective chemicals to enhance physical and mental capacity suggest that there will be few limits to intervention in the human body in the future.

In our attempts to overcome disease and illness, we have always stretched the boundaries of intervention into the human body. In many ways, this continual expansion of our ability to intervene has, in fact, defined progress and, therefore, seldom has been ques-tioned. However, the rapid developments outlined above directed at giving us greater control over what it means to be human have taken on a new urgency but to date have been met with little assessment as to where there are all leading. Our unrealistic dependence on tech-nology to cure human problems, many of which have complex social causes, has translated into a potent desire to find quick technologi-cal fixes to our perceived shortcomings. Moreover, the search for cures for diseases readily gives way to demands for improvements on nature and for control over the aging process through a technologi-cal fountain of youth. We strive for perfect bodies through chemicals and cosmetic surgery, for enhanced mental powers through "smart" drugs, and for replacement of worn out body parts. In all these cases, technology becomes the perceived liberator of human problems.

According to David (1993) our limitless appetite for medical technology is intensified by three factors: deification of doctors, medicalization of social problems, and exaggeration of minor ailments. We expect physicians with their armamentum of technologies to confer immortality and freedom from pain, to rescue us from death, even though both death and some degree of suffering is inevitable in the human condition. The deification of medicine is reinforced by our belief that "tears in the social fabric" such as violence, economic oppression, and racism have medical solutions and is reflected in our exaggeration of minor ailments (David 1993:32). Moreover, it is to the advantage of the medical profession to perpetuate these beliefs, and technology becomes the bridge.

As Reiser (1984:171) cautions, however, technology can be addictive and compelling because it takes on a life of its own. Because they have powerful symbolic meaning, medical devices such as the artificial heart are difficult to limit once they are introduced. Reiser (1985:173) contends that the technological fix approach is generally wrong because it does not adequately account for the complex consequences of technology on the way we think. Furthermore, our heavy faith in technological solutions often has the added danger of diverting attention and resources from more appropriate nontechnological actions.

This continuous development of new medical technologies has the potential to lead to large increases in health care expenditures. More than any other factor, this proliferation of medical technology explains the growth of health spending. "It is often quite possible to push these technologies in a cost-reducing direction, but financial incentives, as well as social and professional pressures in affluent societies, traditionally have pushed them in other directions" (Gelijns and Rosenberg 1994:32).

Medical technology affects outlays by adding to the arsenal of feasible treatments and by reducing the invasiveness of existing interventions, thus increasing the number of patients who might enjoy net gains from diagnosis and treatment. In addition to leading to significant increases in the utilization and intensity of care, many new treatments are expensive. Although not all technological advances necessarily lead to increased expenditures, the net effect has tended to be cost-increasing due to extensions in the range and intensity of care. Even relatively inexpensive advances, such as antibiotics, which appear to reduce health care costs by treating common diseases at a lower cost than past approaches, add significantly to medical spending.

> First, since death from infectious disease is relatively inexpensive and comparatively painless—pneumonia was long known as "the widow's friend"—those spared death by antibiotics have an increased chance of succumbing later to more protracted, painful, and costly illnesses, such as cancer or Alzheimer's disease. Second, antibiotics are an essential part of standard protocols for treating cancer. Cytotoxic drugs frequently undermine natural defences against infection and can be used only if artificial barriers to infection are created. Thus antibiotics enable costly therapies that would be lethal without them.
>
> *(Aaron 1991:48)*

Therefore, even if cost-savings occur at the per patient level, they are usually more than offset by the increase in the use of a new technology (Gelijns and Rosenberg 1994:39).

The impact of technological advances is likely to be aggravated by increases in the number of very elderly people who often become the heaviest users of many medical innovations. This is particularly true in the United States where the tendency to expand application to older and sicker populations usually follows initial narrower uses. It is also possible that increased life spans will be accompanied by a rise in the prevalence of chronic disease as medical interventions and life-sustaining technologies allow persons suffering from these conditions to survive longer. Advances in technology have enabled the prolongation of life of persons with illnesses that would have been untreatable in the recent past.

Moreover, while much curative treatment is beneficial to patients, the marginal gain in terms of length of survival and quality of life is difficult to judge (OECD 1988:67). The reason for this uncertainty is that most medical procedures have not been subject to controlled assessment to determine their effectiveness in particular cases and how they compare in outcome to less expensive alternative approaches. It has been estimated that elimination of care that produces little or no benefit could reduce health care expenditures by as much as 30 percent (Brook and Vaiana 1989). The difficulty is to be able to determine what interventions in what cases will produce little or no benefit. The all too often approach of U.S. society is to use the technologies whenever in doubt.

There is also concern that a large proportion of technological activity is what Lewis Thomas terms half-way technologies. Half-way technologies neither prevent nor cure disease but instead rescue the patient. While they might in some way compensate for the disease's effect on the patient, they often serve only to postpone death or to prolong life but at a much-reduced quality. In contrast definitive medical technologies are those that prevent disease (i.e., immunizations) or represent a genuine cure. Because of limited knowledge and capacities, half-way interventions are often the best that can be done for a patient but they are often very costly and might divert resources from basic research that could lead to definitive technologies.

Half-way technologies often form the "ragged edge" between life and death that will never be eliminated because "No matter how far we push the frontiers of medical progress we are always left with a ragged edge—with poor outcomes, with cases as bad as those we have succeeded in curing, with the inexorable decline of the body however much we seem to have arrested the process" (Callahan 1990:63).

A danger for Thomas (1987) is that in the public's mind half-way technologies become the equivalent of the high technologies of the physical sciences. Despite the major threats of half-way technologies being misrepresented, Bronzino et al. (1990) argue that they may in fact lead to definitive technologies. In other words, the line between the two is never as clear as the critics imply. Some half-way technologies of today are the cures in the future. Therefore, it is wrong to assume that the benefits of such efforts are short-run only. Furthermore, "such technologies often do ameliorate suffering, compensate in some measure for impaired function, and avert premature death even when means of genuine prevention and cure are not available" (Bronzino et al. 1990:522).

Showstack and associates (1985) conclude that the debate over the cost implications of medical technology is too narrowly focused because it frequently emphasizes hardware costs and omits new surgical procedures and other services which are the very factors they found to be responsible for increased treatment costs. They also found that many of these clinical innovations had little immediate effect on health outcomes. This reinforces the view that many technologies and procedures have been put into widespread use before their effectiveness and safety were established.

Revelations that apparent advances in the treatment of lung cancer are nothing but statistical illusions demonstrate this problem (Feinstein et al. 1985). Researchers found no statistically significant difference in the survival rates of patients treated for lung cancer over the last thirty years, despite the introduction of sophisticated diagnostic tools such as CAT scans, nuclear scans, and ultrasound during that period. Data that show that one-half of all patients now survive for five years as compared with one-third in the 1950s are misleading in making it appear that treatment has been successful. In fact, the improvement is spurious; it results from the introduction of diagnostic tests that spot the disease sooner than was before possible. Because their cancer was detected earlier, more recent patients could be followed longer, producing the illusion that they lived longer. Even though the real odds of dying of lung cancer are the same now as they were a generation ago, the model wrongly implied a substantial reduction in the chances of dying within five years. The researchers concluded that while they had expected newer cancer treatments to have improved survival rates, it actually appeared likely that these therapies have helped some patients but harmed others, so that their opposing effects on different patients have counterbalanced one another.

One of the researchers, Daniel Sosin, notes that this false confidence in a treatment could affect physicians' decisions as they attempt to weigh the benefits of chemotherapy or surgical therapy against the risks they pose for a particular patient. Overestimating the benefits on the basis of false inferences concerning survival rates might lead physicians to accept greater risks, at substantial personal and societal cost. Within a context where producers are trained to use all treatments that are of any benefit to the patient despite the cost, accurate data on patient benefit and risk are essential. In the case of lung cancer treatment, it appears that considerable resources have been wasted with little, if any, positive impact on health—resources that could have been better directed elsewhere. A critical question is how many additional widely used treatments for cancer and other diseases are ineffectual.

The implications of the rapid advance of diagnostic and therapeutic medical technologies for health policy are considerable. Even though debate continues and evidence on the effect of specific innovations is inconclusive, overall technology is viewed by many observers as the most critical factor in the growth of health care costs. It is also seen as one of the most difficult factors to control because of its unlimited potential for change. According to Aaron: "Even if all of the inflation arising from fear of malpractice litigation, the extension of insurance, and care providing negligible benefits could somehow be eliminated, the dominant underlying force responsible for rising medical outlays—technological advances—would remain" (1991:52).

Finally, the unrealistic faith in and dependence on technological medicine diverts attention and resources from disease prevention, health promotion, and nonmedical health strategies (Mechanic 1994:8). Callahan argues that it is at the borderline where individual needs become enormously expensive and begin to threaten the welfare of the community as a whole that the most difficult moral problems are encountered: "No doubt the effort to meet individual curative needs often leads to more and more expensive solutions; and it is proper enough to note that we ought not morally reject the meeting of those needs simply on the grounds that they are expensive. But in setting overall priorities for a health care system, making certain that public health needs are reasonably well met before giving a high priority to the more expensive individual curative needs seems important" (Callahan 1992:156). In conflict with this technological imperative mentality it is becoming clear that we can no longer afford the " 'luxury' of expensive, high technology treatments for infertility." (Baird 1993:581)

American patients also expect a different standard of care. Unlike Japan, where physicians spend little time with patients, in the United States such conduct would be unacceptable. Moreover, one is struck by the spartan conditions in hospitals in other nations where amenities are limited. Color TVs, stereo systems, bedside phones, electrical beds, wide menu choices, private and semiprivate accommodations, and fancy lobbies and decorated rooms add substantially to the costs of care without any appreciable impact on health. In an era where hospitals compete for patients these become part of the bargaining chips. It is questionable which of these amenities would be demanded if they were optional and their reimbursement withdrawn from third-party coverage, but the point is that Americans expect hotel amenities and considerably higher levels of personal contact as patients. Also because many of these services are already spent as capital, they must be paid. Seldom do patients or payers have the choice to refuse first class amenities in American hospitals, but because patients now expect such services it is unlikely that major savings could be expected.

MEDICALIZATION OF PREFERENCES

One critical distinction that underlies all potential interventions in the human body centers on the motivation behind a particular application. One the one hand, these techniques can be directed at ameliorating or overcoming disease, illness, or deficiencies in the body. Transplantation of organs, gene therapy, and use of human growth hormone to correct a natural deficiency are examples of such applications. One the other hand, intervention can be initiated to enhance normal body structure and function in the absence of disease or illness. These interventions are based on individual preferences which, in turn, often reflect the social value put on specific characteristics, for instance physical appearance. Frequently, these applications are motivated by simple vanity, although this always occurs within the broader social and cultural context. Moreover, the line between these two categories of intervention is obscure. For instance, cosmetic surgery can be used to correct physical deformities or to give a normal person the features he or she desires. Likewise, although orthodontics can be used to ameliorate dental problems, frequently its use is motivated by the desire to improve physical appearance according to cultural expectations. Despite this ambiguity, a broad array of interventions are undertaken without medical indications in the more narrow sense.

American society especially is obsessed with the search for the perfect body. Our athlete and movie star heroes are clearly rewarded for their physical prowess and looks. Although the purported extensive physical remaking of Michael Jackson may be an extreme manifestation of this obsession, reconstruction of the human body is a multi-billion dollar industry, representing a rapidly growing sector of "health care." Furthermore, countless young women starve themselves to achieve the model body as espoused by the popular media. Crash weight loss diets are marketed less for health reasons than for appearance—advertisements idealize the thin look, often with little or no mention of health benefits, or risks. Moreover, quick technological fixes, not long-term behavioral changes are marketed to mass consumers, many times under the rubric of "medical" solutions.

Extensions of this mode of thinking into the realm of cosmetic surgery are natural. Although many of the applications of cosmetic surgery do not address health problems, by packaging it as health care, we in effect have medicalized physical appearance. In the process, we have also trivialized the human body and the uniqueness of individual identity. Biological diversity and variation in appearance gives way to socially defined or perceived correctness. The selection of model noses, breasts, pectorals, and buttocks is made through the use of computer imagery which allows potential customers a view of what they will look like with their new "enhanced" features. Likewise, widespread use of anabolic steroids and other body-building substances promise a technological short-cut to remolding the body. "Smart" drugs promise to do the same for the brain in the near future. Immediate effects are desired and in many cases apparently delivered by an expanding arsenal of innovative procedures and substances.

Growing evidence of long-term problems with these technological fixes, for instance silicone breast implants and steroid use, appears simply to shift the demand to alternative interventions which promise the same immediate benefits without the proven dangers. Rather than questioning whether there might be something inherently risky in such intrusions into the human body, the tendency is to replace one type with another. Reinforcing this approach is that element of the medical establishment that caters to these demands for the perfect body and which has a significant financial stake in the continued use of these interventions.

It might be argued that the diffusion of new methods of enhancing the body will have an egalitarian impact by allowing those persons less endowed naturally to become more competitive. However, in reality, the vast inequalities in resources in U.S. society make it more likely that those persons who are already advantaged will have access to interventions and become more so at the expense of the least well off. With pectoral implants averaging $7000, calf implants $5000, and buttock implants $7500, they will be available only for those individuals with substantial resources. So far as a society actually rewards individuals with these characteristics, the people who will benefit largely will be those who have sufficient wealth to begin with. Although pressures might be exerted on society to pay for these techniques, this should be avoided because it will divert resources from treating genuine matters of health as opposed to those of preference.

Questions have also been raised as to whether intensive intrusions into the body can deliver what they promise. A recent study by Olshansky, Carnes, and Cassel (1990), for instance, casts doubt that stretching the boundaries of intervention into the human body will give us the reductions in mortality (and morbidity) we have come to expect. Barring major advances in the development of life-extending technologies or the alteration of human aging at the molecular level, the period of rapid increases in life expectancy has come to an end in developed nations. Although the size of the older population will continue to grow even if death rates remain at current levels as result of the large baby boom cohorts, it will take increasingly larger reductions in mortality to produce equivalent increases in life expectancy, according to Olshansky and associates (1990:438). The data indicate that average life expectancy will not exceed 85 years at birth or 35 years at age 50, implying that the upper limit to longevity has already been approached. Further significant declines in mortality are unlikely because the "dramatic age shifts in mortality required for increases in life expectancy beyond 85 years appear unlikely" (Olshansky et al. 1990:638).

Rising Public Expectations and Demands

The primary forces behind this emphasis on technological medicine are found in the health care community and the public. Providers are trained to do what is best for their patients. According to Fuller, medical students and residents "are taught to rely heavily on medical technology, most of it expensive and some of it dangerous. This is because those who teach and do research lead an insular medical career that effectively prevents them from experiencing the realities of medical practice in a community. Yet, they control medical education" (Fuller 1994:22).

In societies that emphasize technological progress, it is not surprising that a maximal model of usage will be predominant. Unless constrained by government or other third-party actions, the health care community will embrace the technological imperative. It will for this reason object to any outside attempts to place limits on the practice of medicine especially when it threatens their interests and the interests of the patients. There is also a strong aversion by the medical community to serve as gatekeepers when it is viewed to the detriment of individual patients even though such a provision is essential to reducing consumption (Wallner 1993:7). As noted by Drummond (1993:17) most professional codes of ethics deny the existence of scarcity of resources.

Likewise, the expectations and demands of the public for health care are potentially insatiable. Health care costs have increased in part because citizens expect and often demand higher and higher levels of medical intervention—levels undreamed of several decades ago. Until recently this expanded view of health care has been encouraged by politicians, governments, and other third party payers by placing heavy emphasis on the rights or entitlements of individuals to health care with few apparent limits. Furthermore, there has been a clear shift toward the notion of positive rights to health care which place a moral duty on society to provide the resources necessary to exercise those rights. Although this shift in itself is not bad, the long-term results in light of expanding medical technology mean that setting limits becomes increasingly difficult politically once the population takes health care rights for granted.

The emphasis on the individual's right to medical care is also reflected in the patient-physician relationship, which has been seen largely as a private one, beyond the public realm. Although in the aggregate citizens are willing to cut costs, when it comes to the individual patient, they are ready to expend all resources without consideration of costs. There is a not-so-implicit assumption that every person has a right to unlimited expenditure on his or her behalf, despite the knowledge that in the aggregate this is unfeasible. This is reinforced by our belief that doing something is better than doing nothing and the failure to understand that marginal benefits can be too meagre to pursue or too costly to justify (Kassler 1994:130). According to Eddy (1993) the difference in cost between the attitude of "when in doubt do it" and that of "when in doubt stop" could add up to $100 billion annually. The problem of unlimited individual claims in the context of limited societal resources produces the dilemma of health care today.

The suggestion that we somehow limit medical expenditures on an individual in order to benefit the community, however, contradicts the traditional patient-oriented mores of medicine. There are strong pressures for intensive intervention on an individual basis even in the last days of life; this, despite the enormous cost for very little return in terms of prolonging the patient's life. In addition to supporting the maximalist approach to medical care, we have created mechanisms to effectively insulate individuals from bearing the costs of expensive medical treatment.

> The comprehensive benefits introduced in the 1960s sowed the seeds of the current financial crisis by insulating Americans from the true cost of health care. Over the next thirty years, Americans would come to view health care at any cost as an entitlement, an inalienable right. It is no accident that national health expenditures began to skyrocket in the 1960s just as individual's out-of-pocket expenses began to plummet. It is also no coincidence that now, when an increasing number of insurance companies are demanding higher co-payments and deductibles and attempting to screen out expensive patients with "exclusion riders" and outright coverage denial, the public has suddenly awakened, demanding that Washington solve the health care crisis.
>
> *(Cundiff and McCarthy 1994:6).*

While third-party coverage is beneficent, insulating the individual patient from cost encourages the maximalist approach and supports the presumption that cost should not be a concern in the treatment of a patient. When costs do become high, the tendency is to demand more front-end insurance coverage to pay for high-cost medical care not to reduce the care itself. We have come to expect the best that medical science can offer when it comes to care for ourselves or our loved ones. Although we complain about the high cost, when our health or life is at stake, we expect no expense to be spared. For us we feel that medicine should not have a price tag.

The belief that individuals have the right to unlimited medical care should they so choose it; the traditional acceptance of the maximalist approach by the medical community; and the insulation of the individual from feeling the cost of treatment, then, together have placed severe limits on the extent to which proscription of expensive and often ineffective intervention is possible. Arguments in favor of containing the costs of health care, while acceptable at the societal level, tend to be rejected when applied at the individual level. Although a large proportion of the population supports some type of cost containment in theory, traditional beliefs in the maximalist approach remain strong. It is little wonder that most elected officials are unwilling to make allocation decisions that conflict with these strongly held values.

It has been suggested that no matter to what extent health care facilities are expanded, there will remain a steady pool of unmet demands. Additional facilities and money, then, are not the answer to the health care crisis. Instead of resolving the problems, this approach increases the demand for medical solutions to an ever-expanding range of problems. Although wealthier countries devote substantially higher proportions of their resources to health services than do poorer countries, demand for even more services does not abate. Instead, the public comes to expect a level of medical care not imagined by persons in less affluent countries. Moreover, as more of these expectations are met, demand for expanded health services actually escalates.

In a system where third-party reimbursement insulates much of the public from the real cost of meeting these higher expectations, it is not surprising that the public strongly supports increased development of medical technologies. The situation is even more complex, however, because seldom does the public create the initial demand for more advanced technology. Instead, the initiative for medical research and development comes from the medical scientists themselves. The liver transplant, for instance, was never demanded by the public, not even by an interested segment of it. Instead, it was developed to meet a need perceived by the medical community that holds out promises that can be fulfilled only if new resources are made available.

> Moreover, once these technologies are introduced, there is strong incentive for maintaining their use for both the medical manufacturers and the professionals who use the products. Thus, we have woven a pattern of interests and incentives that makes it difficult to forgo technical hardware and procedures.
>
> *(Mechanic 1994:7)*

Once developed, however, media attention dramatizes medical innovation, and demand increases among both physicians and patients. Even before an innovation passes out of the experimental stage, consumers come to expect that it will become available for their benefit.

According to Franz Ingelfinger (1980), organized medicine is at blame for the overselling of medicine because as a whole it has encouraged the belief in the omniscience, rather than the ignorance, of the medical profession. He also criticizes politicians who promise too much and voluntary health groups that suggest in their fund-raising campaigns that if only more money were thrown in to the research mill, the major diseases would be contained. For instance: "That elusive cure for cancer is just over the hill, if only . . . . meanwhile, cancer rates among baby boomers appear to be higher than among their among their grandparents, and $25 billion spent in the war against cancer has left 'victory' nowhere in sight" (Barer et al. 1994:9495).

Despite the failure of medicine to deliver on many counts, as a whole the public continues to support the search for ultimate solutions to health problems through technology.

THE MEDIA, MEDICINE, AND PUBLIC EXPECTATIONS

Public expectations are also elevated unrealistically because of a tendency to oversell medical innovation and overestimate the capacities of new medical technologies for resolving health problems. Frequently, the initial response of the media, often encouraged by medical spokespersons, is to report innovations as medical "breakthroughs." Because most health care is routine and not newsworthy, the media naturally focus attention on techniques that can be easily dramatized. This is especially true in the United States.

The mass media are predisposed toward focusing on the more spectacular achievements of medicine and, in the process, have a tendency to simplify and sensationalize technological developments. Seldom is there the time or inclination to temper optimism with realism, or to qualify claims for these medical breakthroughs with caveats about their limitations, complexity, and social implications. As a consequence, expectations frequently are falsely raised. By dwelling on technologies, procedures, and health programs that promise the quick fix, the press and particularly the electronic media promote a "disease of the weak" mentality. This tendency is aggravated by the public's apparently short attention span for news. As a result, the search goes on for newsworthy events to give the public a continual flow of dramatic yet superficial stories about medical developments.

A substantial proportion of the content of the mass media news stories that reaches the public is in the form of summaries of studies from medical journals, particularly the *New England Journal of*

Medicine or *JAMA*. Again, however, these extracts tend to emphasize the news aspects, thus failing to analyze the "breakthrough" fully. The discovery of the AIDS antibodies becomes a potential cure to that disease; artificial heart transplants become a promise of a mechanical fountain of youth; and the war on cancer portends a cure. What are not stressed are the facts that identifying antibodies to the HIV virus, although significant, does not represent a cure for AIDS; artificial heart transplants raise severe questions concerning the quality of life and the use of scarce resources; and no all-encompassing cure for cancer will ever exist. Without exposure to the negative aspects and the uncertainty of medical science, the public is given a narrow vision of medical technology.

In contrast public health issues and nonmedical health-related issues are less dramatic and receive considerably less attention, thus reinforcing in the public's mind the distorted view that medical technology equals health. This pattern results in part from the fact that a large proportion of health stories, perhaps as high as 90 percent (Kassler 1994:122), are initiated by public relations firms funded by the medical establishment. Press releases and video news releases launching new procedures are often presented as objective news stories without investigative analysis. Local evening news shows with limited budgets are particularly likely to run these promotional stories without challenge because they lack staff capable of putting the release in proper perspective. However even the networks and major daily newspapers have become dependent on this new form of advertising. According to Cundiff and McCarthy, "The press dutifully complies and well-timed *Wall Street Journal* and *New York Times* articles announce the advent of new drugs and devices along with testimonials from doctors and glowing forecasts of success from stock analysts" (1994:26).

Public expectations and perceptions of medicine are also shaped by television medical dramas especially the new breed of "reality-based" series such as *Chicago Hope* and *ER*. The public comes to believe that CPR virtually always saves lives and that heroic measures taken by the medical profession are likely to succeed. For instance, in one episode the chief of surgery informs the hospital board that he will defy their order and separate co-joined twins despite the costs and the poor odds because "he has held them." His surgical team of highly trained and confident specialists conducts the surgery, and the result is two beautiful babies who apparently are cured and will live normal healthy lives. Medicine triumphs again and those who question the costs are the bad guys. Hope is alive and well in Chicago. In these series viewers are rewarded by a string of heroic, life-saving interventions and the failures are seen as unfortunate exceptions. Moreover, such programs are advertised as realistic portrayals and watched by huge audiences. As such they reinforce the belief that if given enough resources, medical miracles will follow. Scarcity is viewed as unacceptable and the major barrier to success (see Annas 1995). It is also significant that there are no television series on public health nurses, family practitioners, preventive medicine, or midwives. Perhaps they would make for boring watching.

Despite these limitations, the mass media, particularly television, are for most of the public the most constant and powerful sources of information. Because of the directed coverage of medicine by the media, with few exceptions the public is not exposed to comprehensive, systematic, and critical analysis of medical developments. The media coverage heightens the public's already strong trust in the technological fix.

> The media has certainly heightened public awareness of medicine. American patients are often well informed—not because they learn from their doctors, but because they read the press and watch television. But medical news also stimulates their appetite for new, expensive, high technology procedures. . . . Americans, at least partly because of the media, are getting hungrier for health care   (Kassler 1994:126).

Media coverage solidifies the view that if we as a society would only put our collective mind and resources to a task, we will achieve it. Often cited as support for this assumption are the elimination of small pox, polio, and other communicable diseases. The presumptions that diagnosis of a disease will lead to treatment and treatment to a cure are also central to news coverage of medicine. One danger in this overoptimism is that the public comes to expect near-miracles that medicine cannot deliver. Eventually, this must lead to a reaction against a medical community that delivers much less than it supposedly promised. Public resentment against the amount of resources put into the cancer program reflects in part the perceived lack of progress in what the media portrayed as the effort to eradicate cancer. By reporting only the positive and sensational aspects of medical research and development, the media is in effect creating unrealistic expectations about the power of medicine. In the end, this pattern of coverage is counterproductive and obscures the difficult real decisions that must eventually be made. It also tends to undermine any possibility of a serious national dialogue over the need to set limits by allocating medical resources.

Another problem with America's reaction to health issues is that it tends to be fadish, often based on spurious or oversimplified assumptions. The near obsession with cholesterol screening in the 1980s led to considerable health concerns among otherwise healthy Americans. In an often near-hysterical setting, cholesterol reduction was perceived as a cure all for heart disease risk. Testing programs proliferated and industry geared to cash in by marketing low cholesterol products. Although cholesterol reduction is valuable for those persons at high-risk, the costs of screening and, more importantly, the focus on one risk factor above all others perpetuated the belief in finding a quick fix to a more complicated problem. Moreover, there are questions whether most individuals who participated in cholesterol screening actually changed their long-term dietary habits.

On a grander scale, the government's response to the health risks of asbestos demonstrates this tendency to overreact in ways that ultimately are counterproductive. First, the Environmental Protection Agency (EPA) arbitrarily lumped together disparate materials as asbestos and fostered the spurious view that a single fiber can cause cancer (Abelson 1990:1017). Second, the EPA required schools to inspect for asbestos and submit plans as to how to deal with it. It required that asbestos be removed from buildings before they are demolished or renovated. It has been estimated that the removal of asbestos from buildings could cost as much as $50 to $150 billion spawning an active asbestos-removal industry. The problem is that the "content of asbestos fibers in the air of buildings containing asbestos is harmlessly small and essentially the same as in outdoor air" (Abelson 1990:1017). Also, since asbestos in buildings does not shed fibers unless damaged, ironically the removal process itself releases fibers that could result in more cancer in the workers than could have accrued to the usual occupants of the buildings had the asbestos been left in place. Good intentions based on unsubstantiated assumptions have created increased health hazards and consumed billions of dollars that could have been better spent on proven preventive programs.

PUBLIC OPINION AND HEALTH POLICY

Although the public does not make health policy in any traditional democratic sense, it is a key to any meaningful reform of the health care system. This major shaping function is reflected in the values which dictate what is expected from medicine, the scope of individual rights, and perceptions of the role of the government and society in general in health care. While the latter two elements are reflected by individualism and the technological fix, the role the government takes is clearly shaped by the ambivalence to government which largely favors expanded benefits and protections but rejects any appearance of strong state control (Jacobs 1993:234). In health care, the desire for more services and for security together with the suspicion of government "continues to trump concerns over high costs and the embarrassing lack of access to medical services for the working poor" (Churchill 1994:6).

To some extent the U.S. health care system is in a democratic Catch-22 situation. Needed major changes cannot occur without public support. However, the individualistic value system itself rejects setting limits to health care for individuals, limits that are essential for meaningful health care reform. The key then is the public but the public is spoiled. The public rejects limits to their individual health care even though such limits are necessary for the good of the community now and especially in the future. The public seems willing to support government involvement only if someone else pays the costs.

A 1993 survey by the Harvard School of Public Health found that while moral concern for the uninsured is a strong public value, it itself it is not enough to generate popular support for a national health program. It is more likely that support will come from worries of the middle class that the problems of the uninsured one day will be their problems (Blendon et al. 1994:283). The survey found a fear by Americans that their own health coverage may some time prove to be inadequate. Moreover Americans do not believe that they as individuals are responsible for the nation's health care problems. Only 4 percent identified patients as major contributors through their behavior as consumers of health care. Thus, changes in patterns of use by patients have little support as a means of reform.

The Harvard survey also found that the public is unwilling to make more than moderate sacrifices for the sake of reform nor to pay higher taxes or premiums to fund the changes. This reinforces past studies which found that few persons are willing to pay the costs of a major reform or accept reductions in health care services. Most studies indicate that only a small minority are willing to pay even a modest $200 a year in taxes to support national health insurance (22 percent in Blendon and Donelan 1990). Table 2.1 shows that even at the height of its popularity only about 40 percent of the public favored a tax increase to enact President Clinton's Health Security Act even though support for the Act was near 60 percent.

The public is more likely to support reform if someone else pays for it. This view is reflected in surveys that demonstrate that a majority support requiring employers to pay all or most of the cost of health care coverage. In response to the statement that "all businesses should be required to pay at least 80 percent of medical coverage for their employees," 65 percent agreed and 29 percent disagreed (NBC News/Wall Street Journal 12.14.93). Lost to some of the respondents is the fact that if employers are forced to pay, employees will eventually pay through reduced salaries, higher prices, or possibly layoffs.

Table 2.2 shows strong support in principle for a government responsibility to pay for health care. In 1993, 50 percent either agreed or strongly agreed while less than 15 percent felt that people should take care of it themselves. Despite this rather consistent support for a governmental responsibility since 1975, however, other surveys show distrust of a broadened government role in control of health care. Furthermore, although large majorities perceive a health care crisis, most are satisfied with the current care they receive and favor more rather than less health spending. Although the public wants the problem of health care costs addressed by the policymakers, it appears unwilling to support a solution that would dramatically alter the present health care arrangements.

TABLE 2.1
Support for Tax Increase to Fund Health Security Act

	Sep. 19, 1993	Oct. 10, 1993	Jan. 23, 1994
Favor	39	40	41
Oppose	58	57	54
Don't know	3	3	5

SOURCE: ABC News/*Washington Post.*

The public does perceive a health care crisis. A 1994 Harris Survey found 84 percent agreeing that there was a crisis and 15 percent saying no. Similarly, a 1994 Princeton survey found those agreeing at 79 percent. However, the crisis the public sees is different from that of the experts. While the experts see the problem as one of out-of-control costs and the need to reduce deficit and boost productivity, the public sees the problem on a more personal basis. People want to spend less of their own money, have more security in coverage, and have access to high technology care. Although there is undoubtedly some sympathy for the uninsured the public when asked what is the bigger problem, health costs are too high or coverage is not available to all take the former over the latter 67 to 27 percent (Yankelovich/Time/CNN, 2/10/94). Furthermore, the problem of high costs is personalized to mean high costs to individuals, not the high proportion of the GDP used by health care. Therefore, while 86 percent agree that "we need health reform that will guarantee universal health insurance for all Americans" this support dissipates when details are provided (Harris, 2/6/94). For instance, 84 percent agree that whatever system we have, some people will always get more and better health care than others (Minnesota 1995).

As President Clinton found out, the public is suspicious of any changes to the health care system that might adversely affect their own health care. As soon as it became clear that the President could not provide universal coverage without increased costs or reduced

TABLE 2.2
Government Responsibility to Pay Health Care Bills

	1975	1983	1984	1986	1987	1988	1989	1990	1991	1993
Government is responsible										
Strongly agree	36%	26%	24%	28%	26%	27%	30%	30%	32%	28%
Generally agree	13	19	19	20	20	22	22	26	25	22
Agree with both answers	29	32	35	32	35	35	30	30	27	32
People should care for themselves										
Agree	8	10	12	11	9	9	8	7	9	9
Strongly agree	13	10	8	6	8	6	7	4	6	6

SOURCE: Jacobs et al. 1993.

services to the already insured, support dissipated. Abstract support for health care reform is consistent with the American values of fair play. However, most think that the problems we face can be solved by cutting waste, fraud, and by taxing others (Kosterlitz 1993:127). When confronted with even the possibility that change means sacrifice, however, the public becomes anxious about reform. Additional costs or reduced services or choices are opposed by much of the public. Even an extra measure of security might not be worth the costs.

There is little acknowledgement by the public that constraints are needed. Rationing continues to elicit vehement condemnation as anti-American because it explicitly deals with scarcity and the need for trade-offs. To some extent this public refusal to accept limits is understandable since to date public officials have masked the truth. Like President Clinton, they have promised workable reform without hard choices (see chapter 4 discussion). Churchill summarizes the dilemma this situation creates:

> American culture is ideologically committed to expanded opportunity, progress, and abundance. These cultural traits do not dispose us to contemplate shortages, limits, and hard decisions. . . . Unfortunately, it is not clear that as a society we are ready either to acknowledge limits or to claim responsibility for how the health care system functions   *(1994:7)*.

Although the United States is far from the ideal model of democracy, public opinion traditionally has been a major factor for shaping the political boundaries within which public policy is made. Decision makers enjoy considerable discretion as long as they remain inside the broad parameters of public opinion. However, should they dare violate the public trust and transgress the opinion boundaries, they will find that challenge to the status quo comes only with considerable difficulty and at heavy political cost. Any alterations of the health care system, particularly alterations that might involve possible intervention into individual choice and lifestyle, must necessarily be tempered by the perceptions and expectations of the health care consumers themselves.

Without doubt, these public expectations and perceptions of medicine have resulted in an overutilization of and reliance on technology. Patients demand access to the newest technologies because they are convinced of their value. Popular health-oriented magazines and television shows extol the virtues of medical innovations. Physicians have been trained in the technological imperative which holds that a technology should be used despite its cost if it offers any possibility of benefit. Whether to protect themselves from malpractice suits, to provide the most thorough workup for their patients, or to increase profits, many physicians would rather err heavily on the side of overusing diagnostic and therapeutic technologies. The heavy investment of medical providers in expensive diagnostic equipment such as CAT scanners and MRIs, often merely to stay ahead of the competition, encourages their use even in situations where their benefit is marginal or nonexistent. Third-party retrospective reimbursement provides no disincentive against this overutilization of medical technology. Any limits on the allocation of medical technologies, then, must come from outside the health care system. The only agent with the power to effectuate such limits is the government, but it can do so only within the context of rising public expectations and demands.

To some extent the present American health care crisis is a result of excessive public expectations. The dynamics of the U.S. political process and the medical community have generated expectations which can no longer be realized, thus producing a gap between promise and performance. In health policy this tendency is aggravated because the health care system itself generates excessive expectations among consumers eager to see each new medical "breakthrough" as corroboration of the technological progress whose benefits they expect to share, despite the costs. The difficult task facing policymakers is to devise a system that is more cost-effective, comprehensive and universal while "remaining sensitive to the desire of most Americans for a system that is consistent with their values and unique culture" (Lemco 1994:273).

CHAPTER 3

MEDICINE AND HEALTH
Only One Piece of the Puzzle

The great expectations of the American public concerning what medicine can accomplish in ameliorating illness, disease, and suffering has, therefore, produced unrealistic and unrealizable dependence on medical technologies to make it healthier. Medical care has become synonymous with health care and health care has become the preferred linkage to health itself. This view has been reinforced by a medical industry built upon finding cures to an ever expanding number of diseases. Because the medical profession has both an exclusive power over defining what constitutes a disease and a stake in responding to new disease categories, there is a tendency for continuous expansion of the boundaries of medicine. The resultant medical model of health assumes that health is to be pursued by increasing intensity of medical intervention.

While there is no doubt that medical care can be decisive in individual cases, there is substantial evidence to demonstrate that it is but a relative minor determinant of the health of populations. If the goal of health care is to improve the health of populations, then the medical model must be reassessed. This chapter critically analyses this relationship of medicine and health and reiterates the call by many observers to move to more complex and inclusive models of health. It begins by reviewing what perhaps has been the harshest attack on medicine, that of Ivan Illich two decades ago (Illich 1976). It then attempts to reexamine the role of medicine in health and to put health itself in a broader social context. The chapter concludes by discussing the wide array of social, economic, and physical determinants of health and illustrating that American society especially has been deceived into believing that medicine can provide health.

MEDICAL NEMESIS: AN EXTREME VIEW OF MEDICINE AND HEALTH

For Ivan Illich, health is "simply an every day word" used to designate the intensity with which individuals are able to cope with their internal states and their environmental conditions (1976:14). Health levels are at their optimum when the environment brings out autonomous personal, responsible coping ability. Health levels are reduced when survival depends on outside control of the individuals. A healthy society, then, is one of minimal and only occasional medical intervention. "Healthy people are those who live in healthy homes on a healthy diet in an environment equally fit for birth, growth, work, healing, and dying; they are sustained by a culture that enhances the conscious acceptance of limits to population, of aging, of incomplete recovery and ever-imminent death" (1976:275). Beyond a certain level of intensity institutional health care no matter what form it takes is "equivalent to systematic health denial." In his attack on modern medicine Illich argues that it is imposing increasing and irreparable damage through iatrogenesis.

> Iatrogenesis is clinical when pain, sickness, and death result from medical care; it is social when health policies reinforce an industrial organization that generates ill-health; it is cultural and symbolic when medically sponsored behavior and delusions restrict the vital autonomy of people by undermining their competence in growing up, caring for each other, and ageing, or when medical intervention cripples personal responses to pain, disability, impairment, anguish, and death. *(1976:271)*.

Contrary to contemporary wisdom, according to Illich, medical services have not been important in producing the changes in life-expectancy. The vast amount of medicine is incidental to curing disease. The effectiveness of physicians is an illusion; epidemics come and go and are not modified any more by medical rituals than religious ones. Not only is there no evidence that the improvement in health status can be attributed to medical science but the damage done by medicine to the health of individuals and populations is enormous (476:23). The general state of health of any population is determined primarily by environmental factors including food, water, air, housing and by cultural mechanisms that make it possible to keep the population stable. In contrast to environmental improvements and nonprofessional health measures such as water treatment and antibacterial procedures, the "specifically medical treatment of people is never significantly related to a decline in the compound disease burden or to a rise in life expectancy" (1976:29). Although "awe-inspiring medical technology has combined with egalitarian rhetoric to create the impression that contemporary medicine is highly effective," only a limited number of procedures have become extremely useful and these are with few exceptions very inexpensive and nontechnical. "In contrast, most of today's skyrocketing medical expenditures are destined for the kind of diagnosis and treatment whose effectiveness at best is doubtful" (1976:30).

In addition to its questionable effectiveness and the clinical iatrogenesis that medicine causes, the medicalization of life itself is a social iatrogenesis. Medical bureaucracies create ill health by increasing stress, multiplying disabling dependence, generating new painful needs, lowering levels of tolerance for discomfort or pain, reducing the leeway given a person when he suffers, and abolishing the right of self-care. For Illich: "Social iatrogenesis is at work when health care is turned into a standardized item, a staple; when all suffering is 'hospitalized' and homes become inhospitable to both, sickness, and death; . . . or when suffering, mourning, and healing outside the patient role are labelled a form of deviance" (1976:49).

Although each culture has its own characteristic perception of disease, medicine breeds new categories of patients and creates illness as a social state. It has the authority to label who is sick and who is not and creates a new group of outsiders with each new diagnosis. Social labeling becomes medicalized to the point where all deviance has to have a medical label thus creating evermore distinct categories of demand, supply, and unmet needs. The result is that people come to believe that they cannot cope with their condition unless they see the doctor, a belief that is fostered by the medical system which has become a principle mechanism of social control and economic activity.

For Illich, cultural iatrogenesis sets in when medicine undermines the ability of individuals to face their reality, express their own values, and "accept inevitable and often irremediable pain, impairment, decline and death" (1976:133). To be in good health means not only to cope with reality but also to enjoy it. It means to be able to feel alive in pleasure and in pain and to cherish but risk survival. Both health and suffering are phenomena that distinguish humans from other animals. The most insidious product of medicine, therefore, is the weakening of an individual's capacity to cope, to heal themselves when ill, and to alter their environment. It undermines traditional cultural ways of consoling, caring, and comforting people while they heal and the tolerance extended to the afflicted by denying each person's need to deal with pain, sickness, and death. Instead, medicine is organized to kill pain, eliminate sickness, and abolish the need for an art of suffering and dying. As a result people are deprived of their traditional notions of what constitutes health or death. The medicalization of society has brought the epoch of natural death to an end by substituting mechanical death for all other notions of death. As a result, "Western man has lost the right to preside at his act of dying" (1976:210).

> Suffering, healing, and dying, which are essentially intransitive activities the culture taught each man, are now claimed by technocracy as new areas of policymaking and are treated as malfunctions from which populations ought to be institutionally relieved. The goals of metropolitan medical civilization are thus in opposition to every single cultural health programme they encounter in the process of progressive colonization.
>
> *(Illich 1976:138)*

Although I believe Illich's criticisms of medicine are unduly harsh, especially in that they see the causal direction of harm from medicine to society, he raises many legitimate questions and forces us to place medicine in a social context. Like Kennedy (1981), Mechanic (1993) and many others, Illich concludes that major improvements in health derive from changes in the way in which people are able to live. This suggests the need to replace the medical model with one based in subjective reality. Illich also argues that control over the production side of the medical complex can only work toward better health if it leads to a "very sizable reduction of its total output" rather than to simple technical improvements in the medical arsenal (1976:239).

Too much medicine is not good for health. Not only does it divert resources from more useful endeavors, but it also produces ill health and disrupts traditional social and cultural institutions and values that are central to good health in the broader sense. Finally, Illich concludes that because inherited myths have ceased to provide limits for action, politically established constraints to industrial growth are essential in order to cope with the "materialization of greedy, envious, murderous dreams" (1976:264). Again, although Illich's rhetoric is too strong, I agree that government action is necessary to restrain our unrealistic dependence on the medical model and that maximization of personal responsibility needs to be a central goal.

DEFINING HEALTH: A BALANCE

The first question flowing from critiques such as Illich's is what is meant by the term "health." The medical model is primarily founded on defining health as the absence of disease or illness. A person is healthy under this definition if he or she is not suffering from an illness or disease. The goal of curative medicine is largely to diagnose the illness and restore the health of the patient, who is by definition unhealthy. Inherent in medicine has been the expansion of categories of disease to attribute for a broader range of conditions deemed unhealthy. Such labeling of a condition as a disease has tended to ingrain in medicine the notion that disease is the enemy (Seedhouse 1991:43).

Another definition of health is the coping theory where health is essentially an ability to adapt to the problems life gives us. Under this definition individuals can be healthy even if they are diseased or ill so long as they have the personal strength and resilience to cope with life. The tension with the not-ill theory is manifested in Illich's concern that the latter interferes with individuals' ability to cope with their internal states and environment. Under this definition a person without disease or illness is still unhealthy if they are unable to cope.

The third definition of health, that of the World Health Organization (WHO), defines it as "a state of complete physical, mental and social well-being and not merely the absence of disease or infirmity" (1947). According to Drummond (1993) this definition could also include a dignified death as a dimension of health. This ambitious ideal has been widely criticized because if taken literally it means that individuals are unhealthy if they are unhappy with their lot in life or even just unfulfilled. Moreover, in contrast with the coping theory, individuals with any defined disease, illness, or disability cannot be healthy. Although this definition is so broad as to make it meaningless, this is unfortunate because it does incorporate the need to expand the definition of health beyond the situation where a person has a medically defined illness or disease. To the extent it does broaden ill health beyond the notion of biological dysfunction, the WHO definition is useful despite its operational problems.

One problem with all of these definitions is their failure to explicitly bring in the social and cultural dimensions of health and ill health. Health has both a personal and a public dimension. Although pain and suffering, and disappointment and regret under the WHO definition, are personal, their effect on the lives of others might be severe. Moreover, health and illness are social constructs and culturally influenced. For Callahan (1990:103), illness itself is as much social as individual in its characteristics since tolerability will depend on the kind of care and support provided by others and by the social meaning of the disease. Good health, therefore, requires social networks and systems which in the least are obscured by these definitions of health. According to Lagasse et al.

> Disease has to be considered in a cultural context . . . We define "healthy culture" as a set of rules — either implicit or explicit — which determine the behavior of social subjects in relation to their health. Those rules may be obligations or interdictions, repulsions or desires, likes or dislikes. They may be determinants for the body's use or the body's perceptual status, the distribution of the roles inside the family concerning health and disease, the choice of alternative ways to solve health problems . . . the definition of the limits between normal and abnormal situations in the somatic, psychological, psychosocial, familial or other domains   (1990:238).

Even within particular social systems health can be a very relative term. Seedhouse (1991:40), for instance, sees disease and health akin to the analogy of weeds and flowers. As with plants, what counts as undesirable in one case might be wanted in another. Pneumonia in an otherwise active 20 year old is undesirable and it is appropriate to say she is suffering from a disease. In contrast, pneumonia in a 90 year old victim of a severe stroke might be welcomed as offering an easier death. Although in clinical terms pneumonia in both cases is termed a disease, the ambiguity of the disease label requires clarification of the specific context. Moreover, in an era of increased genetic testing for susceptibilities and traits, the definitions of health and disease require even more clarification (see Nelkin and Tancredi 1989).

Increasingly, it is evident that health must encompass not only the physical and mental aspects of personal well-being but also the social (Babcock and Belotti 1994:209). Adverse conditions in any one of the dimensions can affect the other two. Although there are many models that incorporate this broader view of health (see Evans and Stoddart 1990), I have chosen here to use a model derived from the indigenous people of New Zealand, the Maori. Like many of the more highly integrated Eastern world views, the Maori refuse to segment the world into discrete parts. The Maori health perspective reflects this world view and has been described through the health construct known as the four-sided house (whare tapa wha) by Durie (1994:69). This model compares health to the four walls of a house, each representing a different dimension but all of which are necessary to ensure strength and symmetry. The four dimensions include the spiritual, the mental, the physical, and the extended family (see table 3.1). Critical to the model is the notion of balance among the four dimensions.

For Maori, the most essential requirement for health is the spiritual which implies a capacity to have faith and the capacity to understand the links between the human condition and the environment. Without a spiritual awareness and a mauri (a spirit or vitality, sometimes called a life-force), an individual cannot be healthy and is more prone to illness. The spiritual dimension might involve religious beliefs and practices and might involve a belief in a god, but it is most clearly manifested in relationships with the environment. Interestingly, while the spiritual dimension of health is not apparent in modern medicine it is an integral part of twelve-step programs and some alternative medicine.

TABLE 3.1
The Maori Model of Health

	Taha Wairua	Taha Hinengaro	Taha Tinana	Taha Whanau
Focus	Spiritual	Mental	Physical	Extended family
Key aspects	A capacity for faith and wider communion	A capacity to communicate, to think, and to feel	A capacity for physical growth and development	A capacity to belong, to care, and to share
Themes	Health is related to unseen and unspoken energies	Mind and body inseparable	Good physical health is necessary for optimal development	Individuals are part of wider social systems

SOURCE: Durie 1994:70.

The second dimension is about the expression of thoughts and feelings which in Maori nomenclature derive from the same source within the individual and are vital to health. Health is viewed as an interrelated phenomenon rather than an intra-personal one. Poor health is regarded as a breakdown of harmony between the individual and the wider environment. Also, while Western cultures distinguish between the spoken word and emotions, communication for Maori depends on more than overt messages. Emotional communication is often conveyed through subtle gestures, eye movement or bland expression and can assume an importance as meaningful and valued as an exchange of words. The mind and the body thus become inseparable. This dimension of health goes beyond the Western view of mental health as the absence of mental illness and instead merges with physical health which is complementary. This dimension is implicit in the coping definition but not in the not-ill definition of health.

The third dimension of the Maori model of health is the central relevance of the extended family or social structure to health. This dimension addresses Callahan's (1990) contention that health is social in characteristic and must be defined in that setting. For Maori the family is the prime support system, not only providing physical care but also emotional and cultural. "Maori still maintain that ill health in an individual is a reflection on the family and may well blame a family for allowing a person to become ill or to die, even when there is no direct casual link" (Durie 1994:73). In cases of child neglect or abuse, for instance, the extended family may remove the child from the parents and take over the custodial role. Moreover, a failure to turn to the family when warranted is regarded as immaturity not strength, because the problem is perceived as beyond the individual and social in nature. Interdependence not independence is the healthier goal.

This dimension addresses findings of studies that have demonstrated the importance of kinship structure for good health status. Mechanic (1994:122) for example argues that Mormons and other groups with good health indices share a strong kinship structure that emphasizes the importance of the family, parenthood, and family relationships. Mormons have good health not simply because they value health and abstain from smoking and drinking, but also because of the presence of a "well-knit group structure that demands a person's loyalty and commitment" (1994:123).

Although acknowledging physical health as a critical dimension (one of the four walls), the Maori model of health requires a relative deemphasis of the dominance of the physical aspects of health and the pre-occupation with biological constructs so central to American health care. Underlying this model is the consistent theme of integration of the four dimensions of health. Individual health is a natural part of the wider system, and the artificial boundary between personal and family identity is rejected. Similarly, the divisions between temporal and spiritual, thoughts and feelings, and mental and physical are no longer acceptable. Good health, therefore, cannot be gauged solely by medically bound measures such as blood pressure, cholesterol levels, or the absence of physical disease. Spiritual, emotional, and sexual factors are equally important. This model would seem to reflect the concern of contemporary critics of American medicine, for instance, "We have no lasting hope of devising a decent understanding of health—and thus of fashioning a viable health care system—unless we learn better how to attend to the social dimension of health, indeed unless we learn how to shift our priorities sharply in a societal direction" (Callahan 1990:105).

Putting health into this broader context also raises the question of why we value health in the narrow sense—freedom from disease—so highly in the United States. Although health, of course, should be highly valued since it is central to the completion of one's plan of life, health is better viewed as a means to broader goals and purposes in life. "Good health is not a substitute for a good life, and good health does not guarantee a good life. A good life, individually or societally, can be had without perfect health" (Callahan 1990:114). We seek good health to avoid pain and suffering and at times death and to provide us the opportunity to pursue other life goals. Good health in itself, however, cannot guarantee achievement of our goals, give us a reason to live, or maximize our potential to the highest order. Unfortunately, it is easier to medicalize social problems than to address the core causes of ill health when we have elevated curing ill health as the major social good (Churchill 1994:28). Good health in the physical sense absent the other three dimensions of health is unlikely to assure contentment.

Health, therefore, must be put into perspective along with a wide array of elements of an enjoyable life including art, entertainment, music, work, as well as family and social interaction. To place health above everything else risks underestimating the contribution of these many other factors to the fulfillment of our goals and the enhancement of the human condition. According to Lamm (1993:17) we cannot live by health alone, but must invest in education, infrastructure, and other essential components. Fitzgerald decries the confusion of the ideal of health with the norm for health where "We now act as if we really believe that disease, aging and death are unnatural acts and all things are remediable. All we have to do, we think, is know enough (or spend enough), and disease and death can be prevented or fixed" (1994:197). She sees this leading to a tyranny of health where if ideal health is normal then lack of it must be wrong.

Although health is important it is not all important. It makes little sense to invest disproportionate amounts of societal resources into health at the sacrifice of those things which make life worth living. It is illuminating that at the personal level we are willing to expend significant resources on activities that give us pleasure some of which entail significant health risk, while at the societal level we have refused to muzzle our expenditures on health care. It appears that while we accept the notion that health is but one aspect of well-being at the personal level, as a society we expect medical care to resolve all manner of problems. "In the end we all will die; the question is which allocation of resources will allow the best living of life" (Elhauge 1994:1461).

Medicine and Health Status

The emphasis on medical care in the United States is flawed because it tends to focus on only one dimension of health and because it elevates health as a primary goal instead of a means to broader life goals. Implicit in the conventional health care model is the assumption that improved health status is achieved primarily by higher and higher levels and expenditures on medical care, i.e., we are healthy because we pursue health care without limits. Such thinking, however, conflicts with a preponderance of evidence that shows that it is but another illusion of U.S. health care.

Although the health status of individuals is influenced by medical care and it has the potential to improve quality of life for some persons particularly through relief of pain and suffering, there is little correlation between how much money we spend on doctors and hospitals and how healthy we are as a society. Any relationship between medical care and health, even in its narrow physical sense, is minimal compared to other determinants of health status such as heredity, personal behavior, and the physical and social environment. Health status is more closely correlated with many nonmedical factors including adequate water and sanitation, good nutrition, decent housing and socioeconomic factors (McKeown 1979).

The impact of medical care is further limited because many health conditions are self-limiting, some are incurable, and for many others there is little or no effective treatment. The cases where health care is effective and significantly affects health outcomes "comprise only a small proportion of total medical care—too small to make a discernible impact on the statistics in populations" (Fuchs 1994:109). For Frum, "the tragedies counted among America's most horrific health problems—from premature underweight babies to AIDS-infected drug addicts to the twelve-year-old gunshot victims . . . are not really health problems any more than the plight of the homeless is a housing problem" (1995:33). Nor are the solutions to the underlying causes medical ones.

Figure 3.1 casts doubt on the assumption that more spending on health care is the answer. It shows that the almost exponential increases in the United States over the last decades have not been accompanied by corresponding decreases in mortality rates. Although gross mortality rates are not the optimum measure of health status, the vast discrepancies here raise critical concerns. (More in-

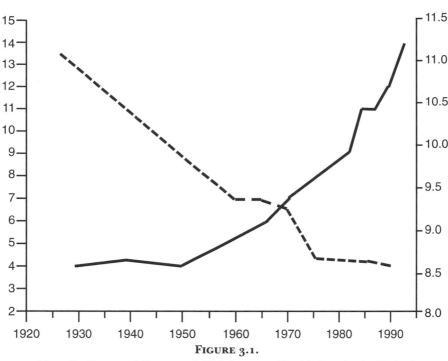

FIGURE 3.1.
Mortality Rates and Percent of GDP Spent on Health Care in the United
States, 1900–1987
—— Health spending as a percentage of GDP (left scale).
- - - Crude mortality rate/1000 population (right scale)
SOURCES: OECD 1989, 1990; LUNDBERG 1992:2522; FRIES ET AL. 1993:321.

depth comparative nation analysis, discussed in chapter 6, reinforces
this.) Expending additional resources on medical care is likely not to
pay dividends in terms of health status.

Moreover, where health gains have presumably been the result of
medical care, data indicates that medical technology has in fact not
played a major role. For instance, it has been estimated that at least
two-thirds of the reduction in mortality rates during the 1970s and 98
percent of the modest mortality rate improvement in the 1980s was
tied to the reduction in death from cardiovascular disease (Drake
1994:133). Under the medical model the reduction in deaths from
cardiovascular disease is assumed to be the result of impressive innovations in treatment, especially coronary by-pass surgery and angio-
plasty. However, evidence suggests that most if not all of this drop is

attributable to lifestyle changes reflected in the decline in smoking, increase in exercise, and decreases in saturated fat consumption. "Only a small part, if any, can be attributed to medical technology" (Cundiff and McCarthy 1994:18). Similarly, while Bunker et al. argue that medical care improves health, they admit that it is difficult to determine its achievements as opposed to benefits emerging from social changes. They conclude that "current data provide no evidence that medical care has reduced mortality when all cancers are added together" (1994:233).

These findings regarding the inadequacy of explaining health status by medical care have significant implications for any efforts to restructure the health care system. If we really want to achieve the goal of maximizing the health of the population, resources would better be directed toward alleviating poverty, reducing crime, changing lifestyles, and so forth. A healthy person does not need medical care. "Good health often does not require access to medical care and is largely dependent on the condition of society" (Hurowitz 1993:130). Although the medical care system can be useful in the management of certain diseases, "people don't get sick because they lack medical care" (David 1993:31).

On these grounds, recent efforts to reform the U.S. health care system are misguided because no amount of restructuring health care along the lines proposed by the reformers will have a major impact on the health of the U.S. community. Reforms for universal access, improved quality of care, and cost containment might improve the medical care system, but they cannot be expected to improve substantially the health of the population. According to Fuchs, "there is little evidence either in this country or abroad to suggest that providing universal coverage or changing the delivery system will have significant favorable effects on health, either in the aggregate or for particular socio-economic groups" (1994:109).

Therefore, reform or restructuring the health care system in itself at best will have a minor impact on health status. Even though we have been conditioned to instinctively look to the medical system to provide higher levels of health, the facts show otherwise. It is illusory that there is an effective medical response to what are in reality social problems and that alterations in the health care system will provide the means to do so. The remainder of this chapter looks at evidence as to what factors influence health and what implications this has for U.S. health policy.

Social Determinants of Health

There is substantial evidence that health status is highly correlated with socioeconomic status. If a primary goal of health policy is to improve the health status of the population it is essential to focus on economic and social determinants of health. The interactive model of health requires a shift away from the dominance of the medical care system toward this more inclusive model of health. "Social problems are resolved primarily through non-medical means, signifying a shift away from the current practice of defining and treating them as medical illnesses" (Hurowitz 1993:132).

Although Evans (1994:4) suggests that "thoughtful clinicians, past and present" know that health of the population is related less to health care than the factors examined here, the American public and its policymakers as well as the health care community have been unwilling to face the consequences that such data imply. Although there is a wide variation in health status across nations, there is often an even wider variation between groups within particular nations which cannot be explained by differences in health systems. Lower social class, as measured by income, education, or other SES indicators, is related with higher death rates overall and higher rates of most diseases that are the common causes of death. Moreover, social class differences in mortality and morbidity are widening (Nuthall 1992:15). For instance, Pappas and associates (1993) found a strong inverse relationship between social class and mortality. "Despite an overall decline in death rates in the United States since 1960, poor and poorly educated people still die at higher rate than those with higher incomes or better education, *and this disparity increased between 1960 and 1986*" (Pappas et al. 1993:103; emphasis added).

Health status disparities linked to SES are most likely the result of a complicated mix of factors suggested by three distinct theories. The first, natural and social selection, contends that one of the key determinants of social class is health status. This theory assumes that those persons with poor health, high-risk behavior, and social pathologies are concentrated in the lower social class. If good health is indeed necessary in order to pursue life goals and affords one the opportunity to succeed in meeting them, it should not be surprising to find that persons in poor health would tend to attain lower SES. Although this might explain the disparity at the margins, however, it is not generally seen as a major explanation.

A second theory, the structuralist, attributes class differences in health to structural factors such as the production and consumption of wealth. Lower SES persons generally live in less healthy environments, both at home and work. In contrast higher SES persons enjoy healthier homes, safer appliances and automobiles, and less hazardous jobs. Moreover, in the United States the working poor have inadequate or no health insurance and less access to the health care system. Whitehead (1987:304) concludes that general living conditions and the environment of the poor are important determinants of health status.

The third theory, a cultural and behavioral one, sees disparities in health among social classes as the result of differences in behavior. Often the culture of the lower classes leads to engagement in many high-risk behaviors that in turn, lead to poor health. Smoking, alcohol and drug abuse, violence, sedentary life styles, poor diet, and other unhealthy behaviors are disproportionately present in lower SES groupings. Many observers have concluded that this last theory is most explanatory, but most conclude that it must be accompanied by the structuralist theory because the behavior occurs within this broader social context. Mechanic concludes that SES is "perhaps the single most important influence on health outcomes, in part through its direct influence, but more importantly, through the many indirect effects it has on factors that directly shape health outcomes" (1994:149). These indirect factors are most apparent when one examines the several components of SES:income; education, and race.

Income

Income has been found to be a critical variable in determining health status at two levels. At the national level research consistently shows that the distribution of income has more to do with the health of the population than does the medical care system. The best health results are achieved in those societies that minimize the gap between the rich and the poor (Kassler 1994:174). Wilkinson (1992) found that approximately two-thirds of the variation in mortality rates in developed nations is related to the distribution of income in the population. This includes the United Kingdom where, despite universal access to health care, mortality rates among the working class population has increased as the income distribution widened in the 1980s

(Wilkinson 1992:167). In contrast, Japan has the most equal income distribution and the highest life expectancy.

At the individual level as well low income is consistently related to ill health, although it is not clear how it operates to produce this result. Low income families are more likely to assess their health status as poor (Rice 1991). In 1991, 7 percent of Americans with incomes below $10,000 reported themselves to be in poor health as compared to less than 1 percent of those with incomes over $30,000 (Angell 1993:126). Figure 3.2 demonstrates that this subjective perception of poor health is supported by objective measures. Low income adults are significantly more likely to have preventable hospitalizations than high income adults. Data for poor children are comparable to that of adults. Another study found that the group with the lowest income was four times as likely to be hospitalized as the highest-income group (see Angell 1993:126).

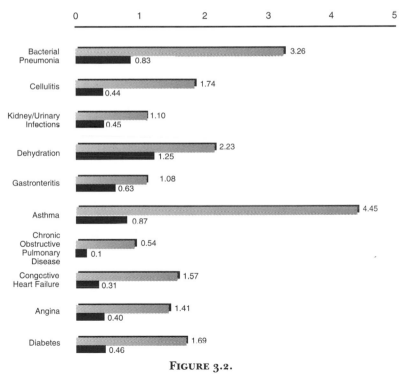

FIGURE 3.2.
Preventable Hospitalizations, Per 1000 Adults Under Age 65, 1989
SOURCE: CHER 1993.

Explanation of these disparities is most likely found in some combination of the theories discussed above, but its implication for health is significant. The impact of any efforts to constrain health care costs will be most severe on the groups who are not only most likely to need the care but also least likely to have other options. It has been apparent for decades that emergency and episodic treatment characterizing so much of the care of disadvantaged groups is extraordinarily wasteful, because continuity in care is important in dealing with their complex sociomedical problems (Mechanic 1994:21). The data in table 3.2 indicate that despite greater need, larger proportions of the poor have difficulty in gaining access to health services that might avert poor health.

Education

Not surprisingly given its close association with income, education is significantly related with health status: "For all the measures of health status included in this report, low levels of education were highly associated with poor health and relatively higher levels of education were associated with good to excellent health" (National Center of Health Statistics 1991:2).

Persons with less education have more frequent short-stay hospitalizations, they have a higher prevalence of chronic conditions and are significantly more limited in activity due to such conditions, and they have significantly lower self-assessments of their health. One study found that of all indicators, education had the strongest and

TABLE 3.2
Access to Health Care Services, Percent by Income Grouping

	Poor	Near Poor	Nonpoor
Unintended births	59%	43%	32%
Problem obtaining prenatal care	19.9%	17.2%	6.6%
Women >50 who obtained mammogram in past year	22%	30%	46%
Children aged 5–7 with dental visit in last year	52.9%	61.7%	83.3%
Adults aged 18–64 with dental visit in past year	41.4%	47.1%	70.8%

SOURCE: Center for Health Economics Research 1993.

most consistent relationship with health and was the single most consistent predictor of good health (Winkleby et al. 1992). Mechanic, too, concluded that education is the "single most important predictor across a broad range of health outcome measures" (1994:123). In part he attributes this to the fact that persons with more education seek out information about health more aggressively and understand and retain it.

Race

Although it is often postulated that race differences might have an independent effect on health status, most studies have found that it is likely indirect and the result of other socioeconomic indicators, particularly education. Pappas et al. conclude that while race has often been understood as a proxy for social class, the gap between black and white health status is affected significantly by low income and poor education (1993:107). Several recent studies have found that education is more strongly associated with mortality from coronary disease and life expectancy than race (Kcil et al. 1993, Guralnik et al. 1993). Haan and Kaplan (1985) found that when adjusted for income, marital status, and household size, the differences in mortality according to race were eliminated. Except for a few conditions, such as hypertension, that affect blacks disproportionately, the poorer health of black Americans probably reflects other correlates of lower SES rather than race itself (Angell 1993:126). Whatever the core reasons, however, table 3.3 illustrates the significant variation in selected health outcomes by race.

TABLE 3.3
Health Indicators, by Race

	White	Black	Hispanic
Low birthweight/1000 live births			
> 18	56.3	127.6	58.4
< 18	83.3	138.3	80.1
Neonatal deaths/1000 births	4.8	11.6	5.8
Postneonatal deaths/1000 live births	2.8	5.8	—
Life expectancy (at birth)			
Male	72.7	64.5	—
Female	79.4	73.6	—

Indirect Influences

Health status then is intimately related to various measures of SES, particularly education and income. These differences are critical in understanding the social and cultural context of health and require considerably more research on how these factors operate. The interactive model of health care attributes poor health outcomes to a broad range of social factors which are bound up in the SES construct. Although SES might have a direct impact on health, it is more likely that it operates indirectly through other factors. In addition to inequitable access to primary care, health promotion and disease prevention efforts, other critical factors include unemployment, violence, breakdown of family support structures, and inadequate housing. Although no attempt is made here to detail the contribution of these factors to poor health, the evidence is reviewed.

Unemployment can influence health by reducing income level and standard of living. Moreover, the importance of work to one's well-being over and above the financial aspects is well documented. The unemployed have less self-esteem and experience significant psychological stress which is linked to higher levels of both subjective and objective assessed levels of physical and mental ill-health. Unemployed men have a significantly higher mortality rate than the male population as a whole. Suicide and deliberate self-harm are more prevalent among the unemployed as are smoking and alcohol and drug abuse, particularly among the unemployable youth. At the community level, death rates have been found to increase during times of economic depression and joblessness and decrease during times of economic growth (Barwick 1992). Although the full dynamics are unclear, the assumption that employment is crucial to both mental and physical health is supported by a broad array of studies. Reduction of unemployment has significant health benefits for the population as well as the individual.

The family has traditionally played an important role in integrating health promoting routines into the daily lives of the members. It has also served as an important facilitator of self-esteem and a social setting that provides critical contributions to psychological and physical development. While reality has often fallen short of this ideal, the decline first of the extended family and more recently the nuclear family has had adverse effects on health. Studies consistently find that marriage is associated with lower levels of mortality, better overall health status and healthier behavior patterns. Moreover, data demonstrate that children in single parent families are at greater health risk than other children, although here again the impact of economic factors is probably instrumental in explaining much of the variation. Family relationships, however, in whatever form do appear to encourage good health practices and provide strong social links that reduce the likelihood of ill health.

Violence and Health

In 1994, there were 38,317 firearm-related fatalities in the United States making it the second most frequent cause of death for persons aged 15–34. Individuals armed with firearms committed a record 930,700 violent crimes in 1992, 50 percent more than the average for the previous five years (Cundiff and McCarthy 1994:165). Based on recent trends it is projected that firearms will become the leading cause of injury deaths for the entire U.S. population within the next decade (CDCP 1994). Moreover, for every fatality it is estimated that there are seven non-fatal injuries that require hospitalization or outpatient treatment. The cost of health care and lost production from firearm related injuries is put in excess of $20 billion per year. One study found that the mean hospital charges per admission of such injuries was $52,271 compared to overall mean hospital charges per admission of $13,974. Twelve percent of the patients had charges in excess of $100,000 (Kizer et al. 1995:1771). Because the population with firearms related injuries tends to be disproportionately poor, a large proportion of the costs is borne by the public. Moreover, such injuries are skewed by race with blacks over-represented by 3.6 times their proportion in the population. Reduction of firearm related injuries, however, is difficult in an environment where the number of firearms is proliferating.

Firearm related injuries are just one evidence of the health impact of violence. Incidence of reported family-related violence continues to rise in the forms of child abuse, spousal abuse, and elder abuse. The Institute of Medicine (1993:133) concludes that battering is a major factor in illness and injury among women, although it often is overlooked by medical professionals. Studies show that between 17 and 25 percent of all emergency department visits involve battered women, but again emergency care providers typically identify less than 5 percent of all women with injuries or illness suggestive of abuse (McLeer and Anwar 1989). The actual health impact is likely significantly higher than the health care costs because battered women often do not receive care because their access to the health care system is often controlled and blocked by their abusers. In addition to this structural barrier, financial and cultural barriers to health care deny battered women, children and elders access to needed care and, thus, a full accounting of the problem (Institute of Medicine 1993:134).

Homelessness and Inadequate Housing

Another factor which is virtually ignored by the medical model but which takes on significance in the more inclusive social model is housing. Lack of housing obviously puts people, particularly children, at serious health risk. While the homeless suffer from the same acute and chronic illnesses as those in the general population, they do so at a much higher rate (Brickner et al. 1990). "Because the homeless have little or no access to adequate bathing and hygienic facilities, survive on the streets or in unsafe and generally unsanitary shelters, smoke and drink to excess, and suffer from inadequate diets, their physical health is compromised (Institute of Medicine 1993:210).

As a result upper respiratory tract infections, trauma and skin ailments are commonplace. A major study of homeless patients found that 37 percent of returning patients had at least one chronic condition, and overall the homeless had rates of tuberculosis and AIDS significantly higher than the general population (Wright and Weber 1987). They estimated that 38 percent of these patients abused alcohol, 13 percent drugs, and 37 percent were mentally ill. Again, the direction of cause and effect between ill health and homelessness is unclear, but the long-term health effects on the homeless are not in question.

Although the health impact of a lack of housing is most severe, poor or inadequate housing can also lead to poor health. Overcrowded living conditions are linked with a wide array of physical and mental health problems. Substandard housing is related to house fires and increased accidents. Furthermore, damp and cold living conditions are associated with respiratory ailments, while improperly ventilated housing is linked to heat-related health problems. In combination with overall poverty, unemployment, poor education, and violence and crime, inadequate housing remains a health hazard for many citizens. These factors share in common their isolation from the medical model. Although medical care is beneficial for many individuals affected by these health-threatening factors, "medical care cannot compensate for economic deprivation, social disorganization, personal alienation, and low levels of education and social integration" (Mechanic 1994:3). In the end solutions to these problems lie fully outside the medical community. Unfortunately, as argued by Kassler (1994:166) health care reformers have focused so much on medical care that they have ignored those factors that ultimately make the biggest difference in people's health.

ENVIRONMENTAL CHANGE AND HEALTH

Global environmental change is ultimately a matter of health, however, the health effects of environmental change have received little attention in the United States. Training and research on environmental health issues is a low priority. In the last decade, for instance, the National Institute of Environmental Health Sciences has ranked last in funding of the 23 institutes in the National Institutes of Health. Medical students in the United States on average receive only six hours of education on environmental and occupational health over their four years of medical school and virtually no exposure to the impact of global issues such as population growth, climate change, and ozone depletion on human health (Chivian 1994:36). For all practical purposes, then, neither the American public nor the medical profession places health within a global environment perspective despite increasing evidence of substantial health effects.

For instance, global climate change resulting from the accumulation of greenhouse gases is likely to have a significant impact on the health of the population. Recent heat waves are viewed as anomalies, but if global warming trends are accurate the increase in the number of days with temperatures over 100° F will produce a sharp rise in heat-related mortality from heat strokes, heart attacks, and cerebral strokes especially among the very young and the elderly and those persons with chronic respiratory diseases. Moreover, the Environmental Protection Agency has warned that global warming and changing patterns of rainfall could result in the spread of infectious diseases as insects carrying the agents move to areas that until now were too cold for their survival. Although the full health impact of global climate change and yet unanticipated outcomes is unlikely in the near future, evidence suggests that commitment is now needed to avert these threats and prevent major health problems (Haines 1993).

Similarly, depletion of the ozone layer poses severe health risks that appear to be emerging already. Higher levels of ultraviolet B radiation (UVB) reaching the earth's surface can damage DNA and proteins and kill cells in all living organisms. There is solid evidence that heightened exposure of humans to UVB leads to an increase in all forms of skin cancer. The incidence of malignant melanomas, with mortality rates of 25 percent, increased in the United States by 83 percent between 1982 and 1989, faster than any other cancer (Leaf 1993). One out of six Americans will be diagnosed with skin cancer during their lifetime producing 700,000 new cases and 9,000 deaths per year. Cataracts represent an even wider health effect of UVB radiation. Already about 1.25 million cataract surgeries are performed annually in the United States at a cost of billions of dollars and cataracts are the third leading cause of preventable blindness. Because UVB exposure can be reduced by 90 percent through a combination of the use of plastic-lensed glasses and a hat, this is one area where health promotion could avert considerable health problems and costs with only minor changes in behavior.

There is also evidence the UVB exposure impairs the cellular immune system which normally recognizes a cancer or a parasitic cell and mounts an immune response to destroy it. Heightened exposure to UVB therefore will not only increase the risk of skin cancer initiation, but also reduce the capacity of a cellular immune response to stop or slow its proliferation. Likewise, the impaired immune response of individuals exposed to infections will heighten the incidence of infections in the population and make them more lethal (Leaf 1993:148).

In addition to the health threats of long-term environmental changes, more immediate and localized conditions can have considerable adverse health consequences for exposed populations. Despite efforts at reducing their impact, air and water pollution levels remain high in many locales and continue to put large numbers of persons at risk. Respiratory problems in urban areas caused or aggravated by air pollution are also likely to be exacerbated by global warming and population concentration (Christiani 1993). Drinking water systems are not only threatened by industrial and waste disposal contamination, but also by the methods used for disinfecting them due to the toxic effects of the disinfectants and their by-products (Hu and Kim 1993:46). The imminent breakdown of old and deteriorating water and sewage systems in some of the larger urban centers represents a growing health concern that requires urgent attention. Unfortunately, infrastructure funding in the United States has decreased as medical care consumes larger shares of state and local budgets.

OCCUPATIONAL DISEASE

Occupational disease encompasses a broad range of human illness. Estimates suggest that as many as 100,000 deaths and 390,000 new cases of work-related disease are identified annually (Baker and Landrigan 1993:73). In addition to direct hazards in the workplace, toxic hazards may be released into the environment or transported to the home on clothing of contaminated workers. Still, the full magnitude of occupational disease is obscured because many such diseases are misdiagnosed or incorrectly attributed to other causes. The long latency period between exposure and onset of symptoms also helps mask occupational diseases. For instance, the latency period for asbestos-related lung cancer can be 25 years or more (Baker and Landrigan 1993:72). While as many as 9 million workers are currently exposed to known or suspected carcinogens, there are no overall estimates of the size of the population with past exposure and thus still at risk to suffer health consequences.

These data demonstrate an urgent need to fund extensive research on occupational disease if our goal is to maximize the health of the population. Health promotion in the workplace, likewise, should be expanded in order to reduce the health risks and educate workers concerning early signs of those illnesses which may be linked to their jobs so that early treatment is possible. Occupation illness represents an area where preventive programs and anticipatory health policy are warranted. While workplaces will never be risk-free, the more we know about possible hazards in each workplace setting the better we are placed to minimize their impact.

What follows is a list of ten leading work-related diseases and injuries, as defined by the National Institute on Occupational Health and Safety

1. Occupational lung diseases: asbestosis, byssinosis, silicosis, coal workers' pneumoconiosis, lung cancer, occupational asthma
2. Musculoskeletal injuries: disorders of the back, trunk, upper extremity, neck, lower extremity; traumatically induced Raynaud's phenomenon
3. Occupational cancers (other than lung): leukemia; mesothelioma; cancers of the bladder, nose, and liver
4. Severe occupation traumatic injuries: amputation, fracture, eye loss, laceration and traumatic death
5. Occupational cardiovascular diseases: hypertension, coronary artery disease, acute myocardial infarction
6. Disorders of reproduction: infertility, spontaneous abortion, teratogenesis
7. Neurotoxic disorders: peripheral neuropathy, toxic encephalitis, psychoses, extreme personality changes (exposure-related)
8. Noise-induced loss of hearing
9. Dermatologic conditions: dermatoses, burns (scaldings), chemical burns, contusions (abrasions)
10. Psychological disorders: neuroses, personality disorders, alcoholism, drug dependency

SOURCE: Baker and Landrigan 1993:74.

We as a society need to pay much closer attention to the social determinants of health if we are serious about improving the health of the population. Unfortunately, many indicators demonstrate that in this broader sense the health of the population might be in a state of decline. Workplace shootings, domestic violence, child abuse, and the breakdown of families and other social structures both reflect and contribute to poor health. Ill health is also manifested by the increasing prevalence of stress-related dysfunction, job-related illness, and mental illness and addictive behaviors, which in turn are linked to the feelings of powerlessness, frustration, and isolation that appear to accompany modern human life. In the Maori model many of these patterns might be identified as a failure of the spiritual dimension of health. These afflictions cannot be addressed by the medical model of health.

In addition there is reason to believe that socioeconomic inequities will worsen in the coming decades in the United States. The gap in income differentials especially between the working poor and rich shows no evidence of narrowing. Job patterns favor the skilled and technologically astute worker, while the unskilled labor force will continue to shrink. Chronic unemployment, particularly among urban minorities is especially troubling in light of the impact of joblessness on health. Ironically, uncontrolled spending on health care and the increased burden of Medicaid on the states is siphoning off badly needed resources from education and social services that are sorely needed to deal with these broader problems that solidify social inequities. The education system has failed to keep up with vast technological changes in the workplace particularly for those who most need it, the lower socioeconomic groups. The potential intergenerational tensions brought on by shifts in budget priorities to medical care and pensions for the aging population are likely to intensify social conflicts.

These social problems are not an indictment of medicine but rather of a society that equates health to medicine and looks first to medical solutions. Individual-oriented medicine is but a manifestation of an individual-oriented society that for too long has neglected broader community spirituality. The United States is overdue for a return to a balance in its conception of health. It must incorporate the near lost dimensions of a more inclusive health model as represented by the concepts of feelings/emotion, family, and spirituality embodied by Maori. Although health policy cannot ignore the physical dimension and those individuals who need medical intervention, the health of the population depends on the notion of community. It is the sense of community that binds populations together and gives them collective, common goals including that of health. The medical model with its focus on the individual "is not inevitable or necessarily the most efficient or effective way of promoting individual health" (Mechanic 1994:105) nor the health of the community as whole. Given the strong social, economic, and cultural determinants of health, it is an illusion that an individual-oriented medical model of health care can succeed in the long run.

CHAPTER 4

AVOIDING HARD CHOICES
A Need for Rationing

One of the messages of the Clinton Health Security Act was that the cost explosion in health spending could be controlled without rationing resources that held some hope of benefit for individual patients. This would be accomplished through efficiency improvements brought about by managed competition, reduction of administrative costs, and elimination of unnecessary and wasteful care. Presumably part of the care to be eliminated was that deemed futile therapy given to terminal patients. Such a message was reassuring in a culture that disdains making hard choices and detests the notion of rationing. It is, of course, much less painful to eliminate waste, administrative costs, and unneeded care than to ration care from identifiable persons who might benefit.

Surveys have found that the American public believes that the critical problems are caused by waste, inefficiency, and greed of insurance companies, hospitals, physicians and malpractice lawyers (Blendon et al. 1994:283). Because of this myopia, the public is unlikely to embrace proposals that meaningfully address the overuse of medical technologies by the public, itself, the cost of using highly trained medical specialists, and the realities of the aging population. However, while all efforts should be made to eliminate waste and inefficiency in the health system, there is considerable evidence that we delude ourselves by believing that such steps alone will be sufficient and will allow us to avoid setting limits on our appetite for and dependence on sophisticated medical interventions.

Any attempts to establish allocation priorities through public policy, therefore, will encounter intense opposition. Some observers also suggest that by shifting societal priorities, we would have more than sufficient funds to resolve health care funding problems. It is argued that this myth of a crisis could be obviated by a transfusion of dollars from the defense budget; a transformation of missiles into medicine. These critics contend that the only crisis in health care is the one imposed by a government that is unwilling or unable to set the "proper" spending priorities. A reordering of these priorities, accompanied by the selection of health care for special emphasis, would provide adequate funds to handle the problems of health care allocation (see White and Waithe 1995).

Contentions that the solutions lie solely in shifting funds from other areas of public spending to health care belies two factors. First, whether or not one approves, there is little evidence of a large cache of national defense funds to be transferred to social programs. Even if there was, health would have to compete with other potential recipient areas. Under current deficit budgetary conditions, cuts, not increases in health care spending as a proportion of the federal budget are likely. Second, assuming the improbable happened and the government decided to trade defense priorities for health care, history indicates that the appropriation of additional funds to medicine often exacerbates rather than resolves the problems. Because health care needs and demands are virtually unlimited and funding sources are finite, shifting higher proportions of the GDP or the federal budget to medical ends simply serves to postpone that inevitable point at which constraints must be imposed. Although the government alone has the means to initiate and coordinate necessary action, it cannot succeed without the explicit support of health care providers and the consumer public.

SAVINGS BY REDUCING COSTS OF DYING

Dying in the United States is expensive compared to other nations. Considerable evidence demonstrates that we are willing to expend more medical resources on terminally ill patients and to intervene more aggressively. The result is that in the United States on average 18 percent of one's lifetime health care costs are spent during the last year of life. Of this proportion, 77 percent is spent in the last six months and almost one-third in the last 30 days. Moreover, 29 percent of Medicare/Medicaid payments are made on behalf of the 5 percent of beneficiaries who die in a given year. Expenditures for health care in the last year of life are 3 to 8 times that of other years (Roos et al. 1989:365). Other measures show that of all the patients who enter ICUs, a significant number die either during their stay or shortly after discharge, often at great expense (Schapira et al. 1993).

Using statistics of this sort some observers have argued that we can save huge amounts of health dollars if only we limit care for terminally ill patients. By eliminating intensive and expensive treatment for terminal patients resources could be released for patients who can benefit more. For instance:

> Intensive care units across the country are overflowing, often crowded with hopeless patients who will derive no long-term benefit from their stays while short-changing the people they were intended to serve, critically ill patients who need temporary support to survive a medical crisis.   *(Rosenthal 1989)*

It is often contended that we can accomplish these savings by encouraging advance directives to withhold technological interventions, emphasizing hospice care, and curtailing futile therapies. By doing so it is assumed we will be able to avoid explicit rationing of beneficial or needed treatments. This section discusses some of the problems with this line of thinking.

Allocation Issues at End of Life

Because the United States lacks the structural mechanisms and public will to set limits on allocation of health care resources we look to other more politically feasible approaches to rationing at the end of life. Recently, these have included encouragement of advance directives and the curtailment of futile treatment for terminal patients. The assumption is that we can save significant resources by withholding treatment from terminal patients and that this can be accomplished without sacrificing appropriate treatment.

One major trend that has intensified over the last several decades is the emphasis on advance directives (AD) initially in the form of living wills and more recently in durable powers of attorney (see Emanuel et al. 1991). Although advance directives have been created ostensibly to empower patients to take control over medical decision making on their behalf and ensure patient autonomy, the resource allocation dimension is readily apparent in the laws and in the literature. Advance directives are not designed to encourage persons to demand all treatment. Rather the presumption of an AD is that individuals will voluntarily forgo certain treatment regimens. In fact, it is unlikely that ADs specifying a demand for all possible life-saving efforts to be used would be necessary under the current medical model where this is standard practice. By definition, then, ADs are designed as a means of rejecting available medical interventions for terminal patients who do not desire certain types of aggressive treatment. Table 4.1 illustrates findings of one study regarding preferences for no treatment.

One problem with the use of advance directives for terminal patients is that terminal illness is an imprecise and ambiguous term. In many cases the uncertainty of medical prognosis makes it impossible to predict with accuracy which patients will live with a particular treatment and which will die. Therefore, a conservative approach to ADs will keep some patients alive beyond the desired time. In contrast, a liberal approach will end treatment for some patients whose lives could have been saved. If the sole goal is to empower patients to take control of their death process, this fact causes problems only

TABLE 4.1
Treatment Preferences for Medical Directive, Dementia, and Terminal Illness

Treatment	Want	Do Not Want	Undecided
CPR	8	84	8
Mechanical respiration	8	84	6
Intravenous fluids	10	82	6
Artificial nutrition	9	82	7
Blood transfusion	9	82	7
Antibiotics	15	79	6
Renal dialysis	8	83	6
Major surgery	8	85	6
Minor surgery	13	81	6
Simple diagnostic procedures	20	75	4
Complex diagnostic procedures	11	83	6

SOURCE: Adapted from Emanuel et al. 1991:893.

when they are unable to understand the uncertainties that surround execution of their decisions. If, however, another motivation for the proliferation of ADs is to reduce futile treatment and save resources, the implications of the inability to ascertain what is a terminal condition are considerable.

Contrary to commonly stated presumptions, a relatively small amount of high technology medicine is expended at the end of life by excessively aggressive care of clearly terminal patients. The problem is that there is an overlap between terminally and critically ill patients often based on probabilities. Terminally ill patients are those with a high probability that they will die in a short period of time no matter what is done. Although critically ill patients may die even with aggressive treatment, the prognosis is that death is possible but not probable. Therefore, if we really want to save significant medical resources, rationing must be extended to critically ill but not necessarily dying patients who cumulatively account for far more resources. Often these are frail, debilitated elderly patients who are not in imminent danger of dying. Importantly, this category of patients is expected to increase significantly over the next decades. Furthermore, as table 4.2 demonstrates, while a large proportion of families of unambiguously terminal patients would prefer nontreatment this does not extend to patients in the critical category.

One question then is how far we extend advance directives into the critically ill category. Furthermore, if we do extend ADs what do we do in situations where the patient does not have an AD (speculative) or in those instances where the patient has expressed a desire to

TABLE 4.2

Preferences of Family Members Regarding Use or No Use of Life-Sustaining Treatment for Incompetent Nursing Home Residents

Intervention	Critical		Degree of Illness Terminal		Permanent Unconscious	
	use	no use	use	no use	use	no use
Hospitalization	41	8	12	33	10	55
Intensive care	35	27	8	53	6	67
CPR	27	47	9	66	0	83
Surgery	10	41	6	69	0	90
Artificial ventilation	19	45	4	69	6	88

SOURCE: Adapted from Danis et al. 1991:885.

have all aggressive treatment? Do we deny such care for patients who demand it even though the treatment is judged to be futile by the medical professionals?

This leads to the consideration of under what conditions it is proper to curtail futile treatment and, more basically, what constitutes a futile treatment. As with ADs, the debate over futile treatment demonstrates potentially conflicting motivations (Brody and Halevy 1955). The first motivation is that curtailing futile treatment protects patient autonomy and the integrity of the physicians as moral and professional agents. To force truly futile treatment on a patient is dehumanizing.

A second motivation behind curtailing futile treatment is to save resources since an inherent aspect of futility is that the benefit of such treatment cannot be worth the investment because it is bound to fail. The notion of futility as wasteful can be used therefore to sanction restrictions on the allocation of resources under the guise of patient autonomy. Patients cannot demand futile therapy and society and the medical community are under no obligation to provide it. For instance, even the Child Abuse Amendment's mandate for treatment of all newborns made exceptions for futile interventions. Futility considerations, although often presented as patient empowerment, contain critical resource allocation dimensions. One study of such treatment decisions at two California hospitals concluded: "Although the allocation of resources was discussed frequently among the physicians caring for the patients, concerns about resources was never cited as the reason for withholding or withdrawing support" (Smedira et al. 1990:313).

Like terminal illness, futility is an elusive concept because it is difficult to predict with certainty that a treatment will be of no benefit to a particular patient. This has led some observers to conclude that futility claims can rarely justify abdication of the physician's obligation to discuss such alternatives with the patient: "Rather than being a discrete and definable entity, futile therapy is merely the end of the spectrum of therapies with very low efficacy. Ambiguity in determining futility . . . undermines the force of futility claims" (Lantos et al. 1989:81).

In contrast some observers believe that on grounds of futility universal application of cardiopulmonary resuscitation (CPR) is indefensible (Saunders 1992). For most patients, CPR is a desperate measure with slender prospects of success. One study found that: "Older patients readily understand prognostic information, which influences their preferences with respect of CPR. Most do not want to undergo CPR once a clinician explains the probability of survival after the procedure" (Murphy et al. 1994:545). At best futility is a controversial concept but one which will receive greater attention as the health crisis escalates.

The Costs of Dying

The aggregate data presented earlier on the costs of dying indicate that persons who die consume a disproportionate amount of medical resources. This is not surprising because costs will always be highest for those persons who are sickest. All these data, however, are based on retrospective studies, which tend to inflate costs at the end of life. They do this because instead of representing the costs involved in treating only those persons known in advance to be dying, they include many patients receiving expensive care who are expected to live but who die. In other words, the data fail to distinguish between clearly terminal patients and those who might be critically ill or where clinical uncertainty leads to a decision to treat aggressively in order to save their life—treatment that ultimately fails, thus placing them retrospectively in the terminal category.

Three sets of questions are crucial concerning the costs of death. First, what is the magnitude of the problem: are the costs excessive and is the situation worsening? Second, how much money actually could be saved by withholding life-saving therapies from dying patients? And third, what specific steps could be taken, if any, to reduce expenditures at the end of life and realize these savings?

Despite the heightened attention placed on the high expenditures for dying patients, recent studies demonstrate that the situation has been relatively stable since 1976. Lubitz and Riley (1993) found that while the costs of treating the dying has increased in dollar terms, as has all health care, as a proportion of total Medicare budget there has been little change. Table 4.3 shows that the adjusted percentage for decedents has fluctuated between 28 and 30 percent. In 1988, the 1.49 million decedents represented 5.1 percent of all Medicare beneficiaries and accounted for 28.6 percent of all expenditures. Also payment for care in the last 60 days as a percent of last year's payment held steady at 52 percent over this period.

TABLE 4.3
Medicare Enrollment and Payments, by Survival Status

Enrollment	1976	1980	1985	1988
All beneficiaries (millions)	23.4	25.2	27.2	29.1
Decedents				
No. (millions)	1.22	1.35	1.45	1.49
Percent	5.2	5.4	5.3	5.1
Payments				
Total ($ billion)	15.2	31.0	57.2	73.0
Percentage for decedents				
Unadjusted	28.2	30.6	26.9	27.2
Adjusted	28.2	30.8	27.4	28.6

SOURCE: Lubitz and Riley 1993:1093.

Moreover, when Scitovsky (1988) controlled for age of decedent she found that hospital cost for the last year of life drops dramatically for those patients 80 and over. Table 4.4 demonstrates that the mean Medicare payments for decedents declines after age 75.

Reinforcing this decline in expenditures per age of decedent is a corresponding pattern when functional status is considered (see table 4.5). Although total expenditures do not vary significantly across categories based on extent of imparity, hospital expenditures decline sharply especially for totally impaired patients. The decrease in hospital costs is offset by large increases in nursing home care. These data demonstrate that high technology hospital services are

TABLE 4.4
Medicare Payments, by Survival Status and Age, 1988

Age	Mean Payments per Person Year	
	Decedents	Survivors
65–69	$15,346	$1,455
70–74	15,778	1,845
75–79	14,902	2,176
80–84	12,838	2,403
85–89	11,422	2,578
90+	8,888	2,258
Total	$13,316	$1,924

SOURCE: Scitovsky 1994:564.

already allocated in a more rational manner than is often assumed. Elderly patients who get hospital care in the last year of life tend to be those with good functional status, especially the younger old. Partially impaired patients, who are likely to have uncertain prognoses, had a relatively high rate of hospital services but they did not receive the intensive care given the unimpaired. Finally, the totally impaired, especially very old patients, received very little high-technology intervention. These data also indicate, however, that nonhospital supportive care can also be very costly when hospital care is avoided. If significant money is to be saved, efforts must be targeted at the younger and relatively unimpaired patients and at supportive health care services.

How much can be saved by rationing care to end-of-life patients? Emanuel and Emanuel (1994) suggest that savings are modest. Even in the best case scenario, where everyone has an advance directive, refuses aggressive treatment at the end of life, and elects to receive hospice care at home, we would reduce health care expenditure by only 3.3 percent. Medicare savings under this scenario are estimated to be 6.1 percent. In 1993 the total savings would have represented approximately $29.7 billion out of an estimated budget of $800 billion. Using different assumptions, Singer and Lowy (1992) found that rationing by patient preference with advance directives could save as much as $55 billion per year (although they admit it could be as low as $5 billion). However, they assume that Medicare figures hold for the entire population although in reality less than 1 percent of the population as opposed to 5 percent of Medicare beneficiaries die each year.

TABLE 4.5
Mean Medical Expenses of Decedents Over 65, by Functional Status

Expenditure Category	Unimpaired	Partially Impaired	Totally Impaired
Hospital	18,000	11,600	3,700
Physician	4,000	4,500	1,600
Nursing home	<100	1,800	11,000
Home health care	<100	3,100	3,900
Other	800	1,000	1,200
Total	23,000	22,000	21,400

SOURCE: Scitovsky 1988:649–50.

With regard to advance directives, most studies have found that they generally do not significantly reduce the cost of care for terminal patients, although the results are disparate. For instance, Schneiderman et al. (1992) found that the average cost for patients without an AD was $56,300 as compared to $61,584 with a living will and $58,346 with a durable power of attorney. Moreover, the authors found no evidence that this could be explained by physicians' refusal to abide by the patients' wishes. Another study found the ICU patients with "do not resuscitate" (DNR) orders used a disproportionate share of resources, but this could be because these patients were older and sicker than those without a DNR order (Jayes et al. 1993).

In contrast, Chambers et al. (1994) found significantly lower costs for terminal patients with an advance directive. Mean hospital charges for patients without documentation of ADs were $95,305 as compared to $30,478 for those with ADs. Some of the wide discrepancies in these findings might be explained by the timing of the directive. Maksoud, Jahnigen, and Skibinski (1993) for instance found that the mean charges of patients who died with a preadmission DNR order were significantly lower than those patients with no DNR order ($10,631 versus $57,334). Charges for those patients who obtained the DNR order in the hospital, however, averaged $73,055.

Scitovsky (1994) suggests that one reason for the high costs associated with patients who obtained the DNR in the hospital is that the orders are often written only a few days before death, after the patient may have undergone considerable treatment. Again, this reflects the difficulty of predicting death for any particular patient at an earlier time and suggests that savings from the use of ADs are unlikely to reach the levels predicted by some observers. These data also demonstrate that high-quality palliative care can also be very expensive. Although it might reduce high technology costs, it is very labor intensive.

Another alternative that has been promised by some observers to produce huge savings is hospice care. As with ADs, however, available data suggest that savings are likely to be more modest. Although at least one study found no significant differences between hospice and conventional care costs (Kane et al. 1984), most studies have found savings averaging about 25 percent for home hospice care and approximately 15 percent for hospital-based hospice care (Greer et al. 1986). In a major study of the Medicare hospice program, Kidder (1992) found that hospice expenditures were lower than expenditures for conventional care only in free-standing hospices. In contrast, expenditures in home health-agency based hospices were about the same as conventional care while those in hospital and skilled nursing-home facility-based hospices were actually slightly higher. As a result Kidder concluded that it is not likely that the hospice benefit will be an important mechanism for containing the costs of terminally ill Medicare beneficiaries (1992:213).

Summary

A growing body of evidence suggests that the idea that we can avoid hard rationing decisions by empowering terminal patients to forgo heroic life-saving attempts and by moving care from a high-technology medical to a hospice setting is largely an illusion. Although savings might accrue from such changes, it is unlikely that they will make significant inroads into the continually escalating health care costs. In order to approach savings of the magnitude needed, such care would have to be withheld from a substantially broadened population of critically ill patients, those who are at risk of dying but who in no way can be described as terminal in the conventional sense.

Scitovsky goes even further in stating that the most difficult decisions center on chronically ill patients, primarily the frail and disabled elderly population in need of long-term supportive care. "Chronically ill patients present us with the dilemma not so much to forgo 'heroics,' but rather of when to halt ordinary care (such as treatment with antibiotics in case of infection) and sustenance" (1994:589). Temkin-Greener et al. come to similar conclusion that, in the end, excessive, high-technology care for the elderly in their last year of life may be much less of a problem than the overall long-term needs of the expanding chronically ill elderly population (1992:200).

Empowerment of patients by allowing them more control over their dying process has been a consistent theme in discussions of advance directives. Likewise, the notion of futile treatment is often applied to those interventions which do not benefit the dying patient and which should, therefore, be withheld. As noted earlier, while many proponents of empowerment are serious about protecting patient autonomy and see these developments as returning control to patients, the resource allocation dimensions of these approaches are obvious (see figure 4.1).. Living wills and durable powers of attorney are viewed by some persons as means of avoiding more explicit rationing of health care resources. While this analysis shows that by themselves such devices will not significantly reduce spending on health care, ironically they incorporate a form of surreptitious rationing by hiding it beneath the veneer of empowerment.

ELIMINATING INEFFICIENCY AND WASTE

Some observers of the American health care system argue that difficult allocation choices can be avoided if we would only eliminate the inefficiency from the current system. For instance: "It is an unconscionable cop-out to resort to rationing by any means . . . . when we can have care for all people with a little efficiency, prudence, and prevention. Studies indicate that at least 25% of the money we spend on health care is wasted" (Califano 1992:1526). Califano goes on to argue that instead of restricting care we can expand access if we shrink overcapacity, streamline the health care bureaucracy and eliminate perverse incentives for hospitals and doctors (1992:1527).

Others have estimated that 30 percent or more of the health care services currently rendered in the United States might be safely forgone, although Hadorn and Brook conclude that the issue of whether elimination of unnecessary services would save enough money to provide all necessary services is yet unresolved (1991:3329). As noted earlier this appears to be an attractive course because "waste cutting, unlike rationing, does not connote the cruel denial of necessary care" (Blustein and Marmor 1992:1544).

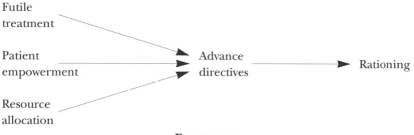

FIGURE 4.1

Inefficient Procedures

Clearly, there are innumerable examples of savings that could be made by eliminating care that some observers would deem unnecessary. Patrick and Erickson for instance suggest the savings of millions of dollars simply be reusing cardiac pacemakers: "Approximately 35 percent of patients receiving a new pacemaker die within 18 months of the procedure. Thus about 35,000 pacemakers are potential candidates for reuse. Not all of these candidates could be accessed, but even if 'wastage' were as high as 70 percent, 10,000 pacemakers could be reused each year" (1993:172).

Similarly, treating coronary thrombosis using Streptokinase rather than the newer Tissue Plasminogen Activator could save $2,000 per dose although ten lives less per thousand would be saved (Wallner 1993:9). Blustein and Marmor (1992), however, suggest that so-called wasteful practice is a "conceptual hodgepodge" encompassing treatments that are ineffective, of uncertain effectiveness, ethically troublesome, and not allocationally efficient. Furthermore, what might be wasteful to one observer might be considered necessary by others, particularly the medical specialists whose practice is based on the procedure in question. So while there is no doubt that much medical care might be of questionable efficiency and that the United States health system has enormous waste and inefficiency, it would be most difficult based on current data to make discrete distinctions. Moreover, patients and their physicians are unlikely to acquiesce to elimination of existing diagnostic and therapeutic procedures despite questions of efficacy.

> However untested, therapies will always be sought by patients wanting to improve their lives, while doctors themselves will want to employ them. Monetary incentives certainly play a role, but physicians are also guided by a special professional ethic . . . there is little likelihood that either of the intimate partners in the doctor-patient relationship will ever perceive a significant proportion of medical treatments as "wasteful."
>
> *(Marmor and Boyum 1994:131)*

In addition there are critical questions as to whether such savings could forestall difficult allocation decisions for more than a short time, given the near limitless expandability of the medical industry (Elhauge 1994:1462). Although large gross savings many result if outcome studies result in the elimination of wasteful practices and the system is made more efficient, the dominant underlying force responsible for rising medical expenditures, technological advances would remain (Aaron 1991:52). Schwartz and Mendelson (1994) estimate that efficiency gains are not likely to reduce the rise in costs between 1994 and 2000 by more than 1.5 percent annually, and they conclude that much more stringent measures are necessary to make substantial reductions.

> Some portion of the increase in costs due to technology may be restrained by devices and drugs that can accomplish a given task at a lower cost. But unless fiscal constraints are severe enough to discourage innovation, the flood of new technologies is likely to overwhelm any savings resulting from a new concern for cost-effectiveness over the next decade.
>
> *(Schwartz and Mendelson 1994:233)*

Any such measures short of rationing beneficial services are unlikely to resolve the problem of rising acute care costs.

Similarly, Aaron (1991) does not see moves to cut waste and inefficiency as materially slowing the growth of overall health care spending on these grounds. First, even if inappropriate therapies are eliminated, the symptoms that occasioned therapy in the first place call for some other form of treatment. Second, effectiveness research itself is costly, complex and time consuming. Although clear-cut results might emerge, many outcomes studies will reveal mixed results in which a therapy is superior in some respects and inferior in others: "Furthermore, the results of such studies will become available slowly over a number of years. At the same time, large numbers of new medical devices and procedures will come into use, most of which will tend to drive up overall costs" (Aaron 1991:50).

And, finally, some efficacy studies will identify procedures which are underused. Although outcomes research is justified in order to eliminate unnecessary and perhaps dangerous therapy, it is unlikely to provide the long-term savings necessary to avoid rationing.

Administrative Costs

Another area targeted by some observers for huge savings is the waste and inefficiency of our fragmented payer system and of the administrative costs it foists on hospitals. Data clearly demonstrate that the cost of our health insurance system is high. For every dollar the insurance industry paid in claims in 1988, 33.5 cents was spent on marketing, administration, and other overhead expenses. This percentage is estimated by Brandon and associates to be 14 times more than Medicare's administrative costs (2.3 percent) and 11 times more than Canada's national health system (3 percent; 1992:73). As illustrated in table 4.6, over $13 billion could have been saved in such costs alone had the same level of care been provided under the single payer system of Canada simply by reducing the waste and inefficiency of the commercial insurance industry. Moreover, between 1970 and 1982 while all health personnel grew by 57 percent, administrative personnel grew by 171 percent (Mechanic 1994:28).

In addition estimates of hospital administrative costs, in part driven by the need to meet reporting requirements of managed care organizations and insurance carriers, range from $41 billion to $47 billion per year (Schwartz and Mendelson 1994:228). However, dramatic reductions are difficult to achieve because administrative costs already have been reduced over the last decade. Schwartz and Mendelsohn estimate that hospital administrative costs could realistically save approximately $5 billion, a large amount but certainly not enough to

TABLE 4.6
Estimated Insurance Expenses for the U.S. Under Different Health Care Financing Systems

	Expenses-to-premiums ratio	U.S. $1000	Individual coverage $	Family policy $
Premiums collected by commercial insurers		55,245,526	1,176	2,508
Estimated expenses under different systems				
Commercial	26.9%	14,914,400	316	675
Medicare	2.3%	1,024,142	27	58
Canada	3.0%	1,335,837	35	75
Difference between Canada and commercial insurers	23.9%	13,578,563	281	599

SOURCE: Brandon et al. 1992:87.

make a dent in the escalation of health care costs. Although they cite other studies that show larger savings particularly as compared to Canada (see Brandon et al. 1992), they argue that such reports "dramatically understated" costs in Canada. In fact, Danzon concludes that administrative costs in Canada are roughly equal to those in the United States (Danzon 1992). Similarly, Kassler challenges reports of Medicare's low administrative costs as deceptive: "Although the Health Care Financing Administration may have spent a low 2.1 percent on the administration of Medicare, that was just to transfer the money to each state's fiscal intermediary that then had the responsibility of distributing funds to providers and patients" (1994:178).

Although lowering administrative costs should receive high priority, promises of huge savings should be met with skepticism. More importantly, even at the most optimistic levels, the savings are unlikely in themselves to curtail large long-term increases in health care expenses driven by medical technology and increased demands by an older population.

PREVENTION STRATEGIES AND HEALTH CARE COSTS

One of the major themes of this book is the need to shift medical care back toward prevention and health promotion in order to restore a balance in the system. If the goal of the health care system is to improve the health of the population, prevention programs particularly those which effect changes toward healthier lifestyles are critical (see Cundiff and McCarthy 1994, and Fox 1993). The most significant improvements in health have come from preventive, not curative or supportive efforts, even though these latter efforts are the most dramatic and are therefore more readily funded. Furthermore, most advances in the preventive area have come from outside medicine, primarily in the areas of improved sanitation, nutrition, housing, and education. Despite this evidence, America at present spends less than 3 percent of its health care dollars on preventive care.

Many observers have argued that a reallocation toward disease prevention and health promotion would not only enhance health but also save money. For instance: "It is essential that preventive medicine be emphasized if costs are to be contained while overall quality of care is improved . . . The right preventive programs can work to reduce disease and cut costs." (Cundiff and McCarthy 1994:11,68).

Similarly: "Public policies designed to provide opportunities to change behavior and/or receive preventive services are expanding access to health care services. The three goals of health policy—cost containment, quality, and access—can all be well served by policies related to promoting health. Those policies will not achieve one goal at the expense of others" (Mueller 1993:152).

Richmond and Fein (1995:71) conclude that efforts toward prevention and promotion have "borne much fruit" and that we are on the threshold of being able to do much better. A modest increase, they argue, would yield significant benefits. The Clinton Health Security Act too placed emphasis on the cost-saving aspects of prevention.

Other observers however are more skeptical of the savings from preventive strategies. According to Leutwyler (1995) lawmakers embraced the notion that increased use of prevention would help cut medical spending because they bought the logic that suggested that if fewer people got sick, fewer would require medical care, and society would pay fewer bills. Russell (1993), however, concludes that while the ideas that prevention saves money has "enduring appeal"—it is more efficient to avoid a disease than try to repair the damage later —cost effectiveness studies provide little evidence of savings. In fact, a growing array of studies on programs for hypertension screening, reducing high blood cholesterol by either diet or drugs, major screening tests for cancer, and routine mammography tests indicate that the net costs per year of life saved are exceedingly high. For Elhauge:

> But the problem lies with the claim that the amount it would have cost to treat those illnesses has been "saved." As discussed above, given the inevitable degeneration of the human body, those saved from one illness almost always go on to experience another. And the illness they go on to experience is generally (though not always) *more* expensive to treat. It is thus not at all clear that preventive medicine actually reduces long-run financial costs. *(1994:1463)*

A review of available data by the Office of Technology Assessment reported that of all the preventive services they evaluated, only three were potentially cost-saving (childhood immunizations, prenatal care for poor women, and several neonatal tests for congenital disorders). Screening for cancer, unless carefully targeted to high-risk individuals costs more than therapy. Similarly, screening for high blood pressure generally costs more than treating heart attack and stroke victims (Leutwyler 1995:124)

High costs arise when diagnostic procedures are used on the population at large to identify those at risk from a condition which is not widespread (i.e. Pap smears to detect cervical cancer, or breast cancer screening), or when procedures whose per unit cost is high are used on patients in the hospital (i.e., preoperative skull or chest x-rays). The low per unit cost of some population screening procedures may obscure their true cost, which is the cost of achieving the desired outcome for the few who will benefit. Although technologically we could reduce the frequency of death from breast cancer by screening, of the birth of surviving bifida babies by prenatal screening, and of brain damage by means of skull radiology, the total costs of each procedure is exceedingly high. For instance, Eddy (1991) found that annual screening for cervical cancer costs about $1.8 million for each additional year of life. For Russell,

> That common theme, played out in its many variations, is simple, direct, and misleading. The straightforward recommendations about screening tests and the information that usually accompanies them are pseudo-truths. They convey rules of thumb developed by experts and leave out the complexities and tradeoffs, the mixture of solid information and educated guesses, that have gone into their development. *(1994:2)*

Although prevention is often assumed to rely on inexpensive low-technology interventions, many prevention approaches concentrate on the use of increasingly sophisticated diagnostic procedures which allow for the identification of rare conditions. Serious outcomes that require major medical intervention can often be avoided by early diagnosis and treatment, but only if large numbers of persons at risk are screened. Examples of this type of preventive effort include cervical cancer screening, blood pressure screening, preoperative chest x-rays, whole body scans, and alpha-fetoprotein tests for spina bifida, to name a few. The problem with these efforts, however, is that because the risk of such problems is so low, extensive screening will avert only a small number of cases at substantial expense.

Within the context of scarce medical resources, diagnostic services might be too expensive under some circumstances even through effective techniques are available to avoid severe disability or even death. In a study for the British National Health Service, Roberts, Farrow, and Charny (1985) contend that here too as well as in curative medicine, difficult choices must be made that may preclude use of certain preventive or early diagnostic services, thereby denying benefits which are technically feasible. They explain that the clinical effectiveness of a service is no longer the only dimension which has to be considered before allocating resources for that purpose. Also considered are the prevalence of the outcome to be avoided in the population at large and the cost of the procedure itself. As noted above, even though the cost of a single procedure might be reasonable, if the condition is rare, a large number of such procedures might be necessary to identify and prevent one case.

A final reason why prevention might not be cost-effective is because of an alteration in the nature of preventive medicine itself. Most of the benefits expected to accrue from traditional public health measures have already been achieved, thus subjecting present and future efforts to the law of diminishing returns. As a result, prevention now must focus on changing lifestyles and identifying the early signs of serious disease through screening and education. Under these conditions, any preventive measure must be evaluated in terms of how successful it is in actually changing behavior that might avert a future disease.

Furthermore, as discussed earlier, many of the ties between lifestyle and health remain speculative and are based on statistical data, not on rigorous clinical trials. Even where evidence of danger is strong, there is considerable debate over how effective any preventive measure might be. "Existing studies suggest that successful behavior modification requires appropriate knowledge, coping skills to overcome barriers to the enactment of the desired behavior, and continuing reinforcement for the emergent behavioral changes" (Mechanic 1994:12). To effect these changes requires investment of considerable resources both to fund research on behavior modification and to carry out the preventive programs.

According to the National Center for Health Services Research (1984:3), one of the reasons health counseling is not more commonly practiced by primary care providers may be the belief that patients will not follow their advice. The results of lifestyle changes can be only stated to the individual patient in terms of probability. Moreover, any illness resulting from potentially harmful behavior is

pletely unlimited health care resources for all of its citizens (Wiener 1992:12). Furthermore, despite the recent heightened pressures on health care systems, rationing has always been a part of medical decision making. Table 4.7 illustrates the wide range of ways in which health care can be rationed. Whether imposed by a market system in which price determines access, a triage system where care is distributed on the basis of need defined largely by the medical community, or a queue system in which time and the waiting process become the major rationing device, medical resources have always been distributed according to criteria that contain varying degrees of subjectivity. In almost all instances, rationing criteria are grounded in a par-

TABLE 4.7
Forms of Health Care Rationing

Form	Criteria Used
Physician discretion	Medical benefit to patient Medical risk to patient Social class or mental capacity
Competitive marketplace	Ability to pay
Insurance marketplace	Ability to pay for insurance Group membership Employment
Socialized insurance (i.e., Medicaid)	Entitlement Means test
Legal	Litigation to gain access & treatment
Personal fund-raising	Support of social organizations Skill in public relations Willingness to appeal to public
Implicit rationing	Queuing Limited manpower and facilities Medical benefits to patient with consideration of social costs
Explicit rationing	Triage Medical benefits to patient with emphasis on social costs and benefits
Controlled rationing	Government control of medicine Equity in access to primary care Social benefit over specific patient benefits Costs to society

ticular value context that results in an inequitable distribution of resources based on social as well as strictly medical considerations.

Although a variety of types of rationing occur in every country, different health care systems place emphasis on particular forms. Those countries with national health services have an easier time using more explicit rationing mechanisms through their control of the supply of resources. In countries with socially determined health budgets, constraints in one area can be justified on grounds that the money will be spent on higher-priority services. According to Wiener (1992:15), this closed system of funding provides a "moral underpinning for resource allocation across a range of potentially unlimited demands." By contrast in the fragmented U.S. health care environment it is considerably more difficult to refuse additional services for patients because there is no certainty the funds will be put to better use elsewhere. The lack of a fixed budget either for government funding or overall national health care spending makes it impossible to say where money "saved" from rationing will go.

Supply-side rationing of the type practiced in the United Kingdom and other national health system (NHS) countries depends upon strict limits set on medical facilities, equipment, and staffs. "The availability of resources inevitably affects clinical decisions. Either some decisions are prohibited because the necessary resources are not available at the right time or some rationing occurs when priorities are set for the use of available resources" (McPherson 1990:21).

General practitioners serve a gatekeeper role and deflect patients from overloading the system. In contrast, the United States must depend on some form of demand-side rationing which is more contentious. The United States begins with excess hospital capacity and an oversupply of specialists, to whom patients have direct access. As a result, the health care system has the capacity to perform any available procedure, including those that the public system does not cover. Persons with adequate insurance or resources, therefore, are unlikely to acquiesce to artificially imposed constraints on their access. Moreover, "demand-side rationing in this environment will be susceptible to a great many poignant personal appeals for coverage and will be extremely difficult to sustain politically" (Wiener 1992:19).

As a result of these systematic differences across countries there is substantially more rationing of high technologies in other countries than would be politically feasible in U.S. culture with its emphasis on individual rights in a medical marketplace. As discussed in greater detail elsewhere, however, this does not mean that rationing is less endemic to the United States only that it takes less systematic and explicit forms (Blank 1992).

Another distinction is between price and nonprice rationing. Price rationing, which is common to the United States, denies health care resources to persons who cannot afford them or who have inadequate third-party coverage. In contrast, nonprice health care rationing, which is common in national health systems, denies medical resources to persons who have the means to afford them. Nonprice rationing depends on limiting the availability of certain health services. According to Aaron (1992:54) services that require specialized capital equipment (e.g. CAT scanners) are easier to ration than are those that rely on multiple use inputs and could be controlled only by infringing on each physician's clinical freedom (e.g., parenteral nutrition). Although nonprice rationing is unlikely to ever be as severe as it is in the United Kingdom, it is inevitable in the United States (Aaron 1992:60).

A final dimension of rationing is that some forms necessitate government involvement, either direct or indirect, while others fail to clearly distinguish between public and private sector choices. Although rationing in the United States is still heavily influenced by the marketplace, litigation, and personal fund-raising, continued dependence on these less explicit forms is not sufficient to resolve health care dilemmas we will face. As a result, we are now witnessing a shift toward the bottom end of table 4.7 possibly culminating in a more central role for the government in the allocation of increasingly scarce medical resources. Although explicit rationing under the authority of the government is but one form of rationing, there are many forces that, concurrently, are now moving even American society in that direction. At the same time, however, explicit public rationing is feared by many observers who continue to argue that rationing is unnecessary or an anathema to be avoided at all costs.

Once rationing is accepted as fact, no matter how disparagingly, the question becomes one of how to implement it. Furthermore, if resources are to be focused on the provision of appropriate health care, who defines this and how is it defined? And what are the criteria for rationing—total lives saved, life-years saved, or quality of life years saved? Because there are no clear answers and because rationing is so entangled with problems of cost containment and efficiency, its implementation is potentially very divisive. As a result, each system will use a different combination of mechanisms. Although unavoidable, rationing remains a highly charged and controversial term in all developed nations. Ultimately, conflicts in rationing health care can be managed only when societal goals and priorities are clarified and acceptable mechanisms are identified.

Some of the approaches to rationing that are widely used are "first come, first serviced" systems of queues, triage systems based on medical urgency, and, more recently, systems based on computation of quality adjusted life years (QALY) used to compare patient and treatment priorities. Jennett (1986) has presented a set of criteria used to determine if treatment is inappropriate. Treatment should be withheld if it is likely to prove *unsuccessful, unsafe, unkind* or *unwise.* According to the Australian National Health and Medical Research Council, however, even if these criteria were applied universally, "there would remain insufficient funds for the care of those who are not excluded by these 'tests' " (1990:9).

Rationing is also often proposed as a means of guaranteeing every citizen a basic level of health care by excluding from coverage those treatments outside this package (see Eddy 1991a). The trade-off here is between universal access to those services deemed basic on the one hand and unequal access to the full range of technically feasible services on the other. For instance while the Canada Health Act of 1984 guarantees health services to all citizens, it specifically excludes most adult dental services, optometry, physiotherapy, osteopathy, ambulance, dietetics, hearing aids, psychology, pharmaceuticals and other ancillary services except when provided in hospitals. Furthermore, as budgets tighten, descheduling of services is undertaken through negotiation with providers.

In 1992 the Dutch government created an advisory committee to establish guidelines for a set of core health services (Dunning Committee, 1992). The committee recommended that in order for a service to be publicly funded it should meet four criteria. First, it should be regarded by the community as necessary care. Second, the care had to be demonstrated as effective. Third, it had to be efficient and fourth, the care could not be left to individual responsibility. In approaching their task in this manner the committee failed to provide a means of balancing one area of necessary care against another nor specific mechanisms for prioritizing health services.

In many countries a basic level of health care focuses on low-technology, primary care and excludes high-technology services such as liver transplants. If basic care is broadened to include unlimited access to intensive and expensive curative regimes, this will undermine the objectives of universal coverage and cost containment that are at the core of most developed countries' health care policies (Eddy 1991). Not surprisingly, these countries are more successful in covering the uninsured and in maintaining considerably lower per capita costs than the United States, but they do so only by limiting the availability of high technology medicine. The divergence between the U.S. health care system and that of other developed nations is most obvious in their approaches to rationing.

In an age of scarce resources in which medical goods and services are rationed, the debate over lifestyle choice increasingly will focus on the extent to which lifestyle ought to influence rationing decisions. While the ethical controversy over this question will not abate, the economic/policy context necessitates moves toward that end.

More than any other issues surrounding the rationing of medical resources, this aspect of lifestyle promises to be the most poignant. When should lifestyle criteria be expressly entered into the rationing equation? Who is responsible for establishing the criteria? What impact will this selection process have on the practice of medicine? These issues will be examined in more detail in chapter 5.

Despite the strong antipathy toward the concept of rationing in the United States, the rationing of medical technologies will become more prevalent. The customary approach to rationing medicine, where it is practiced by health care providers, but not explicitly acknowledged, gives us the illusion that we do not have to make these choices, but it does so only at the cost of mass deception. Lamm (1992:128) contends that we already ration—chronologically, geographically, economically, politically, scientifically, and by disease by giving the health care dollar to highly dramatic technologies. Moreover, this deception, in turn, has contributed to the misconception that as a society we can avoid explicit rationing decisions because we have managed to do so thus far. It is natural, when faced with such painful choices, to take solace in approaches that appear to free us from those decisions. "Such choices are unavoidable, but in health care they are hedged round by the mystic of medicine and by individual and social reluctance to accept the one certainty in life—death" (Maynard 1994:1).

American society, however, can no longer escape facing head on the problems of rationing. Although some persons remain content in the illusions of the customary approach (Califano 1992), high technology medicine accompanied by the array of technological, demographic and social trends discussed here make that impossible.

Although explicit rationing of medical resources is alien to a rights-oriented value system, ultimately there will be no escape from taking such decisions. In the absence of coordinated, consistent national criteria, rationing decisions will continue to be made on an ad hoc, reactive basis by a combination of public and private mechanisms including legislatures, courts, corporations, insurance companies, public relations firms, ethics committees, and physicians. The most appropriate question is not whether rationing ought to be done but rather, who should establish procedures that are fair and reasonable. To this end, a first order of business is to initiate a public dialogue over societal goals and priorities that includes consideration of the preferred agents for rationing medical resources. This initial enterprise could take the form of Lester Milbrath's (1989) Council for Long Range Societal Guidance, a standing national commission on bioethics (OTA 1993), or other proposed mechanisms. Although direct government control of the deliberations of this autonomous group must be restricted, the effort has to be initiated by the national government and must be viewed as legitimate and credible by public officials.

Although consensus on how medical resources ought to be distributed is unlikely, it might be possible to reach general agreement on the procedures through which society will approach these problems. If we can agree that the decisional criteria are fair, and understand that we are bound by them, specific applications, though difficult, might be perceived as unfortunate, but not unfair. As stated earlier, one of the reasons individuals and health providers tend to reject the notion of rationing or any attempt to withhold treatment in the United States is that there is no guarantee that the resources averted will be used fairly or even more efficiently. If one person forgoes a needed liver transplant, rather than being spent on prenatal care, most likely someone else will have the transplant—someone perhaps who is less "deserving."

Any attempts to ration medicine by edict, particularly if they involve lifestyle changes, will fail in a society such as the United States which stresses the predominance of individual rights over other societal priorities. It is foolish to presume that moderation of the expectations, demands, and behavior of a public that has come to expect unlimited access to technological progress in medicine is an easy task. Moreover, because office holders gain so little political credit for trying to convince people that they are largely responsible for their own health problems, one can hardly expect most elected officials to publicly advocate an explicit rationing policy. Elections and careers are lost, not won, on such issues. The difficulty of the issue, however, does not reduce the need and urgency of facing it.

Chapter 5

An Individual's Responsibility
for Health

In chapter 4 I argued that rationing needs to become more explicit and systematic. Current price rationing fails to provide a fair and equitable way of distributing scarce medical resources. I concluded however, by admitting that rationing will be most difficult where resources are denied individuals who have contributed to their own ill health. Moreover, the most difficult preventive measures are likely to be those in which the individual has prime responsibility: smoking, abuse of alcohol and drugs, diet, sedentary lifestyle, use of seat belts, and so forth.

Collectively, for lack of a better term, these behaviors and habits are labeled "lifestyle" decisions. Attempts by the government to intervene in lifestyle decisions are inherently controversial. For instance, laws requiring motorcyclists to wear safety helmets have been attacked as a paternalistic and unwarranted governmental interference in behavior that is not threatening to the health of others. Many of these mandates have either been rejected by the courts as violations of individual autonomy or rescinded by legislatures under constituency pressure. Pressures emerging from the health care crisis necessitate a much closer look at (1) the role individuals play in contributing to their own health problems, (2) a shift of responsibility for health toward the individual, and (3) a renewed emphasis on the obligation to society of individuals to do those things that maximize health.

Because it is society's scarce resources that are being allocated it seems only fair that society be held responsible ultimately for altering the goals which influence individual behavior. In the least, this requires placing the good of health at least on a par with that of enjoyment. To do this, the incentive structure operating within society must be radically revised to better reward healthful lifestyle choices of individual members. A major part of this effort must be aimed at reducing expectations of the public regarding the availability of health care resources and, thereby, reducing their unrealistic demand for curative medicine. Society must realize the necessity for limits and the end of the fatuous assumption of unlimited resources perpetuated in a consumptive society. Central to this understanding of limits will be the controversial notion of individual responsibility which is so alien to the American value system.

THE ROLE OF THE INDIVIDUAL—PAST AND PRESENT

The debate over the role of individual choice in determining personal health, although now intensifying, is far from new. The ancient Greeks stressed the effects of behavior on health. According to Plato, individuals have a responsibility to live in a manner that prevents illness. Those who do not have no claim on community resources for treatment. A virtuous citizen lives a life of moderation and exercises strict self-control. Likewise, the Greek physician Galen concluded that persons who allow harm to come to their bodies when there exists knowledge and the possibility of life's action to prevent it are morally culpable.

This view of individual blame for illness remained prevalent until the end of nineteenth century. Health was assumed to be within the reach of each person, given a modicum of self-control and motivation. Each person was, in great measure, the guardian and preserver of his or her own health. Illness was a state that individuals brought upon themselves through ignorance or intemperance of habit. The logical extension of this approach was to blame the victim. Even today, there is an assumption among many persons that the victims of illness or disease are being punished for their own failings. As evidence of the currency of this viewpoint, one need not look beyond the reaction of some fundamentalist religious leaders to AIDS.

Although it is doubtful that the concept of individual responsibility for health was ever fully displaced, in the early twentieth century knowledge about the relationship between poor social conditions and disease, and a resulting heightened social awareness, shifted emphasis toward societal responsibility for public health. There emerged the notion that society, not the individual, has the means to overcome poverty and disease, and the responsibility for maintaining the health of its people. To a large extent, this view developed from the fact that much disease in the latter nineteenth century was caused by inadequate water and sewerage systems and by abhorrent working conditions over which individuals had little control. Ironically, this emphasis on social responsibility led to an increased paternalism which assumed that individuals were incapable of controlling their own health. Responsibility for disease prevention measures was placed on patients and their physicians, but public health programs proliferated to ameliorate social conditions deemed unhealthy. Through the 1960s at least, the emphasis was on the social right of the individual to health care. In contrast, individual responsibility for personal health was downplayed and those persons who raised the issue were criticized as lacking a social conscience. Public incursions into matters of individual lifestyle were considered outside the legitimate sphere of government intervention.

In 1974, however, a Canadian report, *A New Perspective on the Health of Canadians*, initiated substantial interest in prevention and focused attention on lifestyle as a major determinant of the population's health. This was followed in 1979 by the U.S. Surgeon General's report titled *Health People* which similarly concluded that the foremost causes of illness lie in individual behavior and could be met most effectively through extensive changes in the lifestyles of many Americans. The tone of the report echoed John Knowles admonition that,

> The idea of individual responsibility has been submerged to individual rights—rights, or demands, to be guaranteed by government and delivered by public and private institutions. The cost of sloth, gluttony, alcoholic intemperance, reckless driving, sexual frenzy, and smoking is now a national, and not just an individual, responsibility. This is justified as individual freedom—but one

man's freedom in health is another man's shackle in taxes and insurance premiums. I believe the idea of a "right" to health should be replaced by the idea of an individual moral obligation to preserve one's health—a public duty if you will.   *(1977:59)*

This new health theme was reiterated in two volumes during the Nixon administration (*Forward Plan for Health*) that contained ambitious plans for constraining unhealthy lifestyle risks and furthered the view that the public's health was a matter of personal responsibility. In his address to Congress unveiling the Health Security Act, President Clinton emphasized responsibility as his sixth principle: "In short, responsibility should apply to anybody who abuses the system and drives up the cost for honest, hard-working citizens. . . . Responsibility also means changing some behaviors in this country that drive up our costs like crazy. And without changing it we'll never have the system we ought to have" (1993).

This reemerging emphasis on lifestyles and health follows from data showing that the major causes of mortality have shifted from infectious diseases to degenerative chronic diseases that are often associated with individual behavior. It is estimated that 50 percent of all premature deaths are associated with choices individuals make (Public Health Service 1995:3). As illustrated in table 5.1, three factors (tobacco, alcohol, diet) account for almost 40 percent of all deaths in the United States. "Alcohol, tobacco, injury risks and gaps in primary prevention accounted for 75 percent of the avoidable life years lost," according to Godfrey (1993:186). Moreover, 50 to 90 percent of all cancers are promoted or caused by various personal and environmental factors (Cundiff and McCarthy 1994:33). Likewise, Sullivan concludes, "Better control of fewer than ten risk factors . . . could prevent between 40 and 70 percent of all premature deaths, a third of all cases of acute disability, and two-thirds of all cases of chronic disability" (1990:1066). Table 5.2 demonstrates the cumulative impact of individual behavior on health.

Reinforcing this trend toward reevaluating the extent of morbidity and mortality that are directly tied to individual behavior is the current concern over the costs of health care. The insurmountable economic burden of medical care, to which the individual right–societal responsibility approach has contributed, is intensifying pressures to reduce or at least contain costs wherever possible. Because the need for the most expensive medical interventions such as long-term intensive care and organ transplantation is frequently a product of unhealthy individual action, it is likely that individual behavior that contributes to the need for these massive expenditures will be scrutinized more and more closely.

Although there are no accurate estimates of the cost of premature mortality or preventable morbidity caused by imprudent behavior, it runs into the tens and perhaps hundreds of billions of dollars (Leichter 1991:77). In 1990 the National Institute of Alcohol Abuse and Alcoholism estimated costs to society of alcohol-related problems to be $136.3 billion of which about $90 billion was for health problems. Although Hadley found that expanding medical care use had a significant impact on mortality rates, he concluded that "Changing personal behavior, as represented by reducing cigarette consumption, is probably more efficient" (1982:177). It is unlikely, given the trends in disease and illness and the massive health costs associated with certain individual behaviors that we can make major inroads on the health financing crisis without altering behavior of many individuals as noted by President Clinton. As stated by Tolley et al., "A major challenge in the area of public health is to encourage people to choose healthier lifestyles" (1994:375).

Moreover, because few persons today pay fully for their own medical care—the burden being shared by third-party payers including the government—"illness nowadays is a social event, a social expense" (Harsanyi and Hutton 1981:258). This means that people who try to

TABLE 5.1
Causes of Death in the United States, 1990

Cause	Estimated Number of Deaths	Percentage of Total Deaths
Tobacco	400,000	19
Diet/activity patterns	300,000	14
Alcohol	100,000	5
Microbial agents	90,000	4
Toxic agents	60,000	3
Firearms	35,000	1
Sexual behavior	30,000	1
Motor vehicles	25,000	1
Illicit use of drugs	20,000	<1
Total	1,060,000	

SOURCE: McGinnis and Foege 1993.

take care of themselves are underwriting the costs incurred by those who fail to do so. Understandably, there is an increasingly vocal demand to shift the monetary burden to those individuals who knowingly take the health risks. Results of this demand can be seen in moves toward lower insurance premiums for nonsmokers, recommendations to raise the tax on alcoholic beverages to pay for alcohol abuse programs, and corporate incentives for participation in physical fitness programs.

TABLE 5.2
Lifestyle and Self-Inflicted Diseases

Lifestyle	Self-Inflicted Diseases
Alcohol abuse	Cirrhosis of the liver Encephalopathy and malnutrition Motor-vehicle accidents Obesity
Cigarette smoking	Chronic bronchitis Emphysema Lung, bladder, and breast cancer Coronary artery disease
Pharmaceutical abuse	Drug dependence Adverse drug reactions
Addiction to psychotropic drugs	Suicide Homicide Malnutrition Accidents
Overeating	Obesity
High fat intake	Arteriosclerosis Coronary artery disease Diabetes
Low-fiber diet	Colorectal cancer
High carbohydrate intake	Dental caries
Lack of exercise	Coronary artery disease
Failure to wear seat belts	Higher incidence of severe automobile injuries and deaths
Sexual promiscuity or "irresponsibility"	Syphilis Gonorrhea Cervical cancer AIDS
Sun tanning	Skin cancer

SOURCE: Leichter 1991:77.

Considerable initiative for these actions comes from distaste at having to pay for someone else's bad habits. This demand for societal action in part reflects a desire for protection from the costs of calamities others bring upon themselves—in other words, it is a demand for fairness (Wikler 1978). The specter of unbounded increases in health care costs, reflected in skyrocketing medical insurance premiums, fuels the demand that persons engaging in a high-risk or unhealthy behavior pay their own way. This individual responsibility model is in direct contrast with the social responsibility model in which the individual is not held personally accountable for the results of his or her actions. Whereas the latter model recoils from placing blame on the victim, the present perspective makes an explicit goal of assigning responsibility, of finding fault in the individual.

According to Sher (1983:11), many medical needs are foreseeable and avoidable consequences of individuals' actions. Where the condition requiring care is predictable and avoidable and the person behaves such as to incur the condition, it might be termed "deserved." Although the medical needs created by such irresponsible behavior may not create valid claims on society for aid, it is unlikely that we would deny medical service even to those who have voluntarily brought on their own conditions. "It seems inhumane, and indeed indecent, to let someone suffer or die for lack of easily available treatment," according to Sher (1983:12). Despite this caveat, Sher concludes that when political and economic constraints make the meeting of all health needs impossible, "even those who accept the ideal of freedom may endorse some restrictions on choice to correct for unavailable distortions of judgment" (Sher 1983:12).

One such person is Robert Veatch:"I reach the conclusion that it is fair, that it is just, if persons in need of health services resulting from true, voluntary risks are treated differently from those in need of the same services for other reasons. In fact, it would be unfair if the two groups were treated equally" (1980:54).

A related matter concerns the disposition of cases involving individuals who have consciously chosen not to purchase health insurance. Although it is irrational in these times not to protect future financial security by purchasing health insurance, many people who can afford such insurance allocate their resources to more immediate and tangible expenditures. Questions arise as to the obligation of society to pay for needed health care for these individuals and the fairness of making others in society assume the risk that they avoided covering. Although it is not realistic to expect people to sacrifice food, clothing, and other necessities to buy medical insurance they may never use, one could argue that health insurance ought to take precedence over video recorders, new automobiles, and so forth. However, as legitimate needs in society have come to encompass a broad array of material goods, any attempts to ensure voluntary participation would fail. As often stated by the Clintons in defense of the Health Security Act, this dilemma could be largely resolved by the creation of a national health insurance plan that would mandate such participation by requiring enrollment of all wage earners.

The individual responsibility model becomes especially appropriate in light of the shift toward viewing health care as a positive right, because positive rights are accompanied by more extensive obligations. While negative rights are correlative only with the negative duty not to interfere with the rights of others, positive rights entail the duty to provide others in society with a minimal level of goods and services. Conversely, the recipient of positive rights has an obligation to other possessors of that right not to waste those goods and services. By transforming the right to health care from a negative to a positive right, considerably more obligations are placed on the recipients of that right.

Furthermore, the social responsibility model for health is less appropriate because of the aforementioned change in the nature of the health problems confronting us. Preventive health care is no longer a matter of mobilizing resources to overcome unavoidable public hazards such as poor sanitation and contaminated water supplies. Most, although certainly not all, health hazards today are avoidable or minimizable by individual action. A model that includes individual responsibility is more appropriate because the individual alone can now avoid many diseases. Whereas in the past, the major causes of disease were out of the individual's hands, today the individual can make a difference.

In an era where social action was necessary to overcome threats to health, it did not make sense to hold the individual responsible. Although society and its agents retain the responsibility to ameliorate where possible the causes of diseases, increasingly individuals can play an important role in their own health. Writes Veatch, "Even for those conditions that do not yet lend themselves to such direct voluntary control, the chronic diseases and even genetic diseases, there exists the possibility of purposive, rational decisions that have an indirect impact on the risk" (1980:52). With that capacity comes a heightened individual responsibility for health. Although we should not abandon the social responsibility model, it must be tempered with a heavy dose of individual responsibility.

There currently are pressures from many interests to broaden the scope of its involvement in personal lifestyle determination. Whether out of concern for fairness, paternalism, strict economics, or a blame-the-victim mentality, momentum is increasing for aggressive efforts to effect changes in individual behavior deemed dangerous to health. This is clearly evident for smoking and drinking. Attempts to ban smoking in public places and to remove the drinker from the highways are being approached with near missionary zeal by an array of organized interest groups that are lobbying hard, particularly in state legislatures. Although their motivations and proposed strategies differ, proponents of government involvement effectively utilize impressive data of the social and economic costs of the targeted behavior to buttress their arguments.

OBJECTIONS TO EMPHASIS ON INDIVIDUAL RESPONSIBILITY

Vigorous debate over public involvement in programs designed to reduce morbidity and mortality rates linked to personal behavior is inevitable. Because this approach confronts, and indeed threatens, the prevailing belief in individual rights and social responsibility, there has been no shortage of critics who view such a pattern as regressive and dangerous. Fitzgerald (1994) argues that this approach to disease prevention can deteriorate into "victim-blaming" if it becomes too strident and one-sided and fails to recognize the responsibility of society and government to develop and execute public policies that ameliorate conditions which help engender the unhealthful behaviors people adopt. If the so-called voluntary behavior of individuals is the result of socioeconomic and cultural factors, then blaming the individual wrongly evades the real cause, which is rooted in underlying social inequities (Chadwick 1993:87). At the base of this criticism, then, is the ideological debate over the extent to which lifestyles are determined by individual or societal forces.

Opposition to the use of lifestyle in rationing or allocating health care resources takes many forms. First, it is argued that in a liberal society with its pluralist traditions there is no one conception of the good life (Elhauge 1994:1520). Whose view then ought to prevail in deciding what is socially acceptable behavior? The threat to individual liberty inherent in allocating resources by lifestyle ironically is perceived by both liberals and conservatives. Civil liberty proponents argue that competent adults have a right to live as they want, even foolishly or self-destructively, as long as they are not an immediate threat to others. Paying the costs of their behavior is one of the costs a society must bear to remain free. In like manner, conservatives view state intrusion in private affairs unacceptable. Overall, the argument here is that individuals should be left with as much leeway as possible in choosing their own lifestyles no matter how foolish. Even if there are cost externalities on others, any state intervention must be non-coercive because any intrusions on personal autonomy are viewed as examples of heavy-handed paternalism. If carried to the extreme, however, this argument would negate all preventive efforts because as noted by Miller, "virtually no public health measure of consequence can be cited that does not in some measure, according to someone's view, limit individual freedoms" (1984:553).

A second, related objection to focusing attention on individual behavior is the concept of blaming the victim. According to Leichter: "The 'sickness as sin' emphasis . . . bares striking resemblance to the nineteenth-century conception of sickness as divine judgment for behavior" (1991:85). Tesh (1981) denounces such emphasis as a political ploy aimed at diverting attention from the core socioeconomic origins of disease and failures of the health care system. We protect industry by blaming the sick. Chadwick (1993) argues that society's notion of desert is not an appropriate factor for allocating health care resources and argues that the problem with the idea of individual responsibility for health is that it gives insignificant weight to social causes of disease and to the context within which individual choices are made. She concludes that we cannot abandon people to their fate on grounds of disapproval of their lifestyle. Fitzgerald, too, warns against a zealotry about healthy lifestyles on grounds of victim blaming. "In this way we can blame patients for their illnesses and deny them both our compassion and our services. The thrust toward rationing of health care is making the association between vice and disease a public policy" (1994:197).

The third criticism flows from the second and argues that victim blaming is especially unfair because much unhealthy behavior stems from uncontrollable characteristics. Genetic predispositions as well as the socioeconomic context often result in behaviors where the individual is neither free to choose nor able to control his or her behavior. As long as our understanding of the scientific bases of self-abuse is so weak, it is unfair to blame the person. In effect, punishing an ill person for characteristics or actions beyond his or her control, makes unhealthy behavior itself a crime. For Etzioni, "health as individual responsibility . . . tends to overlook or misconstrue the nature of the social constraints on the individual will" (1978:65). Moreover, social conditions not only are influential in maintaining unhealthy habits but also might stimulate their initial adoption (Leichter 1991:84).

A final argument leveled against individual responsibility is that any system designed to enforce its role in allocation is unworkable. There is no sharp line between those persons who take health risks and those who do not because we all take risks. Such a system is also susceptible to discriminatory abuse. For instance, despite all the attention targeted at cigarette smokers, it is not clear that a smoker imposes greater financial burdens on society than a nonsmoker. Because smokers die younger, nonsmokers probably end up requiring treatment for a greater number of diseases including expensive ones at the end of life. In addition they draw significantly more resources in pensions. For this reason, Elhauge sees the emphasis on individual responsibility based on prejudicial hostility toward smokers, not on facts, and concludes: "Even if smoking—or some other category of activity—could be shown to impose net societal costs, a more proportionate response would be to impose greater cigarette taxes rather than adopting an allocation scheme that imposes potential capital punishment" (1994: 1523).

SUPPORT FOR INDIVIDUAL RESPONSIBILITY

The strong reaction against a new emphasis on individual responsibility for health by both liberal and conservative critics is neither surprising nor unwarranted. As argued in chapter 2, individual behavior cannot be understood outside a complex social and cultural milieu. Mechanic is correct when he concludes that individual behavior is influenced more by cultural and socially rewarded adaptational behavior than specific health motivations. Most behavior is influenced as much by the "routine organization of everyday settings and activities" as by personal decisions of individuals (Mechanic 1994:119). I argue, however, that rewarding unhealthy behaviors by guaranteeing needed medical interventions to ameliorate the problems they cause simply reinforces such routines. Instead of enabling such behavior we ought to make it socially and culturally unacceptable.

It is interesting, for example, that while the debate over liver transplantation for alcoholic cirrhosis continues (see Starzl et al. 1988) those who know most about alcohol addiction are explicit that alcoholics should not continue to be rescued from their own actions. No matter how well-intentioned such interventions are, they serve only to protect the addict from his or her actions. Enablers do the addict no favor in the long run. The failure of the general medical community to understand the dynamics of addiction and its rescue of the drug or alcohol addict who needs medical treatment as a consequence of his or her own actions in effect enables the addict to deny the consequences and the addiction. While refusing to rescue addicts appears uncaring and cruel, enabling actions are counterproductive in treating the core problem. Enabling perpetuates the illness of addiction and hampers possible recovery (Al-Anon 1989).

Although many of the arguments against instituting individual responsibility for health are important points for debate, the U.S. liberal society has gone too far in downplaying personal responsibility. We need to restore a balance that is now missing because: "A society cannot afford to absolve everyone of personal responsibility, even as it tempers judgments with compassion. From a practical vantage, there simply aren't sufficient resources" (Kassler 1994:176).

Beauchamp (1988:22) sees restrictions on risky individual behaviors as justified because those risks that result in loss of life in the aggregate are risks to the community. He suggests that limiting liberties to promote the public health is to promote a common good, not a private or paternalistic one. "The American insistence on absolute autonomy has a kind of mystic quality that badly needs deflating" if we are to serve the collective interests (Beauchamp 1988:99). Callahan (1990:105) too sees a need to shift priorities toward the collective good even if it involves restricting the behavior of individuals.

Chadwick (1993:87) contends that desert should not be a consideration in allocating health care resources because we all take risks, for instance driving a car. Her analogy however fails to distinguish between the normal risks of driving a car and irresponsible use of the car. Although the notion of no-fault action is attractive in our society, it dilutes the notion of responsibility that is integral to a community. An individual responsibility approach would treat the person who continues to drive recklessly or drunkenly differently than the person who admittedly takes a risk by driving at all but is hit by the reckless, intoxicated driver. While medical ethics may demand equal treatment or in some cases preference for the reckless driver, the signals this sends to individuals reinforces the presumption that society cannot or will not value responsible behavior when it comes to allocating scarce medical resources.

Likewise, Fitzgerald (1994:197) is correct in arguing the dangers of developing a view that if health is normal then sickness and accidents must be faults. In the extreme, such a system is unfair and unrealistic because such a view is simply wrong. Some accidents and illnesses have faults and others do not. However, the opposite view that sickness and accidents can never be someone's responsibility (or fault) is also in error. As discussed earlier, much of what is spent on health care is in fact directed toward situations where the individual has contributed to or caused the problem. To deny responsibility is as dangerous as assuming that someone must always be at fault.

Free Will and Individual Responsibility

Critics who charge that any effort to assign individual responsibility for behaviors that result in ill health amounts to "blaming the victim" appear all too willing to dismiss individual accountability for action. The assumption that persons are victims implies a lack of free will on their part. Individuals, in this approach, are viewed as incapable of making rational decisions when it comes to selecting healthy as opposed to unhealthy practices. Such critics may argue, for instance, that cigarette smokers smoke because of peer pressure as shaped and reinforced by media advertising, and are therefore simply reflecting societal influences. Recent suits against tobacco companies by cigarette smokers whose habit has led to disease exemplify this reasoning, in which the person who made the choice to smoke would be absolved of responsibility.

According to this viewpoint, individuals are unable to make rational choices, because they are products of societal forces that mold their personal behavior. This argument can be heard from both ends of the ideological spectrum. Although the most vocal proponents of this view come from the left, fundamental religions contend that society perpetuates promiscuity, pornography, and so forth through the mass media and assume that individuals have little capacity to act in ways counter to what the media tells them. This environmental determinist view concedes to individuals little free will to choose a healthy lifestyle.

Ironically, this argument against the free will and accountability of individuals for their actions is manifested as well in genetic arguments that would appear to be the antithesis of the environmentalist approach. Increasingly, evidence is offered to support the contention that unhealthy personal habits might be genetically preconditioned. Recently, the heightened genetic susceptibility of persons to alcoholism (Holden 1991) and obesity (Price 1987) has been suggested as a cause of these problems. The search for genetic markers that determine susceptibility is ongoing and undoubtedly will result in the identification of some genes that are found in higher proportions among persons with specific behavioral patterns (Young 1993). As with strict social environmental determinism, if the genetic argument is stated in the extreme, it will suggest that individuals lack the free will to make certain choices concerning their personal behavior because they are, in effect, the product of their genes.

Both of these theoretical perspectives are important contributors to our understanding of personal behavior. Certainly, as humans we are products of both the social environment and our genetic heritage. Many personal practices are shaped by the value system and institutional structure of a particular culture—there is no disputing this. Furthermore, current scientific evidence suggests that a genetic base to behavior is often present, particularly in creating susceptibility to a behavior. Although it is unlikely that alcoholism, for instance, is genetically determined, human twin studies as well as experimental animal research demonstrate a genetic predisposition. Some people, then, might have less resistance than others to alcohol addiction or might have a genetic predisposition toward obesity. In neither case should this negate the dimension of free will or individual responsibility for behavior.

Any policies that ration medicine on the basis of lifestyle choices or that otherwise discriminate against those persons who engage in self-destructive or unhealthy habits must take into account the social and genetic contributions to that behavior. If it is found that people are unable to exercise free choice within the context of the mass media or other societal incentives toward the unhealthy practice, then that incentive structure should be modified. Conversely, until society actually does use lifestyle choices to ration scarce resources, there is little disincentive for such behavior.

Within our technological-fix mentality, it is not uncommon for those persons engaging in unhealthy behaviors to rationalize their actions by assuming that science will provide a cure for problems that might accrue in the long run. "An irony worth noting is that the willingness of individuals to voluntarily jeopardize their health may be due, at least in part, to their faith in the ability of technology to rescue them if and when the harmful consequences of their choices eventuate" (Bronzino et al. 1990:518).

Why should people stop acting in unhealthy ways if they know they will be taken care of in any eventuality—if society and its paramedics, emergency rooms, technological wizardry, and social services will be there to pick up the pieces? Would persons change their behavior if they knew that medical resources would not be available to them because of an explicit social policy against the deployment of scarce resources to individuals who knowingly contribute to their own ill health? If one assumes that social environment is critical to individual choice, then a responsible public policy to alter the current incentive/disincentive structure is necessary.

Unfortunately, many of those observers with a social-environmental determinist leaning reject strong action by the state to discourage deleterious personal behavior. Such efforts, they argue, represent illegitimate state interference in individual choice. Rationing of medicine on lifestyle grounds is bound to be attacked by these individuals as a further attempt to blame the victim. The circularity of their argument is obvious, because unless society takes steps to strongly discourage harmful behaviors, it in effect encourages such behaviors. Particularly if individuals lack the free will to make and thus be responsible for their own decisions, it is up to society to actively work to shape their practices. By denying free will and also rejecting societal intervention, the proponents of this approach offer no logical means out of this dilemma. Although the provision of education programs and adequate social support systems to ensure that a free, informed choice is possible should be a first priority, it is unlikely that the problems of alcohol abuse, smoking, proper diet, and so forth will be overcome by these means alone. More ambitious and intrusive steps by society, however, are destined to be fought by critics who appear to want it both ways.

Similarly, it is difficult to apply the genetic model without severe implications for individual choice. If we accept the assumption that behavior has a significant genetic component, we have several options. We can choose to ignore evidence of genetic propensities, but in the process forfeit any advantages that would accrue from designing social policy that would target these individuals for special education, counseling, or treatment programs. Alternately, we could utilize this information to categorize children on the basis of the genetic markers they carry and establish preventive programs to avert behavioral patterns that, combined with their genetic susceptibility, would put these persons at risk.

The second option can be perceived as either expanding the person's free choice by fully setting forth the risks, or constraining it by defining what is socially responsible action in light of the information. In other words, although such information may or may not be valuable for a particular individual, designing social policy around it might be seen as constrictive of free choice. Furthermore, the social stigma of simply being identified as having heightened genetic susceptibility might be critical enough to impugn the fairness of any such policy, not to mention its questionable effectiveness as a preventive strategy. Once this type of information is available, however, it may be difficult for a society concerned with the health of its citizens not to utilize it. It is feasible that genetic information of this type might be included among the criteria for rationing medicine in the foreseeable future and be an integral part of a preventive program. Both the environmental and genetic models, then, could be used to justify intrusive governmental policies designed to alter individual behavior that is deemed to be unhealthy. By assuming that individual free will and responsibility for behavior are limited by either the societal or genetic factors, these approaches could conceivably lead to severe constraints being imposed upon individual lifestyle choices if used as rationales for public policy.

Balancing Rights and Responsibilities

We need to set reasonable boundaries on the rights to health care and reinstitute the notion of individual responsibility for health.

Every right ought to carry with it a corresponding obligation to those upon whom the claim is levied. This is especially relevant in attempts to tie allocation and rationing criteria to individual lifestyle choice. It could be argued that in order to claim societal health resources, a person should be expected to act responsibly and not unduly contribute to the risk of ill health. Although people have a right to design their own lifestyle, if they choose to engage in practices and behavior that puts them at high risk, they should be prepared to relinquish their claim on societal health care resources. By failing to balance their rights with responsibilities, they would surrender positive extensions of those rights. The concept of responsibility, then, places rights in a social context and allows an observer to set priorities among rights according to the extent to which each interest is affected. In order to determine the rights that are appropriate, each application would have to be analyzed carefully within this more complex and dynamic context. The responsibility of society toward particular individuals or groups would have to be gauged and their freedom of expression and choice balanced against their broader responsibilities to society.

The distinction between positive and negative rights is clear in cases of unhealthy or high-risk lifestyle choices. The right not to wear seat belts, for instance, must be weighed against the positive right to medical resources if one is injured because seat belts were not used despite the substantial burden such injuries place on society in the aggregate. It is necessary to decide how it is most appropriate for society to preempt rights: either pass mandatory seat belt laws and constrain the right not to wear the belt, or refuse to allocate societal resources to treat persons injured because they failed to take this action.

A preventive approach places restrictions on the negative right—the right not to be interfered with—and justifies state intervention on grounds of avoiding the future health costs associated with this behavior. Obviously, this means that the right of many people to choose whether to wear seat belts or not will be constrained in order to protect the health of the few people who are in an accident and would be injured more seriously if they chose not to take this preventive measure. Although this approach seems most reasonable, perhaps the more direct threat of rationing resources away from those injured while not wearing seat belts is also appropriate.

The same approach could be used to penalize persons who fail to take other preventive actions, but only with severe consequences for the concept of positive rights. Using this approach, cigarette smokers could continue to exercise that lifestyle choice, but they would lose their claim upon society for health resources to treat the results of their behavior. The same could be done for voluntary obesity, alcohol consumption, promiscuity, and so forth. Understandably, this approach requires a complete revision of the prevailing notion of rights in the United States. Whereas the conventional notion of rights largely excludes responsibility for personal behavior, this revised concept would shift emphasis heavily toward responsibility. Furthermore, those persons who failed to act responsibly would lose in large portion their claim upon societal health resources.

Problems arise in balancing out negative as well as positive rights and in determining whose rights take precedence in cases of conflict. In addition, any rights must be viewed within a broader social context that includes consideration of other values such as fairness and equity. Although a person might believe he or she has a right to a transplant operation, the realization that expending up to 100 units of blood and tens of thousands of dollars on an operation that has a low chance of restoring the recipient to a reasonable quality of life diverts resources from many other persons who would benefit may make such surgery seem unfair. Questions abound in medicine as to what legitimate claim a person has on health care resources. It is clear that the more broadly we define an individual's positive right to these resources, the more constraints we place on the rights of others. Any policy decision to limit the claims of citizens covered by public health care plans risks discriminating against those persons lacking adequate private resources and raises questions of equity.

The central problem in expanding our notions of a positive right to health care is in setting reasonable boundaries. It is one thing to argue that all persons have a right to primary health care. It is quite another to assume that this right encompasses guaranteed access to a full range of curative or rescue technologies. Within the framework of scarce medical resources and virtually unlimited, though extremely expensive, technological intervention possibilities, constraints on what a right to health care entails must be established and enforced, no matter how difficult that might be. Someone has to pay for each person's claim on medical resources. When these costs become prohibitive, rights must be defined more narrowly.

Moreno and Bayer (1985:37) contend that the critics of health promotion strategies have seized the ideological high ground and

forced the advocates to defend state intervention solely on the basis
of economic costs for society accruing from risky personal behavior.
They argue that proponents of intervention would be on a more
solid ethical ground in asserting the moral primacy of health itself as
a social good (Moreno and Bayer 1985:37). The well-being of the
members of the community is in itself a legitimate concern of public
policy. Certainly health is a critical element of this well-being. Economic arguments alone, they argue, fail to justify ethically aggressive
state intervention and can cut both ways.

Similarly, Russell (1986:112) argues that while good health has
intrinsic value and is worth paying for, by emphasizing cost savings
the most ardent proponents of prevention have put themselves in the
untenable position of arguing that a preventive measure is a good
investment only because it saves money. With this logic, the burden
of proof is placed on the proponents to demonstrate that prevention
is invariably the best monetary investment, which it may not be.
Although the paucity of conclusive scientific data on the deleterious
effects of many lifestyle practices on health and the impracticality of
effective enforcement of intrusive social policy buttress the arguments of the opposition, they do not negate the need for vigorous
debate over the issue.

REINSTATING THE RESPONSIBILITY OF THE INDIVIDUAL

If a shift to individual responsibility is necessary as argued here, what
are the best and most feasible routes to this end in U.S. culture? On
the one hand individuals can be encouraged to take responsibility.
This can be effected by health education and health promotion campaigns and by modifying the social and economic incentive structure
to enable healthy behavior. On the other hand, steps could be taken
to make individuals more financially responsible for unhealthy
behavior or, at the extreme, health care resources could be denied.

Between these extremes are a limitless array of positive and negative incentives. Noncoercive measures to encourage healthful lifestyles might include provision of jogging paths and bicycle lanes and
access to healthful opposed to junk foods. Financial incentives such
as lowered insurance premium rates, decreased taxes, and other
rewards for prudent personal lifestyles easily degenerate into disincentives which, in effect, punish individuals for socially unacceptable

practices. Alcohol and cigarette taxes designed to alter personal behavior are one clear form of disincentive.

In most instances, however, such simplistic approaches are inequitable and regressive in that they are hardest on the poor. A more subtle means of enforcing compliance is by establishing standards of duty under the tort system and assigning liability for personal practices that violate court-enforced societal norms. Any policy to change lifestyles will probably depend on some combination of incentives and disincentives—in other words, rewards or punishments—for socially defined acceptable and unacceptable individual action.

One critical question deserves substantially more attention: how does society set the baseline for incentives and disincentives? There is a latent assumption that the newest technologies somehow ought to set the baseline. Although not surprising given the strength of the technological imperative in our system, this approach must be reevaluated. As noted throughout this book, the finite resources available for health care can never meet the infinite demands which medical innovations seem to foster. By building an incentive/disincentive structure on the baseline of the newest technologies, there is little to discourage continually escalating use of these innovations. A shift toward the individual responsibility model must include an awareness of inconsistencies in the inventive/disincentive structure.

The most coercive mechanisms for controlling personal lifestyle choices are regulations that specifically prohibit certain practices under threat of law. The strength of the outcry against mandatory motorcycle helmet laws in the mid-1970s demonstrates the difficulty of framing regulatory policies that are perceived as impinging upon personal choice in the pluralist United States. Similar difficulties in enforcing mandatory seat belt laws and antismoking ordinances suggest that direct government efforts to regulate individual lifestyle, even to promote health and prevent illness, are likely to withstand neither constitutional tests nor public opinion. As noted in chapter 2, Americans value their freedom to select their own lifestyle and tend to react against direct government intervention, whether based upon economic or paternalistic rationales. Unfortunately, this persuasion will be devastating unless some limits are set, as difficult task as that might be.

In our society, education concerning the potentially harmful effects of personal practices on the individual's health is the most acceptable means of altering behavior. Although it is not as explicitly intrusive as other options discussed above, education can be selective and manipulative. Particularly in the United States, with its emphasis on mass persuasion, education efforts are never completely neutral nor, perhaps, should they be. The effectiveness of an education campaign, whether it be designed to encourage people to quit smoking, to obtain annual dental checkups, or to buckle up their seat belts, is measured by the extent to which individuals alter behavior. To some degree, every educational campaign has a message to sell—it advocates that a particular responsible choice be made.

Not surprisingly, education efforts are criticized from both sides in the lifestyles debate, although for different reasons. Some advocates of reform cite the minimal effectiveness of education programs as evidence that such efforts are a waste of resources and a subterfuge for inaction. In contrast, opponents argue that education efforts are not neutral either by design or effect. They contend that under the guise of education, individuals are manipulated. At the least, they are given the impression that if they do not change their behavior, they are being irresponsible. In spite of these problems, I believe that the most acceptable means for reducing unhealthy and unsafe personal behavior is education and that such education should come before habits are formed, preferably early in youth. Health education in the United States, however, has received little support under the dominant medical model. Well under 1 percent of total health expenditures are allocated to education. Moreover, the quality of existing health education efforts tends to be low and the results discouraging. Although education is the most feasible means of promoting healthy personal lifestyles, it alone is unlikely to drastically alter individual behavior because such behavior, no matter how destructive, has broad attraction to many people. Appeals to the individual's own future health as well as to more general social goals in itself will fail to avert the need for expending a large proportion of the health care budget on conditions and diseases that are preventable.

Taxing Unhealthy Behaviors

For those persons opposed to rationing medicine by lifestyle another option is to make those who engage in high-risk activities contribute proportionately more to the health care budget. "Sin taxes" have become an attractive source of general revenue over and above their use in recouping excess costs linked to the behavior, and their inclusion in the Clinton Health Security Act was among the proposal's most popular aspects (Kahn 1995:181). They are made more attractive because they are viewed as taxing undesirable behavior as well as compensating for external costs caused by persons indulging in it. For most activities, this could be achieved by taxing risky behavior, but only if the taxes collected went directly to health care to subsidize the increase in costs attributed to that behavior. Cundiff and McCarthy for instance: "suggest that under a rebalanced health care system it will be possible to fund health care expenses primarily through taxes on commodities that contribute substantially to the nation's current health care burden" (1994:15).

To do so for alcohol they propose a tax of $2.00 per ounce, meaning the *tax* on a six-pack of beer would be $13.00, a 750 ml bottle of wine $12.00, and a 750 ml bottle of 100 proof liquor, $40.00. While such taxes are likely to shrink alcohol usage, given the political influence of the alcohol industry and the drinking public, it is unlikely that anything near this level will be approached. In addition to the traditional sin taxes of cigarettes and alcohol, Cundiff and McCarthy suggest taxing firearms, the electronic media, nonrenewable energy, and unhealthy food. The actual level of taxes on such commodities should reflect public health care costs.

In addition to using such taxes to fund health care, another goal is to use taxing to increase the costs of these commodities and thus reduce consumption, thereby improving public health, preventing disease, and promoting health. If successful it is argued that this strategy will ultimately reduce the need for medical care. Reduced consumption of course, will also reduce revenues. It is estimated, for instance, that for every 10 percent increase in the price of cigarettes, adult consumption decreases by 4 percent (Kassler 1994:202). Cross-national studies, however, suggest that decreased consumption following heightened taxes on alcohol might be short-lived and that consumption levels will slowly rise to previous levels as consumers become accustomed to the higher prices.

Although the "sin tax" strategy is intuitively attractive, except for tobacco and alcohol users, its operationalization is problematic. To be fair such schemes should include any products or behaviors that lead to ill health. Cundiff and McCarthy (1994) suggest taxes on sky diving, junk food, motorcycles, sports, and other risky activities—but such a list, of course, could be endless. However, our understanding of the scientific basis of health and disease and the relative contributions of individual behaviors changes over time. Furthermore, society's view of acceptable and unacceptable actions clouds the objectivity in determining what might be taxed. Who or what agency will decide where to draw the lines under such circumstances?

Another problem with taxing unhealthy behavior is that many risky behaviors are illegal. Taxing alcohol and cigarettes, but not marijuana, cocaine, crack, or other substances would seem to be counterproductive. Perhaps this supports the case for legalizing these drugs and taxing them at rates commensurate with their health costs, but this seems unlikely to occur. The same can be said for prostitution and other activities that increase the risk and thus the health costs of promiscuous sex.

Equitable implementation of taxing health risk behaviors is not feasible in light of these complexities. In their extensive study of poor health habits, Manning et al. (1991) found that compared to the external costs of cigarette smoking the current excise tax in the United States on cigarettes (one of the lowest in Western democracies) is too high, while external costs of alcohol require at least a doubling of current alcohol taxes. This discrepancy in large part reflects political and social factors that have made cigarettes a popular and easy target for taxation because it is borne by a politically incorrect behavior. Another discrepancy is that instead of taxing tobacco to offset the increased health costs of smokers, the vast proportion of the funds collected go into the general revenue funds of the states.

Another alternative to rationing by lifestyle is to increase the premiums paid into the health system by those individuals who engage in high-risk behaviors. Again, while this approach seems logical and is intuitively attractive as more fair than rationing, like taxation it is inherently selective in nature and by necessity has focused only on several areas, particularly smoking and alcohol use. Moreover, many of those individuals at highest risk fall outside the private insurance system and are unlikely to be affected by higher premiums. Although increased premiums for unhealthy lifestyle enjoy wide support and provide the appearance of fairness, they too fail to deliver needed incentives for individual responsibility.

Rationing by Lifestyle

The most controversial question surrounding individual responsibility is whether individuals who engage in unhealthy behavior should be denied certain types of health care. Although many ethicists and social commentators condemn any suggestions of such explicit rationing, the economic context and realities of where health care resources are used demands consideration that individuals who harm themselves be denied expensive medical technologies in scarce supply. I agree with Engelhardt when he concludes: "It will also be morally acceptable for society, if it pursues expensive life-saving treatment, to exclude persons who through their own choices increase the cost of care . . . . There is no invidious discrimination against persons in setting limits to coverage or in precluding coverage if the costs are increased through free choice" (1984:70).

As individuals in the United States come to pay larger proportions in out-of-pocket costs or insurance premiums, the issue of individual responsibility will intensify. Individuals who try to take care of themselves increasingly will realize that they are paying the costs of the deleterious behavior of a minority of citizens who use a disproportionate amount of health care. At present this cost-shifting is not transparent because the tab is largely borne by third-party payers. With the severe tightening up of Medicare and Medicaid spending and the increased use of managed competition, the extent of the burden of individuals who live unhealthy lifestyles on the health system will become more apparent. Already many medical personnel are aware of the large proportion of their time devoted to individuals who refuse to protect their health and they "find it a particular affront that anyone would deliberately risk it" (Elhauge 1994:1524). Although it is politically incorrect and ethically suspect to call for such rationing, I argue that this is the direction we must move.

While I agree that it is unfair to hold persons responsible for behavior that is not under their control and that health status is most clearly defined by one's environment, I consider that much behavior is conscious and deliberate. Although ultimately the goal should be to eliminate social inequities that cumulatively influence individual health status and behavior, unless we instill the idea of individual responsibility and modify the current incentive structure, any health care reform will fail. Given the discussion of the limits of medical care in chapter 2, pouring more money into fixing the health of persons who endanger their own health, is futile. It would be more effective and humane to shift the resources saved by rationing into social programs designed to reduce poverty, crime, and other manifestations of socioeconomic inequalities.

Those observers opposed to rationing by lifestyle are likely to reject any rationing scheme because all rationing schemes will most adversely affect persons who engage in unhealthy lifestyles simply because it is they who are the high users of such services. If we are serious about controlling the health cost explosion we must ration from high users. Directly or indirectly then rationing will reduce the medical resources going to such individuals. The question, then, is whether to make individual behavior an explicit basis upon which to deny health care. Excluding those situations where such individuals will be denied treatment because they are poorer medical risks or have less optimistic prognosis than individuals with healthy lifestyles, given equal need and equal prognosis should lifestyle count? While I argue that medical ethics excludes the medical community itself from considering lifestyle per se, I also submit that public policy can and should make distinctions.

Despite the difficulties and the problems raised by the critics, I favor explicit policies that ration high-cost medical interventions away from individuals who have clearly contributed to or caused their ill health. We need to make inroads into the high costs of caring for high users although these costs are problematic and understandably difficult of resolution. Such a system should be instituted incrementally over the coming decade, for it would be most unfair to immediately implement it without fair warning. Also, this time lag will give us the opportunity to do more research on the linkage between individual actions and health. Although one result of such rationing might be to save significant resources, the primary goal is to put all citizens on notice that the assumption of unlimited medical support is no longer assured for those persons who refuse to take responsibility for their own health. Also, as noted earlier any resources saved by this policy should be shifted into programs designed to ameliorate social inequities.

Under this policy all persons, no matter what their lifestyle should have access to a basic package of health care, which includes primary care and a limited range of acute/chronic care. Other interventions such as organ transplantation, kidney dialysis, and long-term intensive care should be provided only if resources are available to meet the basic needs of all citizens. We need to draw lines somewhere. A good place to start is to reduce funding for those procedures that are primarily used to rescue people from the results of their own behavior. Such a system would be dependent on a shift from demand-side, price rationing to supply-side, nonprice rationing. Under the current open-ended system a Mickey Mantle or Larry Hagman can always get their transplant because it is rationed by price. This transformation would move the U.S. approach toward those found in other democracies where, not surprisingly, there is greater emphasis on individual responsibility and collective good (see chapter 4).

Prevention and Lifestyle

The preference for curative medicine over prevention in the United States is overwhelming. In 1993, total national expenditures for population-based public health activities was estimated to be $8.4 billion, less than 1 percent of total health care spending (Public Health Service 1995:5). Despite the AIDS epidemic, tuberculosis and measles outbreaks, and increased problems with substance abuse, violence and teenage pregnancy, public health strategies as a proportion of the health care budget fell by 25 percent between 1981 and 1993. In 1992 $34 was spent per person on prevention while $3,007 was spent per person on medical care (Public Health Service 1995:42). Cuts in public health budgets have also been the U.S. norm as well.

Despite a general understanding that it is more cost-effective and humane to avoid a condition in the first place than to have to treat it later, health systems instead continue to place emphasis on curative approaches. As noted earlier, this is not surprising because whereas curative medicine deals with identifiable patients, prevention deals with statistical lives: "When a patient is facing certain death, the individual, his or her family, and society as a whole are willing to pay heavily for any innovation that offers even a small promise of postponing death. By contrast, the healthy population is not willing to pay for preventive innovations that would save many more lives for each dollar of expenditure" (Fuchs 1994:111). Although preventive programs also help individuals, it is difficult to identify who they might be, whereas curative medicine relates to specific patients in "direct, immediate and documentable way" (Baird Commission 1993:347).

Moreover, the medical profession has developed primarily around the search for cures of disease, rather than for preventing disease. Also, most advances in the preventive area have come from outside medicine, particularly through improved sanitation, housing, nutrition, and education. Despite considerable evidence suggesting that the most significant improvements have come from preventive approaches, "many groups (health care workers, physicians, hospital employees, pharmacists, and others employed in the health care industry) have a strong interest in maintaining or increasing funding for treatment" (Baird Commission 1993:348). Any reduction in this emphasis is likely to run into opposition from the health care industry, medical professionals, and consumers who have "grown accustomed to expensive care at low direct cost" (Harrop 1992:159). In combination with potential patients and a public strongly influenced by optimistic media coverage these groups have substantial influence on the priority given curative medicine. Human interest stories and favorable media coverage, naturally follow technological breakthroughs in treatment. Together these forces can provide formidable pressures against a reallocation of scarce resources from curative to preventive strategies.

Despite these problems, evidence suggests that the most significant improvements in health have come from preventive medicine, not curative or supportive, even though these latter efforts are the most dramatic and, therefore, most easily funded (Fries et al. 1993). Elsewhere, Fries (1988) concludes that prevention compresses morbidity by extending a person's healthy years and thereby reducing the individual and social burden of illness. By postponing the time at which we become victims of a chronic disease, prevention allows people to live healthier and more active lives although it might not necessarily extend their life span. Although modern medicine is by no means ineffective, Western cultures have overestimated its effectiveness and underestimated its limitations, according to Palmer and Short (1989:48). Therefore, "reform of the medical delivery system and improvements in access to medical care alone will make possible only limited gains in health, the remaining gains require community-level interventions that public health provides" (Public Health Service 1995:6).

A multifaceted preventive approach would require that substantial attention be given to improving the environment by reducing environmental pollutants; to eliminating unsafe working conditions; and to continuing to improve housing, health education, and early detection programs. Inadequate nutrition continues to contribute to a variety of health problems and would also have to be addressed in a comprehensive health care program.

The goal of primary prevention, then, is to avoid or reduce the onset of disease, thus producing a healthier population. This goal cannot be achieved without altering unhealthy individual behaviors. As discussed in chapter 4, prevention will not reduce health care costs unless it is accompanied by major lifestyle changes in the population. As stated by Bronzino et al.: "for preventive health care and associated technologies to merit much investment of society's health care resources, these sorts of coercive limits on individual choice [i.e. banning use of cigarettes, forcing individuals to exercise] would have to be enacted" (1990:517).

To the extent that such constraints are unlikely in the United States, primary prevention will not be entirely successful. Despite this, prevention must be a central element of health care reform and all efforts should be made to educate, encourage, and motivate essential behavioral changes.

Although I contend that the individual must bear considerably more responsibility for his or her health status, the abrogation of society's responsibility for the health of its members does not follow. If anything, the social responsibility to educate and counsel individuals is heavier. It is in this area of a social responsibility for encouraging healthful behavior where our institutions have failed. Although I agree with Goodman and Goodman (1986) that assigning to the individual the major responsibility for preventive health shifts the onus away from social agencies, I argue that it does so justifiably only after society has made considerable effort to inform and educate individuals. This societal commitment must also include increasing the priority of research into lifestyle choice and health so that the individual has the best information possible upon which to base his or her choices. Instead of reducing social responsibility, prevention, even when targeted at individual lifestyle, primarily redirects responsibility away from the provision of curative technologies toward the provision of information and education.

CHAPTER 6

COMPARATIVE HEALTH POLICY
The United States Stands Alone

The United States is the only Western industrial country that does not guarantee universal health care. As discussed thus far, it is clear that the United States has many health care problems that are unique, or at the least extreme. But all countries, regardless of their health care systems are facing similar problems of rising demands for medical technologies, aging populations, and continuing pressures for increased health care expenditures. Moreover, the recession that hit most Western countries "aggravated cost pressures by squeezing the general tax or employment-based revenues that support health systems worldwide" (Kassler 1994:191). Despite this, most other countries have been able to control inflation of health care costs while providing health care to all their citizens.

Table 6.1 illustrates that the U.S. expenditure as a percentage of Gross Domestic Product (GDP) outstrips that of all other Western countries. More importantly, despite its significantly higher base, the U.S. growth rate is triple the OECD country average and shows no clear signs of abating. "The problem of excess spending on health in comparison to other developed nations is getting worse, not better"

(Drake 1994:131). Other countries have made the hard choices and set limits and the United States does stand largely alone. Per capita spending for health care in the United States on the basis of GDP purchasing power parities is 2.2 times the estimated OECD average and more than 50 percent higher than its nearest competitor, Switzerland (Schieber et al. 1994:102).

In spite of this huge "lead" in health care spending, however, the U.S. population does not generally enjoy higher levels of health. In comparison with six nations (table 6.2) the United States ranks seventh in infant mortality, sixth in female life expectancy at birth, and fourth in male life expectancy at birth. Only in life expectancy at 80 is the United States in the top 3. While these measures certainly do not provide the full picture, on few measures of health does the United States rank near the top despite massive expenditures and

TABLE 6.1

Total Health Expenditures by Selected OECD Countries as a Percentage of GDP

	1980	1985	1986	1987	1988	1989	1990	1991	1992	Growth Rate 1980-92
Australia	7.3%	7.7%	8.0%	7.8%	7.7%	7.8%	8.2%	8.5%	8.8%	1.6%
Austria	7.9	8.1	8.3	8.4	8.4	8.5	8.4	8.6	8.8	0.9
Belgium	6.6	7.4	7.6	7.7	7.7	7.6	7.6	8.1	8.2	1.8
Canada	7.4	8.5	8.8	8.9	8.8	9.0	9.4	10.0	10.3	2.8
Denmark	6.8	6.3	6.0	6.3	6.5	6.5	6.3	6.6	6.5	-0.4
Finland	6.5	7.3	7.4	7.5	7.3	7.4	8.0	9.1	9.4	3.1
France	7.6	8.5	8.5	8.5	8.6	8.7	8.9	9.1	9.4	1.8
Germany	8.4	8.7	8.6	8.7	8.8	8.3	8.3	8.4	8.7	0.3
Iceland	6.4	7.0	7.8	7.9	8.5	8.5	8.2	8.4	8.5	2.4
Ireland	9.2	8.2	8.1	7.7	7.3	6.9	7.0	7.4	7.1	-2.1
Italy	6.9	7.0	6.9	7.4	7.6	7.6	8.1	8.4	8.5	1.8
Japan	6.6	6.5	6.6	7.0	6.8	6.7	6.6	6.7	6.9	0.4
Luxembourg	6.8	8.8	6.7	7.3	7.2	6.9	7.2	7.3	7.4	0.7
Netherlands	8.0	8.0	8.1	8.3	8.2	8.1	8.2	8.4	8.6	0.6
New Zealand	7.2	6.5	6.7	7.0	7.1	7.2	7.3	7.7	7.7	0.6
Norway	6.6	6.4	7.1	7.4	7.7	7.4	7.5	8.0	8.3	1.9
Spain	5.6	5.7	5.6	5.7	6.0	6.3	6.6	6.5	7.0	1.9
Sweden	9.4	8.9	8.6	8.6	8.6	8.6	8.6	8.5	7.9	-1.4
Switzerland	7.3	8.1	8.1	8.3	8.4	8.4	8.4	9.0	9.3	2.0
U.K.	5.8	6.0	6.1	6.1	6.1	6.0	6.2	6.6	7.1	1.3
U.S.	9.3	10.8	10.9	11.1	11.5	11.9	12.6	13.2	13.6	4.2
OECD average	7.0%	7.2%	7.3%	7.4%	7.5%	7.4%	7.6%	7.9%	8.1%	1.2%

SOURCES: OECD Health Data File. Schieber et al. 1994:101.

TABLE 6.2
Health Outcome Indicators for Seven Nations

Country	Infant Mortality per 1,000	Female Life Expectancy (at birth)	Male Life Expectancy (at birth)	Female Life Expectancy (at age 80)	Male Life Expectancy (at age 80)
Canada	7.2	79.7	73.0	8.9	6.9
France	7.7	80.6	72.3	7.5	6.1
Germany	7.6	78.4	71.8	7.6	6.1
Japan	4.8	81.3	75.5	8.4	6.9
Sweden	5.8	80.0	74.2	8.1	6.3
U.K.	9.0	78.1	72.4	8.1	6.4
U.S.	10.0	78.3	71.5	8.7	6.9

SOURCE: Schieber et al. 1991.

great technological progress. Except for female life expectancy at age 80, Japan, which allocates only 54 percent as much of its GDP for health care as the United States, has better or equal health indicators (Drake 1994:133).

This chapter describes how health care systems vary across Western nations, and contrasts the fragmented, market-oriented U.S. system with an array of alternative systems. Although no attempt is made to suggest that the United States would be better off with the system of any other country nor that it would be feasible to even consider such a move, such comparative analysis is valuable in demonstrating what factors appear to be operative in allowing these countries to provide universal health care at a more manageable cost. The analysis generally confirms the conclusion of Barer et al. that the "basic common thread is one form of monetary control over health care budgets, or at least over the most significant segments of them" (1994:91). Although each country has fashioned its own type of control over the mix of recipients and many permit or even encourage competition, nowhere but in the United States are these mechanisms relied on to control overall costs of health care.

CLASSIFICATIONS OF HEALTH CARE SYSTEMS

Despite apparent widespread differences among the health care systems of developed nations, at their base they represent variants or combinations of a limited number of types. Various observers have classified health care systems using different criteria each of which is valuable in simplifying what can be a complicated set of cross-cutting dimensions. One basic classification scheme centers on the dimension of state involvement. On the one extreme is the potential of a completely free market system with no state involvement while on the other is a tax-supported state monopoly of all health care. Neither of these extremes exists, but along the continuum are three models that together represent the core types of health care systems operating across these countries.

As illustrated in figure 6.1 the private insurance model is that with the least state involvement. This type is characterized by employer-based or individual purchase of private health insurance that is financed by individual and/or employer contributions. This system also is based on private ownership of health care providers and the factors of production although it might include a publicly funded safety net for the most vulnerable groups such as the poor, the elderly, or the young. This type is most clearly represented by the United States.

The second type of health system as to state involvement is the social insurance model. Although there is variation as to organization, this type is characterized by a universal coverage health insurance generally within a framework of social security. This compulsory health insurance is funded by employer and individual contributions through nonprofit insurance funds, often regulated and subsidized by the state. Generally provision of services is private on a fee-for-service basis although some public ownership of the factors of production is likely. Germany, France, and Japan represent examples of this type.

The third type and that which might approach the government monopoly in its pure form is the national health service model. Under this model there is universal coverage funded out of general taxation. The provision of health care services under this model is fully administered by the state, which either owns or controls the factors of pro-

FIGURE 6.1
Types of Health Care Systems, by State Involvement

duction. Although they have all moved away from this pure model to varying degrees the United Kingdom, Sweden, New Zealand, and Norway are examples of the national health service model.

A closely related dimension used to categorize health care systems turns on the method and source of financing. On the one extreme are those systems fully dependent on private sources of funding and on the other are those fully funded by public sources. Based on this criterion there are four main approaches to funding:

1. Direct payment by users
2. Private health insurance
3. Social or state insurance
4. Direct tax

With each basic model, however, there are many variants (Maxwell 1988). For instance the direct tax might be based in the central government, in subunits such as states or provinces, or in a combination of governments. Similarly, the social insurance system might be based on a single national scheme or on multiple insurance schemes regulated or controlled by the government. Furthermore, there is a wide array of possible combinations of basic types and their variants often used within a single health care system.

According to Appleby, "all health-care systems are pluralistic with respect to financing (and organisation) with tendencies to one method rather than another" (1992:10). For example in France approximately 70 percent of funding is through social insurance, 20 percent through direct payment by users, and 10 percent through direct government taxation. Similarly, Germany depends heavily on social insurance (over 60 percent), with 14 percent general taxation, 12 percent direct payments, and 5 percent private insurance. In contrast, Sweden's system is 80 percent state-funded, 13 percent by social insurance, and 7 percent direct user payment, while the United Kingdom is 87 percent funded through general taxation (Appleby 1992:12). Table 6.3 indicates not only how the proportion of health care financed through general taxation varies by country but also how it varies across time in each country.

In addition to the wide variety of combinations of these funding methods in each country, different countries apply them in different ways. Some such as the United States use general taxation for particular groups such as the poor and elderly, but depend on private

TABLE 6.3
Public Financing as a Percentage of Total Health Expenditures

	1960	1970	1975	1980	1985	1987
Norway	77.8	91.6	96.2	98.4	97.2	97.6
Luxembourg	—	—	—	—	89.7	91.6
Sweden	72.6	86.0	90.2	92.1	91.1	90.8
Iceland	40.0	47.4	58.4	82.6	83.0	88.5
Ireland	76.0	77.8	82.5	93.5	87.0	87.0
U.K.	85.2	87.0	91.1	89.8	86.0	86.4
Denmark	88.7	86.3	91.9	85.2	85.1	85.5
New Zealand	80.0	80.3	83.9	83.6	82.1	82.5
Italy	83.1	86.4	86.1	82.4	79.6	79.2
Finland	54.9	72.3	78.7	78.3	77.2	78.6
Germany	67.5	74.1	80.2	79.4	78.0	78.4
Belgium	61.6	87.0	79.6	81.5	76.9	76.9
Greece	57.9	53.9	61.6	84.0	98.2	75.2
France	57.8	78.1	78.9	80.8	79.4	74.8
Canada	43.1	70.3	76.5	75.0	75.9	73.9
Netherlands	33.3	84.3	76.5	78.9	79.0	73.9
Japan	60.4	69.3	72.0	70.8	72.5	73.0
Spain	52.1	54.7	70.4	73.5	71.5	71.5
Australia	52.6	52.6	63.9	61.7	72.3	70.5
Switzerland	61.3	63.9	66.5	65.4	68.5	68.2
Austria	66.7	63.0	69.9	68.8	64.7	67.1
Portugal	—	—	58.9	71.7	71.3	60.7
U.S.	24.7	37.0	42.5	42.4	41.4	41.4
Mean	61.8	71.6	75.5	78.2	78.5	77.1

SOURCE: OECD, Measuring Health Care.

insurance or direct payments for the remainder of the population. Other countries distinguish between specific forms of health care. For instance New Zealand heavily funds hospital care through general taxation but depends on direct user payment of most primary care, except for particular categories of patients. When examining health care policy, then, it is critical to examine not only how health care is financed based on these types but under what circumstances it is dependent on particular sources.

THE GOALS OF HEALTH POLICY

As noted in chapter 1, any health policy must be founded on goals and objectives that ought to be clarified early in the policymaking process. Two levels of goals are discernible. The first are broad stated goals that often function symbolically and are more in the realm of political rhetoric than reality. The second level are specific programmatic goals that frame a particular policy. Both are critical in evaluating the success or failure of a policy. Although many goals can be specified and measured with accuracy, generally the broader goals are less amenable to operationalization. Also, problems arise when the goals themselves are in potential conflict. Analysis becomes even more difficult when the goals are defined differently by the various participants or when the goals shift over time. In spite of these problems it is critical to examine the stated goals of the various nations' health policy.

For the two decades following World War II the predominant goals of health policy initiatives in all developed nations were *equity or access* and *quality* of health care. Even though the actual policies varied significantly from country to country, together the goals of access and quality shaped health care priorities. The variation can largely be explained by how much emphasis each nation put on subsidiary competing goals of freedom of choice for consumers, autonomy of the health care providers and insurers, and various notions of common or societal good. The mix of these policy goals in turn were shaped by variations in national cultures, politics, and institutional structures. In the United States for instance, with its strong emphasis on individual freedom both by patients and the health care community and the growing strength of private providers and insurers, universal access was never given the predominance it enjoyed in other nations. In contrast, Britain, with its stronger tradition of common good and its relatively weaker medical community, readily replaced its National Health Insurance with the more comprehensive National Health Service and its central goal of universal access.

Despite these variations, health policy in all developed nations in the postwar period put priority on ensuring access of all citizens to increasing levels of medical intervention. New hospitals were built and many new beds were added to existing structures; significantly expanded investments were made in medical education and research; the supply of medical personnel increased and the boundaries of medicine were extended by new specialities; and many institutional mechanisms for assuring access to these resources were initiated. The postwar boom of medicine in turn was met by heightened expectations and demands of the publics to even greater access to a barrage of new medical innovations.

Two types of access were addressed by health policies of this era: financial access and physical access. Financial access was met by restructuring the health care systems so as to provide universal access to some minimal level of health care for all citizens according to need. In most cases this required some degree of public financing or public coordination of private sickness funds with cover for those who fell through the private system. Other than the United States, all countries were reasonably successful in achieving near universal levels of access despite major variations in the means to that end.

The second type of access has proven more difficult to achieve as health care became more specialized and capital intensive. Geographical inequities in health care, although initially reduced by regional reallocation schemes, have proven difficult to resolve. Isolated, rural areas consistently are undersupplied in health care personnel. The maldistribution of physicians in favor of urban areas reflects both a lack of sufficient numbers of patients in many rural areas and a concentration of health care facilities in core urban populations. Although most countries have created incentives to correct the maldistribution of physicians, financial inducements have not proven able to overcome the problem (Harrop 1992a:161).

Another problem is that the delivery of health care services to rural areas is significantly more expensive on a per capita basis because of the high cost of capital equipment needed to supply state-of-the-art medical care. As a result many specialized services are provided only in urban regional centers. Although patients from isolated geographical locations might well have equal financial access to the same level of medicine as their urban brethren, travel costs, relocation costs, and costs in wasted time produce substantial inequities in effective access.

The goal of high quality of health care, also a hallmark of the 1950s and 1960s, has also proven problematic. The main difficulty with defining quality is a lack of an objective means of measuring quality medicine. Not surprisingly international comparisons seldom address this factor since it is much easier to compare cost figures, usage data, and other readily quantifiable factors. Even within single countries, quality is rarely monitored because there is little agreement on what criteria should be used. Unfortunately, quality has become identified with the latest technological developments, with curative medicine, sophisticated diagnostic technologies, and with specialist services. This emphasis is misleading in that it makes the assumption that quality can be defined by the number of machines, the number of medical specialists, and the number of intensive medical interventions performed.

Quality as defined by technology however is of questionable value when compared to health outcome as measured by a variety of indicators of the health of the population. Table 6.4, for instance, compares the United States, Canada, and Germany in terms of the number of delivery sites for several medical technologies. Although the United States by far has the highest "quality" if measured solely by availability of this type of care, it does not rate as high as either Canada or Germany on many measures of health outcome. Also, when quality is defined in this way, it is likely to conflict with the goal of access, which by necessity requires constraints on the disproportionate investment on a small number of users. While the goal of universal access assumes some minimal level of care available to those persons in need, it cannot allow unlimited amounts of resources to be expended on high-technology interventions.

> The overinvestment in health care reflects the choice of technology that the United States has made and the comprehensiveness with which that technology choice has been applied. Other countries have chosen much less capital-intensive care technologies that utilize fewer resources in aggregate, even though the United States does not have more doctors and hospital beds per capita than the other countries   *(Rublee 1994:115)*.

TABLE 6.4
Care Delivery Sites for Modern Medical Technologies per Million Population

Medical Technology	Country			
	United States 1992	Canada 1993	Germany 1993	U.S. Ratio to second highest
Open heart surgery	3.7	1.3	.8	2.85
Cardiac catheterization	6.4	2.8	3.4	1.88
Organ transplantation	2.4	1.2	.5	2.00
Radiation therapy	10.3	4.8	4.6	2.15
Magnetic resonance imaging	11.2	1.1	3.7	3.03
Extracorporeal shock wave lithotripsy	1.9	.5	1.4	1.36

SOURCE: Rublee 1994:115.

Despite these problems, however, quality along with equity were the most articulated goals of health policy prior to the 1970s.

Escalating costs, in large part fueled by the open-ended goals of access and quality, were aggravated by the worldwide recession and oil crisis of the 1970s. One result was an unmistakable shift in emphasis from access and quality to *cost containment* and the need to constrain health care spending. The aging populations, limitless technological potential, and heightened public expectations have solidified this goal in the 1990s. No country has escaped this highly visible shift toward improving productivity, maximizing efficiency, and incorporating management procedures to health care brought on by the predominant goal of cost containment. Moreover, to date reform efforts in most Western countries, with the notable exception of the United States, have been effective to the extent that they have stopped or slowed the rate of increase of health care spending as a proportion of GDP. Interestingly, the new emphasis on cost containment and system efficiency have forced an evaluation of quality, an effort that was conspicuously absent when quality was a stated goal. This shift in goals has expectedly run into opposition from the health care industry, medical professionals, and health care consumers who have "grown accustomed to expensive care at low direct cost" (Harrop 1992:159).

Cost Containment Strategies

Cost containment strategies vary significantly from one health system to the next and the objective may be to stop costs from rising in real terms, to reduce the costs of health care in real terms, or to slow the rate of increase of costs. The health care sectors over which cost containment policies operate and the type of cost-control strategy also vary as to whether health services are financed on a direct budget basis by the government, indirectly through the private sector, or through contracts with independent providers such as physicians paid on a fee-for-service basis or hospitals paid per item of service provided or per day of service. Although most services fall into the latter category in countries such as Germany, France, the United States, and the Netherlands, those countries with national health services such as Britain, Spain, and New Zealand have direct budget control—at least over most hospitals. The capacity for effective cost containment policies, therefore, varies considerably from one country to the next.

Cost containment strategies can operate on either the demand or the supply side of health care. Additionally, they can be carried out through a direct, regulatory edict (macromanagement) or through indirect incentive systems aimed at providers and patients (micromanagement). Furthermore, depending on the system the major efforts can be initiated and implemented by either public agencies—national or local—or by the private sector. According to Reinhardt (1990:107), European countries tend to emphasize macromanagement strategies such as global budgets to control their health systems, while only the United States, with its fear of centralized control, largely rejects regulatory macromanagement opting instead to fine-tune financial incentives for health care.

Demand-Side Strategies

Demand-side cost containment strategies depend primarily on strategies designed to reduce consumer demand and increase patient consciousness of the costs of providing care. Usually this is accomplished by requiring some form of cost-sharing by the consumers of health care. This might be done through user charges as a flat rate per unit of service (e.g., $50 per hospital night, $20 per doctor visit, $20 per prescription), some proportion of the cost (e.g., 20 percent of outpatient costs, 30 percent of inpatient costs), or some combination. Out-of-pocket costs or co-payments are normally applied at the time of use with the goal of discouraging user demand and by acting indirectly on physicians to reduce services through the knowledge that the patient must share in the cost. Another approach is to require deductibles (e.g., the first $100 per condition).

The major assumption of demand-side cost containment measures is that use of services will decrease when market incentives are implemented which make patients bear part of the costs. Studies have found that cost-sharing through either co-insurance or deductibles does, indeed, reduce health spending. A Rand Corporation study, for instance, found that outpatient spending was 46 percent lower among individuals enrolled in health plans with co-insurance than among those in free care plans. The 25 percent co-insurance plans produced the largest difference from the free care plan (Manning et al. 1987). Similarly, outpatient spending was 30 percent lower and inpatient spending 10 percent lower under individual deductible plans. Moreover, cost-sharing reduces adult hospital admissions by up to 38 percent as compared to free plans (Thorpe 1992:260).

Despite these findings of cost savings, there is some question as to how genuine the benefits of demand-side cost containment are in the long run. The critical question is whether the reduced use of medical resources produced by these policies leads to lower levels of health for those individuals who abstain due to cost considerations? In the Rand study, access to more services did not result in better health among consumers who were young, middle income, and in good health (Brook et al. 1984). In contrast, access to more services did result in better health outcomes among the poor and those persons with initial clinical indicators of poor health. In other words while many healthy people are likely to be able to reduce care without adverse consequences, when ill people forgo needed services health outcomes suffer. Among the latter group, access to free care is associated with reduced mortality rates of about 10 percent annually over a cost-sharing plan. Part of this difference might be explained by the fact that relatively young, healthy, and affluent consumers are able to carry supplemental insurance to cover charges, thus undercutting the goal of cost-sharing. Unless prohibited from doing so, those with insurance resources will counteract the apparent cost savings (OECD 1992:139).

Other demand-side approaches to cost containment include the exclusion of coverage or reducing payment for specific services such as visual aids, dentistry, diagnostic tests, pharmaceuticals, transportation, and mental health or counseling services. Co-payment for pharmaceuticals is a popular demand-side strategy. Some public systems allow extra billing. Other countries such as Japan, Canada, and Germany have either prohibited or strictly limited extra billing because of its impact on equity and its overall inflationary effect. Overall, demand-side approaches are limited by their adverse impact on access and inequitable financial burden across groups in society. While the latter problems can be reduced by providing exemptions to co-payments, this entails a complicated administrative and monitoring system which in turn adds to costs. According to the OECD, "it is doubtful whether anything other than modest charges (with exceptions for poor and high users) will be either equitable or efficient" (1992:139).

Supply-Side Strategies

Supply-side cost containment measures are generally more effective
than demand-side ones, especially when they entail the imposition of
direct central controls on payments to providers. In commenting on
seven European countries, for instance, the OECD concludes:

> The strong suggestion is that any cost containment was achieved
> not by modest increases in cost-sharing that took place . . . but by
> direct action on the supply side either by strengthening the
> hand of third-party payers through, for example, the introduc-
> tion of global budgeting, or by direct central regulation of fees
> and charges   *(1992:148)*.

The major instruments of this regulatory cost containment are fee
and price controls, control over capacity of the system, and control
over wages and salaries. Table 6.5 illustrates the wide range of short-
to long-term controls that are possible.

TABLE 6.5
Supply-Side Controls

Short-Term Direct Controls
 Budget ceilings for hospitals
 Controls on staff numbers in hospitals or clinics
 Controls on levels of remuneration
 Controls on prices (e.g., per bed day)
 Controls on quantities (e.g., per prescription)

Short-Term Indirect Controls
 Changing relative value scales
 A positive/ negative list for pharmaceutical products or
    chemist substitution
 Doctor profiles with or without sanctions for excess use
    of diagnostic tests, visits per patient, prescriptions

Medium-Term Direct Controls and Incentives
 Controls over construction or extension of hospitals
 Controls over the installation of expensive equipment
 Controls and incentives to develop substitutes for
    traditional hospital care

Long-Term Direct Controls on Manpower
 Controls over number of students entering medical or dental school
    passing into the second year
 Controls over entry to specialist training

SOURCE: Abel-Smith 1984:3–4.

The clearest supply-side strategy is to tighten controls over reimbursement or payment schedules. This is easiest to accomplish in an
integrated system where the government has the capacity to set
global budgets. Global budgets for hospitals are more effective than
price or volume controls alone because they cannot be avoided by
raising volume when prices are fixed or prices when volume is fixed.
Usually discretion is given to local managers to spend within the
prospective budget. According to Harrop (1992:163) budget caps
work provided there is the political will to enforce them. Budget caps
are less effective when the government grants additional funds to
those hospitals which overspend and require supplements to their
budgets. Because hospitals consume the majority of health spending,
this single approach is effective. According to the OECD (1992:141),
the analysis of per capita health expenditure across all OECD nations
suggests that hospital global budgets reduce total national health
expenditures by about 13 percent.

One problem with global budgets is that they might effectuate cost
containment by forcing hospitals to cut corners, thus providing a
lower quality of care. Because they do not readily distinguish as to
quality of care there are often no rewards for *good* economical treatment. Although this problem can be minimized by close auditing of
quality, global budgets themselves are not sufficient to protect consumers because the emphasis is on lowering the costs per case.

> The beauty of capitation or global budgets is that they provide
> incentives for cost-saving innovations and eliminate barriers to
> substituting nonmedical for medical services. Unfortunately,
> capitation or global budgets in the absence of other incentives
> and measures for quality assurance can result in mediocre ser-
> vices and poor responsiveness.   *(Mechanic 1994:14)*

In terms of the goal of containing costs, however, any form of
prospective payment will succeed by relating rewards to planned
workload and encouraging awareness of cost per case. In contrast,
any system with open-ended retrospective reimbursement for hospitals will have higher expenditures per capita (Culyer 1990:37).

Although global budgets are easier to implement by a central
authority, single-source funding is not essential. Germany and the
Netherlands for example have been successful in securing cost control
in systems composed of many payers. Germany has accomplished this

through highly decentralized negotiations between sickness funds and providers while the Netherlands has used direct intervention to put controls on premiums and set mandatory open enrollment. Japan, too, has been successful through instituting a rigid uniform fee structure and prohibiting extra billing. Control over medical remuneration, then, can be accomplished without global budgeting. Although direct price and quantity controls may be less effective than global budgets or direct caps, they are applicable to all segments of health care, including pharmaceuticals, and thus potentially more comprehensive.

Lacking the centralized regulatory control found in other countries, the United States implemented the Medicare prospective payment system in the mid 1980s. Diagnosis-related groups (DRGs) were introduced to regulate costs of federal spending for the elderly. The DRGs set prospective limits per diagnostic category on a fixed schedule. It was hoped that the private sector would follow the lead to reduce overall costs, but this has not happened. There is also some question whether DRGs actually have contained hospital costs in the long run. For instance, while hospitals under the DRG system were found to have reduced costs per day by 9.8 percent, costs per admission by 14.1 percent, and average length of stay by 6.5 percent, the effect on total costs was offset by an 11.7 percent increase in admission rates (Culyer, Brazier, and O'Donnell 1988). There is also serious concern over the tendency of DRGs to reinforce the tiered system of health care when they apply only to that portion of the population which is on Medicare.

Another major supply-side approach to cost containment is the strategy of creating market conditions under which the more efficient providers will thrive and the relatively more costly will be driven out of competitive markets. This has been initiated by separating the funder and provider functions and opening competition among providers. In the U.K. for instance self-governing hospital trusts (SGHT) will compete with private sector hospitals for contracts with the district health authorities. The contracts will specify workloads and quality assurance procedures and feature explicit management budgets. It is assumed that by providing market-type incentives for cost-effectiveness at the provider level the health authorities will be able to reduce costs while maintaining overall control through competitive contracts.

Other supply-side approaches include controls over construction of hospitals, the purchase of expensive and often duplicative equipment, and the numbers of medical students entering particular specialities. Centralized health planning with requirements for certificate of need for new construction or expensive equipment have been used by the United States, without major success in controlling costs however. Moves to less expensive health care delivery arrangements might be more useful in the future. Encouragement of outpatient over inpatient facilities and reduction in the oversupply of acute hospital beds are likely to constrain costs as is the shift from more expensive hospital beds to nursing homes or home care.

Although there is some evidence that those systems with strong centralized control over budgets are best positioned to constrain costs, health reforms in many countries include an emphasis on inclusion of market or quasi-market mechanisms. Although there is considerable variation among these countries as to how and what extent they are shifting in this direction, it is critical to examine in more detail the notion of a health care marketplace.

THE GOVERNMENT AND THE MARKETPLACE

One evident trend in many public health systems is toward inclusion of market or quasi-market mechanisms to provide incentives to improve efficiency. Public sector monopolies provide few such incentives and in fact are likely to contain perverse incentives that in effect punish efficiency (Enthoven 1990:62). On the other hand, a totally free market in health insurance cannot produce either equity or efficiency. Therefore, even the United States, clearly the most market-oriented system, exerts considerable regulatory influence over the workings of the market. As with other aspects of health policy, the approach a particular government takes is dependent upon the ideology of past and present governments and the predominant models of health care finance and delivery (OECD 1992:28).

Generally, governments can take one of two main routes in regulating health care systems. The first approach involves regulation in the more conventional sense of setting constraints on the private sector. This detailed command-and-control type of activity is generally designed to supplant and override market forces and institutions. This can be effected by specifying coverage of insurance policies, regulating membership and premiums, controlling the quantity and quality of prices, mandating set-fee structures and schedules, fixing wage rates, and controlling planning capacity. For instance, although the Japanese health system is largely private, both funders and providers are highly regulated by the government through a universal fee structure, centralized billing and payment, standard co-payments, and prohibition of extra billing. Despite the predominance of the private sector in the United States, providers, especially hospitals, face many constraints—the result of regulation from local, state, and the national government. Some observers argue that the major problem in health care today is overregulation (Ricardo-Campbell 1982). If the competitive market were left to operate on its own, they contend, medical care dilemmas would dissipate.

> Policymakers have created a Dante's Hell of regulation and manipulation. Insurance company medical auditors and government bureaucrats push and shove each other to look over the shoulder of every doctor whose bills they are asked to pay. Their monitoring of every patient, provider, procedure, and prescription has forced doctors and nurses to become masters of the universe of regulatory manipulation rather than masters of the universe of medicine.   *(Califano 1992:1528)*

The second approach a government can take is to foster an environment for promoting self-regulation by the health care community. Such measures are generally included under the rubric of pro-market or pro-competitive policies. The goal of these policies is to maximize autonomy for insurers, providers, and consumers through the operation of traditional marketplace principles. The government's role then is to provide an appropriate balance among the various stakeholders such as it would in other areas of the economy. Furthermore, the government has a responsibility to ensure proper incentives for the provision and consumption of health care resources. The major assumption of this approach to regulation is that a free market for health care can regulate itself if given the opportunity by the government. Supporters of this strategy generally contend that the health care system is in effect a large business and that, if left alone to operate according to the principles of supply and demand, it will best serve the consumer public. Regulation, it is contended, interferes with the effective operation of the marketplace and creates artificial inequities in the system.

The fallacy of this approach is that the health care market contains none of the self-selecting mechanisms that work to check market excesses. In fact, if health care operated as a conventional market, "[w]e would be no more concerned about the proportion of the [GNP] consumed by health care than we [would] about the proportion of [GNP] spent on transportation, housing, or shoes" (Eddy 1990:1165). In order for an efficient, market-based health care system to work, several conditions are essential. First decisions must be made by the consumers. Second, the consumers must know the value and costs of the goods they are contemplating purchasing. Third, the consumers must pay the full cost and receive the full benefit of the goods they choose to buy. All three conditions are absent from the current market for health care services (Eddy 1990:1165).

First, medical decisions are seldom made by the patient. Although some discretion is possible, the traditional physician-patient relationship is based on the trust and ultimate dependence of the patient on the expertise of the physician, often under uncertain circumstances. The individual patient's choice is heavily conditioned and constrained by the providers of health care. Health care is not a commodity in any traditional market sense precisely because the patient cannot make his or her choice independent of these nonmarket forces.

Second, most patients have a difficult time judging the care they buy. As a result, health care providers have enormous discretion in deciding both the type and cost of care provided. The specialized knowledge required for the dispensation of health care, in conjunction with the emotional and often urgent nature of medical decisions, undercuts the patient's ability to be a rational shopper. It is unrealistic to expect consumers to become sophisticated, cost-effective purchasers of health care, in part because of the steep learning curve in shopping for value in health care.

Moreover, it does not follow that more informed consumers of health care will buy for lower cost. In fact, evidence suggests that knowledge often leads to higher costs because "patients with more knowledge tend to be more demanding in terms of tests and treatments they want for themselves" (Coddington et al. 1991:271). Demand for health care is inelastic for most consumers because an increase in price does not lead to significant decrease in the amount of services demanded. Patients want the best care regardless of cost and, when given a free choice, usually opt for the most technological and expensive form of health care.

The major reason that patients are unlikely to be frugal consumers, as assumed by marketplace models, results from the failure to meet the third condition. Third-party payment, whether private or public, assures that the potential consumer who receives the value pays only a fraction of the costs, if any. Under this incentive structure, it is "well known that people consume more when they do not pay the full cost of something than they would consume if they did pay the full cost" (Eddy 1990:1169).

Private insurance can spread the risk and the burden of payment, however, private insurers have an incentive to exclude, or raise, premiums against high-risk individuals. Moreover, because those persons who are ill or most at risk for ill health are often least able to pay, the marketplace functions to serve primarily those who can afford to buy into the system, paradoxically those who are least likely to need extensive medical care. Health insurance is typically purchased by healthy people, while most health care is consumed by sick people. In contrast to their purchase of durable goods, sick people cannot replace health insurance that once might have seemed optional but no longer is (Aaron 1991:17). Income redistribution based on market principles therefore is not possible without intervention that negates those very principles of supply and demand.

Unregulated health insurance also brings with it overconsumption because neither the patient nor the physician has an incentive to economize when the amorphous third party is paying the bill. This moral hazard problem is by no means unique to private insurance, and in fact is inherent in any third-party payment system. However, without strict controls and a restructuring of the traditional market functioning both equity and efficiency are lacking. It is highly unlikely, therefore, that self-regulation alone is sufficient to resolve the crisis of health care delivery and financing. Pure market solutions are bound to fail in the long run because they serve to reaffirm claims to unlimited resources by those persons who can afford it and favor acute care regardless of prognosis over preventive and promotion measures which would be more effective in improving the health status of the community as a whole. Although there are steps that can be taken to give the health care community an active role in the regulatory process and incentives to modify the marketplace (i.e., move from retrospective to prospective payment systems), adequate regulation requires inclusion of bureaucratic controls in order to shape the diverse demands of the health care marketplace. Although this does not negate a role for the market, alone it is insufficient to deal with the peculiarities of health care.

In addition to Japan, other countries actively intervene in private health care markets with detailed regulations of the command and control type. In the Netherlands, for instance, insurers are mandated to provide basic insurance at set premiums for certain high-risk individuals who are not eligible for public insurance. Similarly, in Ireland voluntary health insurance is supplied by a single quasi-government insurer which imposes community rating on the private sector insurers (OECD 1992:28). In contrast, in the United Kingdom where private insurance plays only a supplementary role there is little regulation of the private insurance market, while in the United States regulation is widespread but largely uncoordinated, confusing, and often counterproductive.

The fact that all Western nations have shifted emphasis to the goal of cost containment does not justify unquestioned acceptance of its new dominance. Although cost containment has become a central tenet of health policy reforms of the 1980s and 1990s, in itself it is not a sensible objective. The major goal of health policy ought not be to save money, but to promote the health and welfare of the population. To the extent that these cost containment measures undermine this broader goal, they invite condemnation. On the other hand, it is increasingly evident that without successful initiatives to constrain costs, all health care systems continually face funding crises. What is needed then is a balance of the goals of equity, quality, and efficiency—a difficult but not impossible task. Although implementation of policies and mechanisms to constrain health care costs are essential, they must be kept in proper perspective.

GLOBAL BUDGETS, PRIMARY CARE, AND CONTROL OF TECHNOLOGY

Of all Western industrialized nations, the United States stands alone in terms of the power of the private sector to dictate the parameters of health care. Even countries such as Australia, France, and the Netherlands which have clear private/public mixes, have much stronger public involvement. The ability of nearly all other Western nations to cover their entire populations with minimal patient cost, while devoting substantially smaller proportions of their GDP to health care raises serious questions as to whether reliance on market forces and competition, no matter how "managed," is justified. While the health care share of GDP in the United States continues to increase without apparent bounds, it has generally stabilized in most European countries, and actually decreased in several, especially Ireland and Denmark. In addition, the United States continues to lag behind most developed nations in life expectancy at birth and in mortality rates for chronic conditions (Davis 1990:113).

One reason for this discrepancy is the willingness and capacity of other nations to control the supply side by strengthening the hands of insurers and by imposing direct, central controls on payments to providers and on the capacities of their health systems. For instance, during the 1980s Belgium, France, Germany, and the Netherlands introduced systems of global budgeting to replace the daily rates paid to hospitals. These nations joined Ireland, Spain, and the United Kingdom, which already had mechanisms for capping hospital expenditures (Hurst and Poullier 1993:5). Germany also capped payments to physicians as a whole, while Ireland moved from fee-for-service to capitation. According to the OECD (1992:5) the capping of total expenditure did succeed in containing health care costs in these countries. Although Belgium and France were less successful than the others in containing costs in the late 1980s, the evidence suggests this is because ambulatory care in both countries, paid by fee-for service with fee controls but not global budgets, increased significantly. In addition, in France private hospitals, which constitute one-third of all beds, do not operate under the global budget (Hurst and Poullier 1993:5). Ireland was able to reduce its health care expenditures by moving to capitation payments for public patients of GPs and adoption of tough measures to reduce public health care expenditures. Although a reduction in spending for health care in itself is not admirable if health of the population suffers, there is no evidence at this stage this has been the case, although there are arguments by opponents that governments have pushed spending below the optimum.

Several European governments have carried out major reforms toward increased reliance on market or quasi-market mechanisms, but in all cases, the governments have maintained firm control. Germany, the Netherlands, and the United Kingdom have introduced or strengthened competition among the providers in their national health systems without sacrificing cost control and universal coverage. Despite moves toward decentralization and regionalization of services, European countries maintain centralized financial controls over fees, budgets, and capital outlays. Global control of total health spending (not just public spending) seems to be a key to both universal coverage and cost control. Such mechanisms also serve as very powerful rationing mechanisms.

It has been suggested that in comparison with European countries the values upon which the U.S. health care system is based, with its emphasis on personal responsibility, freedom of choice, and pluralism, have obscured goals related to the health of the population and equity of access (Jonsson 1990:87). As a result, centralized health planning and a large government role in health care financing are more acceptable to Europeans. Despite the severe constraints imposed by the European systems as viewed by Americans, citizens of most European countries are "at root very satisfied with their health care systems, and have well-developed channels of accountability through which to express dissatisfaction in specific cases" (Evans and Barer 1990:83). In part this might be because the more comprehensive health systems of Europe have a higher commitment to primary care and prevention. Equity and universal access along with global budgets results in this concentration on non high-technology medicine. Germany, Belgium, Finland, and Switzerland, for instance, stand out as expending large shares of their health care budgets to ambulatory care. A recent OECD study found that those countries which allocate larger shares to inpatient care have higher per capita health spending (1992:64). According to Jonsson (1990:92), the underrepresentation of inexpensive but cost-effective primary/prevention services is a serious inefficiency in a health system.

Despite the lower priority European countries have put on curative medicine, one concern expressed in these countries is that there is too much bias in favor of acute diagnostic tests and high-technology medicine at the expense of prevention and long-term care. As a result some governments have introduced "heavy handed" and detailed regulations in an effort to contain costs in these areas (Hurst and Poullier 1993:6). Although the patterns of introduction, diffusion, and rationing of new technologies differs across all countries, in those with centralized funding and controls, new technologies must be accommodated within the existing systems of resource allocation. Because tradeoffs must be made between the innovations and current treatment and that of other conditions, there is an explicit need to establish priorities. Analysis of the marginal costs and benefits and comparison with existing treatments is critical, and a new procedure might not be accepted unless it is clear that it will have a major impact on health outcomes and/or reduce costs.

> In some countries this is already done—for example, in the Netherlands, the Medical Council vets new procedures and technology, while, in the United Kingdom, various kinds of elective surgery are severely restricted for the very old. Such measures can also provide an important signal to medical research and technology—which has rarely had to face the test of markets— to place greater emphasis on cost savings and effectiveness.
>
> (*OECD 1992:75*).

Japan: Universal Access and Uniform Fee Schedules

Although Japan was the first nation with universal health coverage (1961), it was largely caught unaware by massive increases in costs during the 1970s and fell behind other developed nations in introducing cost containment policies. Since the early 1980s, however, it has made impressive strides in integrating cost containment with its goal of equity in access (Powell and Anesaki 1990:116). Japan's health care system is a complex mixture of public and private funding and provider agents which reflects it unique cultural and social context. Although the health care delivery system is dominated by the private sector, unlike the United States it is not market-oriented. Providers compete for patients and consumers have broad freedom of choice, but all funders and providers are strictly regulated by the government. Furthermore, all health care payments are made on the basis of a national fee schedule with implicit limits on increases in overall expenditures. The result is a system that largely is meeting its two highest priority goals of equal access and control of health care expenditures.

Despite the presence of multiple systems, all billing and payment in Japan is centralized through the payment fund of the National Health Insurance (NHI). It reviews all bills submitted and has the power to reduce payment and minimize fraud. This process also serves as a major mechanism of cost containment, according to Ikegami (1992:704). Reviews by NHI serve as a warning to providers and trigger peer pressures for compliance. Although all insurance plans cover most medical services plus direct cash benefits paid the insured for childbirth, maternity leave, nursing, injury, and sickness, co-payments are required under all plans. Except for the very minimal deductibles under the Geriatric Health Act, the co-payments are large enough to serve as disincentives for overuse of the plans. Moreover, because Japan places heavy emphasis on preventive medicine and ambulatory/primary care, the hospital admission rate is about one-third that of the United States and the surgical procedure rate is only one-quarter that of the United States (Ikegami 1992:700–701).

While universal coverage guarantees access to available health care, Japan has been able to keep cost increases under control. The key to this success appears to be the uniform fee system, which not only controls cost inflation but also enables the government to reward clinic general practitioners engaged in primary care. Providers are paid on a fee-for-service basis with the price of each service determined by a uniform point fee system. The government's Central Social Medical Care Council negotiates changes in the fee schedule with representatives of providers, payers, and public interest groups. The fees are inclusive and fixed. Moreover, extra billing is prohibited by law, thus discouraging supplementary private insurance schemes that could circumvent the system and escalate costs. In large part, therefore, the uniform fee schedule has been effective in containing total health care expenditures.

The universal fee schedule also has a critical role in setting allocation priorities. It serves as an allocation mechanism by providing a financial incentive structure for the provision of selected services (i.e., primary care) by setting the fee allowed higher than the actual costs. In contrast it can discourage medical applications deemed undesirable by setting the allowable fees lower than the actual costs. For Ikegami (1992:691) the schedule is a "powerful tool" for promoting certain services and thus shaping the distribution of health care resources.

The universal fee structure also allows for control over the diffusion of new technologies. Because the fee for a new technology or procedure is set by comparing it to the nearest equivalent service, potentially more expensive innovations are discouraged. Although the very low rate of organ transplantation in Japan might better be explained by cultural veneration of the dead and dislike of invasive technologies, high-cost individual intensive medicine is clearly constrained by the fee structure. Rationing decisions pertaining to such technologies therefore are made through the broader incentive structure determined by societal priorities reflected in the fee levels.

The Japanese system is one of a strong government role in financing and in fixing prices. The government has taken clear steps to ensure equity in financing among the multitude of private and public plans and assured equality of service since providers are always paid the same amount for a service no matter what insurance plan the patient has even if on public assistance. The rationing that occurs has legitimacy because the playing field is level. Although the system has problems with multiple diagnoses and increased volume to make up for fee constraints and no clear mechanism to ensure quality of care, overall Japan has created an effective system for eliminating the necessity of explicit rationing decisions at the individual level.

SETTING SPENDING LIMITS

Thus we have seen that other industrial democracies have been more successful than the United States in providing universal access and constraining medical care costs without appreciable adverse impact on the health of their populations. Despite major variations in health structure, generally they have accomplished this by setting relatively rigid limits on health care spending and constraining development and diffusion of curative medical technologies. The more established traditions of collective health and community good and the narrower notions of individual rights have been instrumental in making these efforts acceptable to the populations. The key however is a willingness to set explicit spending limits through global budgeting, national fee structures, or other mechanisms that will have the effect of constraining individual-oriented medical care.

Although I favor a single-payer plan, this is most unlikely to emerge in the United States at least in the near future. At a minimum, however, some type of centralized and standardized health plan applicable to all persons is necessary to counteract the perverse incentive structure, wasteful administrative system, and unbridled spending pattern that now characterizes the U.S. health care system. We also need a national insurance system in order to spread health risks across the entire population, thereby eliminating cost-shifting—a principal destabilizing factor and the "major culprit" behind the escalating number of uninsured and underinsured Americans (Coddington et al. 1991:23). The experiences of the nations outlined here indicate that this is not only feasible, it is the norm.

It is crucial that U.S. policymakers look at the experiences of other democracies and move toward adapting those mechanisms and strategies that seem to be workable in meeting enlightened health care goals. One mechanism that should be carefully considered is Japan's national fee structure, which has proven very effective in providing universal coverage, restraining costs and, importantly, shaping the incentive structure through which primary care is emphasized. Japan's central billing and payment system within the context of a largely private health care system is more feasible in the United States than the single-payer model of Canada. Although Japan's system is no panacea (see Marmor 1994) it, along with that of Germany and other European nations, should provide valuable lessons as to what is needed. Whatever combination of approaches and mechanisms are ultimately used, the key requirement will be instituting constraints on the supply of high-technology medicine along the lines of other democratic countries.

CHAPTER 7

CONTROLLING MEDICAL TECHNOLOGY

Throughout this book I have viewed the near obsession with medical technology as having a portentous impact on the U.S. health care system. Although technological medicine has expanded in all Western nations, a unique set of values, practices, and structures in the United States has exaggerated the forces driving the diffusion of technology. Jacobs terms this distinctive U.S. commitment to expand the supply of technologically sophisticated medicine the "American supply state" and contrasts it with the higher priority put on access to health care in other nations (1995:143). A combination of faith in technology to provide health care, the influence of a powerful medical research industry, and an incentive structure that rewards individualized medicine and innovation assures dominance of the supply state. In contrast those nations that emphasize access have by necessity limited development and diffusion of medical technologies by constraining facility development, placing greater emphasis on primary care physicians, and exercising governmental planning authority.

I contend that control of the unbridled proliferation of medical technology must be a high priority even if it means some individuals will be denied potential life-saving innovations. As stated cogently by Riegelman, it is "now clear that it will be impossible to control the costs of medical care without taming medical technology" (1991:75). Given the current value system and incentive structure as well as the unwillingness to institute some form of global budgeting, however, this will require not only major structural changes but also an intensified resolve to grasp the severity of the problems we will soon face if changes are not made. Unless we adopt a realistic view of the deleterious influence of the supply state dominance, universal access and cost control will continue to be elusive.

THE INAPPROPRIATE USE OF TECHNOLOGY

According to Perry, the "inappropriate use of technology" is an umbrella phrase used to define the possible misapplication of technology under a variety of circumstances including "use of technology in ignorance or for a marginal benefit to the patient, use of technology in the absence of evidence of its value or in spite of the fact that conclusive studies have not been done" (1989:771). Inappropriate use of technology then goes beyond the medical judgments that inherently lead to applications that are of questionable value to a particular patient and rather addresses systemwide use of technologies under Perry's criteria.

According to the Radical Statistics Group "the idea that market forces should determine medical need in the community is likely to lead to inappropriate care" (1976:18). The fee-for-service retrospective reimbursement system in the United States further distorts the market because it fails to provide any effective mechanisms to constrain these market forces. On the contrary, it creates an incentive structure that rewards overuse of technologies and invasive procedures. The result is that many of the interventions practiced by the medical profession, especially specialties and subspecialties that organize around each innovation, have never been subjected to objective scrutiny nor assessed as to their contribution to health or their cost-effectiveness (Butter 1993). "This leads to the perpetuation of some illogical, expensive and frequently dangerous practices carried on in the name of modern medicine" (RSG 1976:23).

Nowhere is the evidence of a medical marketplace run amuck more obvious than in the United States. Because hospitals must keep up with the latest developments in order to compete for patients in the marketplace, the proliferation of technologies is rapid. As a result, between 1984 and 1988 alone American hospitals added 176 open heart surgery units, 792 CAT scanners, 490 MRI scanners, 287 cardiac catherization units, and 148 organ transplant units (Butter 1993:16). Under this open-ended, multipayer system, the medical community has quickly expanded to incorporate new developments that, although often experimental, are offered to patients as "innovative therapies."

For instance in the six years from 1982 to 1988 liver and heart transplant centers increased from 3 to 74 and 5 to 144, respectively. Similarly, coronary artery bypass grafts grew at a rate of 20 to 40 percent annually in the mid-1980s, despite lingering questions as to their positive contribution to the health of many recipients. Interestingly, the average hospital profit margin for bypass surgery is 40 percent as compared to overall profit margins of 4 percent (Cundiff and McCarthy 1994:25). Not surprisingly, the United States performs bypass surgeries at 5 to 6 times the rate of countries with some form of public control. Moreover, care delivery sites for open heart surgery, cardiac catherization, and organ transplantation are 2 to 6 times those in other countries (Rublee 1994:15).

Although this proliferation of medical technology means that insured Americans have access to the latest innovations, in many cases the interventions are of unproven benefit and in some cases might be dangerous to the patient. Furthermore, the diffusion of unproven interventions consumes ever larger proportions of health care resources, thus diverting resources from universal access to beneficial treatments, primary care, and prevention. As a result, there has been considerable critical analysis of spending patterns on innovative therapy particularly those relating to heart disease and cancer (see Cundiff and McCarthy 1994). The experience with in vitro fertilization (IVF), I believe, serves as another example of what has gone wrong with technological medicine.

The Case of IVF

IVF is an illuminating example of the impact of the U.S. medical market because its evolution from inception to an accepted medical practice has been especially rapid and striking. In one decade the

number of centers practicing IVF jumped from 1 (1981) to over 200
(1989) as hospitals and entrepreneurs attempted to cash in on the
strong desire of infertile (and vulnerable) couples to have children.
IVF has been actively marketed and accompanied by a very effective
media public relations' campaign (see Bonnicksen 1989:26). Furthermore, unlike the United Kingdom where the Human Embryology
and Fertilisation Authority was established to regulate such activities,
control of the practice in the United States has generally been left to
those professions that profit from its use.

Despite the diffusion of IVF and related procedures, there is a clear
lack of scientific evidence to demonstrate that they are effective, that
the treatment is more likely to result in a birth than no treatment.
According to the recent report of the Canadian Royal Commission
on New Reproductive Technologies:

> Unproven and quite possibly ineffective procedures are being
> offered as medical treatment and women are undertaking the
> risks of the procedures without knowing whether they are more
> likely to have a child than if they received no treatment.
> Moreover, treatment is being offered and these risks taken with-
> out any comprehensive and consistent collection and analysis of
> information on outcomes, so that these uncertainties could be
> reduced.   *(Baird 1993:521).*

Declarations that IVF is therapy obscure the fact that still relatively
little is known about the underlying mechanisms of fertilization,
implantation, and development. Caplan adds that the efficacy associated with a particular activity in terms of the probability it will produce the intended outcome is also critical in defining therapy. He
contends that it is "hard to imagine using the label of therapy for
a procedure with a success rate of less than one in ten per trial"
(Caplan 1990:160). Likewise, despite such low success rates, "some
states have mandated insurance coverage for what is, by any standard
(save that of hope and desire), a relatively inefficacious technology"
(Callahan 1990:167). Although deceptive this disassociation with
experimental status serves the needs of clinicians, entrepreneurs,
and patients. Therapy status gives more hope to patients even if they
are aware of the low overall success rates because they assume it will
work for them. Moreover, clinicians naturally prefer to offer therapy
to patients than to recruit subjects for research. Therapy is more

lucrative especially since most third-party payers are unlikely to pay for experimental protocol.

Although determining success rates of IVF would appear to be straightforward, there remains considerable controversy because of the use of different measures of success, misinformation, and wide variation across programs and between patients with certain indications. Although some clinics report pregnancy rates of 25 percent, when measured by live birth per treatment cycle a figure of 10 percent at best seems more accurate. Moreover, this is reduced to 4 percent for women over 40, 5.9 percent for couples with male infertility factor, and 8 percent for women infertile over three years (Haan 1991). There is substantial evidence that even these success rates are exaggerated because of spontaneous pregnancies occurring during treatment. Studies of women accepted for IVF programs show that between 7 and 28 percent conceive naturally either before receiving treatment or within two years after discontinuation (Wagner and St. Clare 1989:1028). The data on women who become pregnant independent of IVF treatment suggest that success rates are masking some births not attributable to the treatment. It is quite possible that the higher pregnancy rates for IVF patients infertile for three or less years reflect independent pregnancies.

While success rates are lower than commonly stated by marketing materials, the costs per live birth are significantly higher than the oft-cited figure of $25,000. In their study Neumann and associates (1994) found costs ranging from a low of $66,667 for the base case where a woman becomes pregnant in cycle 1 to $800,000 for a woman over age 40 or when male factor infertility is present or where 5 cycles are necessary. These higher costs correctly incorporate the costs of failed treatment cycles and subsequent procedures that occur more frequently with IVF pregnancies such as high-risk obstetrical care, cesarean sections, and neonatal care. In the least, these data raise critical questions as to whether extending IVF to older women and couples with male factor infertility can be justified on resource allocation grounds. While the Canadian report recommended IVF be limited to use on women with bilateral fallopian tube blockage, the market in the United States is being continually expanded to other indications.

Another consideration that has been minimized in the IVF marketplace is safety. While all medical interventions carry risks, IVF is not a life-saving procedure and should therefore not pose significant risk to the patients. But IVF includes a series of stages each of which has been linked to specific complications for the woman and potential offspring. Although some of these problems are minimal, some represent serious health risks. It is clear that considerably more data on complications of IVF are necessary in order to fully evaluate the safety of variations that in some cases have been widely diffused in the absence of appropriate trials.

Hyperstimulation of the ovaries (or superovulation) is used in order to attain as many follicles and oocytes as possible and thus maximize the number of embryos produced in a single treatment cycle. Ovarian stimulation has been linked to coagulation abnormalities leading to thromboembolism, stroke, and mycocarial infarction, but the two main complications are the ovarian hyperstimulation syndrome (OHSS) and cancer (OTA 1988:125). Moderate OHSS has an incidence of 3 to 4 percent, while severe (which in several cases has led to death of the woman) has an incidence of .1 to .2 percent (Schenker and Ezra 1994:412). Ovulation induction has also been linked with breast, genital, and hormone-dependent cancer such as melanomas. In addition complications associated with oocyte retrieval procedures include bleeding,infection, and injury to blood vessels, the uterus, the bladder, or intestine (Schenker and Ezra 1994:414).

One well-documented risk associated with all assisted reproduction technologies including IVF is multiple pregnancy (MP). The vast majority of higher-order MPs (63 to 80 percent) are a direct result of the use of these procedures (Callahan et al. 1994:244). While technologically assisted births represent only 2 percent of singleton pregnancies, they produce 35 percent of twin and 77 percent of triplet plus pregnancies. The incidence of MP under IVF is tenfold that of spontaneous reproduction (Collins and Bleyl 1990:1384). MPs are associated with a wide range of complications for both the pregnant women and the fetus/neonate. MP especially for older women undergoing IVF might produce an unbearable overload for the cardiovascular and renal functions (Schenker and Ezra 1994:418). MP is also related to perinatal mortality. The incidence of mortality for triplets (70 to 140 per 1,000 births) and quadruplets (100 to 170 per 1,000 births) is almost ten times that of singletons (7 to 23 per 1,000 births) (Weissman et al. 1991). MP babies are also likely to be premature and vulnerable to the array of problems linked to very low birthweight. Triplets are 32.7 times more likely to be very low birthweight than singletons. Another concern is the cost of MP. One study found that the cost for single births averaged $9,845, twins $37,947, and triplets $109,765 (Callahan et al. 1994: 247).

One response to the increased rates of MPs produced by IVF is the highly controversial procedure of selective reduction or termination of pregnancies. Usually this entails an injection of potassium chloride into the heart of the fetus (or fetuses) to be aborted. This procedure, however, also carries with it medical risks, including the possibility of losing all fetuses being carried and thus a high psychological price particularly for women who have struggled for years to become pregnant only to succeed but then be faced with the prospect of losing it all. The need for selective reduction can be minimized by reducing the number of embryos transferred but this reduces the overall success rates of IVF. A "more prudent intervention" according to Luke (1994:105) would be more judicious use of assisted reproduction technologies.

In addition to the heightened probability of multiple pregnancies with IVF, spontaneous abortion and ectopic pregnancies are also more frequent. The high incidence of abortion with IVF could be attributed to the increased age of the patients which is associated with increased prevalence of chromosomal aberrations or early recognition of these pregnancies and subsequent abortions due to close monitoring. Likewise, ectopic pregnancy is more common in IVF because of the embryo transfer process. In addition to fetal wastage during pregnancy there is an increased incidence of first and second trimester bleeding, toxemia, fetal growth retardation, and anemia, as well as pregnancy-induced hypertension.

This brief review of the efficacy, safety, and costs of IVF demonstrates that this procedure has become accepted medical practice without adequate scientific assessment. Its rapid proliferation has preceded the type of outcomes research that is essential in order to protect both individual patients and the health care system. In addition, concern over the psychological costs borne by the vast majority of women who unsuccessfully pursue pregnancy through these techniques should warrant a caution which to date has not been forthcoming. The question is whether new reproductive technology is increasing women's autonomy or creating the ultimate oppression: that is, taking reproduction out of the hands of women altogether and forever (Morgall 1993:191). The demand for pregnancy, the organization of medical specialities surrounding these procedures, the open-ended reimbursement and incentive structure, and powerful market forces make it unlikely that IVF and a whole range of potentially inappropriate medical technologies can be constrained without some semblance of public control. Moreover this control must come early in the process of development before the intervention becomes a routine part of medical practice. One approach toward this end has been technology assessment.

ASSESSMENT OF MEDICAL TECHNOLOGY

The short history of medical technology assessment (MTA) has been an inconsistent and controversial one. It has been characterized by strong opposition from interests that see it as a threat to their autonomy and by criticism by those observers who feel it has failed to accomplish the objective of critical assessment and thus stem the proliferation of questionable technologies and procedures. In light of this controversy MTA has received considerable attention in the last decade.

The Institute of Medicine has defined technology assessment as the "process of examining and reporting properties of medical technology used in health care, such as safety, efficacy, feasibility and indications for use, cost, and cost-effectiveness, as well as social, economic, and ethical considerations, whether intended or unintended" (1985:2). This definition raises two aspects of MTA which are crucial in its full effectiveness. Most obvious is the broad concern with effects on society. More subtle is the emphasis on second-order consequences: those which are unintended, indirect, or delayed. Any assessment of medical technologies or proposed programs to be built around them must focus on both of these concerns as well as on the strictly technical questions of safety and efficacy, which unfortunately too often receive predominant attention.

The Practice of MTA

The practice of MTA has been widespread in both the private and public sectors. In 1986 Perry estimated that there were at least 45 organizations involved in MTA including the American Medical Association, the American College of Physicians, Blue Cross/Blue

Shield, the American Hospital Association, and a myriad of medical societies, health provider organizations, nonprofit health-related organizations, and manufacturers of drugs and medical devices. However, despite the scope of MTA activities, there was little cooperation, coordination, or even exchange of data among the many assessment efforts. "Although many have realized that better information on the benefits, risks, costs, and social implications of medical technology is essential to guiding the development and use of technology without unnecessarily impeding innovation, progress toward developing a coherent system for assessing medical technologies has been slow" (OTA 1982:91).

Moreover, contemporary assessments are usually narrowly focused and rarely entail the collection of primary data. They largely fail to place the specific assessments in the broader context of the national health crisis. This is not surprising, because each organization has a stake in the results of its assessment. Furthermore, few of these organizations have the resources to support necessary research, including clinical trials. Although there appears to be a realization that a more coherent system of medical technology assessment is essential if we are to make rational decisions concerning health care, genuine collaboration between these groups is problematic without a major initiative from the federal government. Given the current, and most likely long-term, emphasis on cost containment, efforts to strengthen medical technology assessment, even to achieve consensus on its basic objectives and approaches, will be difficult.

Impetus for government involvement in health technology assessment came from a 1976 OTA report, which concluded that assessment should be made before costly new medical technologies and procedures were put into general use (OTA 1976). This report called for the establishment of formal mechanisms for accomplishing that task and played a part in the program of the National Institutes of Health designed to develop a consensus on technical issues. The short-lived National Center for Health Care Technology (NCHCT) was an attempt to strengthen and centralize efforts to assess health care technologies. After NCHCT's demise in 1981, the OTA reiterated the importance to the nation of a rational and systematic approach to medical technology assessment. "The most important policy need is to bring forth a rational, systematic approach from the present multiplicity of agencies and activities to promote and coordinate medical technology assessment" (OTA 1982:18).

In 1984, Congress enacted legislation signed by President Reagan (Public Law 98–551) which revised the existing National Center for Health Services Research and broadened its mandate for assessing new technology to include not only considerations of safety and efficacy, but, as appropriate, cost-effectiveness. The new name of the center became the National Center for Health Services Research Assessment/Health Care Technology Assessment (NCHSR/HCTA). This law also established a council to advise the secretary of DHHS and the director of the center about health care technology assessment, and it instituted a council on health care technology under the sponsorship of the National Academy of Sciences (NAS), with partial governmental support.

The latter provision implemented a recommendation by the Institute of Medicine (IOM 1983) that proposed creation of a private/public organization to assess medical technology as part of the Institute. This Council on Health Care Technology was charged with identifying obsolete or inappropriately applied health care technologies as well as coordinating and commissioning assessments of specific technologies. After considerable problems in soliciting long-term private support to match federal grant monies and gaining cooperation from groups in the private sector concerned with the result of technology assessment, the Council was ultimately abandoned in 1989. Its demise again reflected the uncertain attitudes both in the private and public sectors regarding limiting the diffusion of medical technology.

Another privately sponsored initiative to establish a framework for resolving future issues in medicine was the Health Policy Agenda for the American People instituted by the AMA in 1982. This project involved the combined effort of 172 private and public organizations. Phase 1 of the two-phase project produced 159 principles and 41 issues covering a wide spectrum of health concerns. One of the position statements coming out of stage two was that: "Society must come to grips with the moral and ethical questions posed by rapid developments in health care technology—who should have access to this technology, under what circumstances should technology be applied or withdrawn, and the respective roles of providers and patients in reaching these decisions" (*American Medical News*, March 6, 1987: 1). Despite its emphasis on consensus building across a wide array of groups, the project failed to achieve this goal and its principles and policy recommendations in large measure were not implemented.

The Office of Health Technology Assessment's TA efforts have by and large been narrowly defined studies of safety, efficacy, and costs. Furthermore, the resources available for original assessments of medical technology are limited, thus requiring dependence on published literature or existing assessments provided in some cases by the medical industry.

In an area related to MTA, in 1989 Congress created the Agency for Health-Care Policy and Research (AHCPR) within the Public Health Service to undertake a major new program of research to emphasize both the effectiveness and appropriateness of health care services and procedures. Criteria for AHCPR research priorities include commonly occurring conditions that incur high cost for Medicare where data is available and patterns of care vary widely. To date there has been strong pressure on AHCPR to produce immediate results to improve quality of care. This emphasis might jeopardize a more valuable long-term perspective (Donaldson and Capron 1991).

In 1982, the congressional OTA concluded that emerging drugs and medical devices are adequately and appropriately identified and tested, but that emerging medical and surgical procedures are not. "The most pressing need is for some routine mechanism, e.g., the reimbursement system, to identify new procedures before they are adopted" (OTA 1982:17). Unlike other substantive areas, the reimbursement system, rather than a regulatory agency, may be the prime candidate for assessment because coverage and payment decisions by the government have become critical factors in the diffusion of medical technologies.

Despite the fact that the OTA's critical analysis of the assessment process for medical procedures is over a decade old, its observations remain relevant today. No class of medical technology is adequately evaluated on a continuing basis for either cost-effectiveness or social or ethical implications. Despite efforts at MTA described above, there is no single organization whose mission it is to assure that medical and surgical procedures are fully assessed before their widespread use.

Furthermore, the synthesis phase of MTA continues to be weak at best. Research evidence regarding the safety, efficacy, and effectiveness of emerging technologies is seldom analyzed systematically and objectively. As evidenced by the recent expansion of coverage for heart and liver transplantations and funding of AIDS research and treatment, reimbursement and regulatory decisions continue to be under the heavy influence of the political climate and clearly reflect a value system mired in the technological imperative. The OTA's 1982 statement unfortunately describes the current context of MTA: "Federal agencies and private insurers and organizations set policies, guidelines, regulations, and/or make reimbursement coverage determinations, many of which profoundly affect the adoption and level of use of medical technologies. Yet, their decisions are usually based on informal, subjective, group-generated norms which tend to support the status quo" (OTA 1982, 17). Had these recommendations of OTA (1976 1982) been implemented in a timely fashion, the framework of MTA today would be significantly stronger.

Interestingly, the OTA itself was unable to break through these value constraints and critically assess emerging medical technologies. The power of the status quo, usually stated in terms of maintaining a nonpartisan stance, has led to the practice of presenting a balanced set of policy options, not policy recommendations. For instance, while the OTA report on infertility (1988) includes a detailed and very valuable description of new techniques in human reproduction and of the social, legal, and ethnical implications, it steers clear of recommending any limits on the development or diffusion of these revolutionary new technologies. Although the content of the report would seem to justify the conclusion that we would be better advised to put our scarce resources in preventive approaches instead of costly individual-oriented techniques such as in vitro fertilization, in the name of political objectivity no such recommendation was forthcoming. Instead of stating the Congress "should," a variety of options were presented in the form of Congress "could." The problems of OTA are now academic since it was abolished by Congress in 1995.

Most recently the states, driven by rapidly expanding Medicaid costs have begun to "reevaluate their once-limited role in the assessment of medical technology" (Mendelson et al. 1995:84). States are increasingly becoming involved in MTA and a variety of clinically oriented activities including the development and promulgation of clinical practice guidelines. In a few states, detailed MTAs are being conducted on selected technologies. Leading the way are Minnesota's Health Technology Advisory Committee, Washington State's Health Services Effectiveness Advisory Committee, and Oregon's Medical Technology Assessment Program. The Oregon program was established by the Health Resources Commission to address issues of appropriate allocation and use of health care resources. It is designed to address technology usage and diffusion throughout the state. While a Technical Advisory Panel of experts conducts the technical aspects of the assessment, the Health Resources Commission conducts the social policy aspects "including projecting the overall state cost of providing the technology and assessing the likely net health, social, and economic consequences of the application and use of the technology in Oregon" (Mendelson et al. 1995:87). Whether the effort of Oregon and other states will be successful in these assessment activities will depend on adequate funding as well as private and public cooperation. More critically, the verdict is still out on whether such efforts will in fact achieve the primary goal of containing costs.

Criticisms of MTA

It is understandable that MTA has had opposition from many forces within the medical industry. Because such assessment takes time it threatens to delay new technology applications and thus dampen potential profits. Any attempts to stop or slow development of particular medical innovations, therefore, face vehement criticism from those individuals, interest groups, and economic interests that have a personal stake in continued funding. For instance, Fuchs and Garber conclude that: "Admiration for the new technology assessment is not universal. Many practicing physicians believe it will further erode their ability to practice as they deem best; similarly, medical researchers, pharmaceutical manufacturers, and producers of medical devices fear that it will inhibit the development and diffusion of new forms of technology" (1990:1073).

Ironically, this opposition, in part, has been a factor in shaping MTA efforts such that they are largely ineffective in slowing the proliferation of medical innovations. In turn this has raised another set of criticisms from observers who believe that MTA is bound to fail because it does not challenge assumptions of the medical model and the technological imperative. According to Callahan, the TA movement is just another example of the faith in technology fixes for complex social problems. TA lacks any real value framework by which to make judgments on the moral or social worth or value of different technological goals—it can only assess relative efficacy and economic consequences but it cannot help determine whether it is justifiable to bear these consequences (Callahan 1990:92). Morgall contends that MTA has not moved beyond the status quo and is built upon the assumptions of the medical model. As a result, "the possibility of totally rejecting the technology in question is not really an option in most methods, which do not challenge the technology but rather take it as given" (Morgall 1993:189). To do otherwise, of course, would not only go against the interests of the medical industry but also the strong predisposition among the American public against precluding development of technologies that might benefit individuals, no matter how costly.

The result of these value preferences is an almost universal failure of TA in this area to recommend against development of questionable techniques or to reassess older technologies and consider discontinuing their use (Banta and Thacker 1990:236). Part of this problem might stem from an inherent difficulty of MTA to deal with futuristic problems. Whether because of short-term political pressures, the difficulty of forecasting long-term problems, or some combination of both, the time frame of MTA continues to be limited to the near future. Moreover, the strong preference of the public and leaders for more and more advanced biomedical interventions makes any attempts to restrict their development politically unattractive. The burden these technologies may place on future generations and the negative consequences that might accompany them are thus minimized or absent from most assessments.

The complexity of the interaction between medical technology and values requires considerably more attention to the long-term power of the technologies to alter values, often in unanticipated directions. Much of the current MTA tends to be linear in nature with little appreciation of the interrelationships and dynamics of medical technology, politics, and values. As a result, efforts at assessing medical technologies tend to underestimate technology's impact on public expectations and usage and vice versa. Although it is common for many MTAs today to include a chapter on ethical issues, most ignore or downplay the technology/value dynamics and assume a static ethical framework.

Because MTA lacks the capacity to critically analyze the prevailing value framework itself, it is an inadequate tool for making hard choices. A common assumption of MTAs is that if a technology is safe and effective it should be used and funded. However,

> Efficacy and affordability are two entirely different matters, and
> their implicit conflation in such technology assessment promo-
> tion contributes enormously to the illusion that the key to cost
> containment lies in determining which technologies will be effi-
> cacious. This could well be called the *efficacy fallacy*: if it works,
> we should therefore be able to afford it.   *(Callahan 1990: 94).*

As unlikely as it is for MTA to reject a technology because it is ineffective, it is even less likely that efficacious and safe, but unafford-
able, technologies will be rejected by MTA. As argued earlier, however, elimination of ineffective technologies alone will not resolve
the health care crisis. Hard decisions involve sacrificing clinically useful technologies, technologies that may work but that collectively
might bankrupt the system while contributing very little to the health
of the population. It is here where MTA could be most useful, but it
is here where it falls well short. While Callahan agrees that MTA in
some form is needed he argues that it is a "useless (and expensive)
exercise unless there is a willingness to engage in prospective assessment before technologies are introduced, and to *force* a discontinuation of the use of those technologies that are ineffective or only marginally effective, or effective but too expensive to find social justifi-
cation" (1990:99–100). To date this commitment has been lacking
in MTA.

Another criticism leveled indirectly at MTA is that while it might
free up resources by improving at least marginally the precision of
medical care, it is assumed that the resources saved will be rede-
ployed elsewhere in medical care and not shifted to nonmedical
health initiatives. The result is that no matter what MTA concludes
regarding specific techniques the medical model will continue to
dominate the production of health."The redirection of such resources to alternative (nonmedical) pathways to better population
health is not contemplated, and in the absence of coordination with
public regulation will not occur" (Lomas and Contandriopoulos
1994:255).

Although at its best MTA can tell us whether we are doing things
right within the context of medical care, it cannot tell us whether we
are doing the right things for maintenance and promotion of health,
because it fails to address that dimension. But by focusing only on
the former we leave unexplained nonmedical possibilities for improving health.

MTA: What's Needed

Despite the increasing magnitude and frequency of MTA, most efforts continue to be flawed. Furthermore, the failure of such assessments has less to do with the capabilities of the assessing agents or even the strategies and methods used than it does with the value context underlying medicine. The constraints, then, are political and social and reflect the high personal stakes that are inherent in the life and death issues surrounding medical policy. The failure of most MTA efforts to flatly reject certain directions of research or at least to place a low priority on them is not surprising given the potentially explosive nature of such recommendations. Moreover, in those few cases where such recommendations have been made (e.g., artificial heart), the political response has been predictable and the MTA has been ignored.

On a more practical level, funding commitment to MTA has been haphazard. Many of the assessment bodies have been hampered by the inability to conduct original and independent research, while some have expired due to funding problems. Although the provision of adequate resources will not resolve the underlying problems inherent in conventional MTA, reliable and consistent funding is a prerequisite for broadening MTA to address the core value biases. Fuchs suggests that collection of 1 cent on every $10.00 of premium income would yield $200 million annually to fund an independent technology assessment institute analogous to that of the Electric Power Research Institute (1993:195).

Most needed at this time is a rethinking of these values that now constrain MTA and the setting of social priorities. Again, this is not a new idea. The 1976 OTA report stated that "macroalternatives" to each technology being assessed should be defined. It is critical to consider alternative strategies to solve the same medical problem in very different ways and to consider the effect that the technology in question will have on the development and implementation of those alternatives.

> For example, in assessing a therapeutic technology, one might consider proposals for prevention of the disease in question. It would be legitimate, in this context, to ask how reasonable, feasible, or desirable these alternatives are and whether heavy investment in or implementation of the therapeutic technology

would encourage, discourage, or complement their development and implementation.   *(OTA 1976:52).*

While OTA recognized that excessively detailed assessment of
macroalternatives could lead to undesirable expansion of the scope
of the MTA being performed, ignoring such macroalternatives
might result in obscuring the most desirable policy alternatives by
subordinating the problem at hand to the particular technology.
Because of the process by which technologies are now chosen for
assessment by MTA, and the often narrowly focused requests that
limit the scope of a particular study, however, discussion of macroalternatives, particularly nontechnological ones, is frequently limited
or absent in the final reports. Again, the strong value bias in favor of
technological fixes, combined with the inherent dramatic nature of
many technological interventions, leads to a hesitancy to reject the
technological solutions or to recommend against their development
and proliferation in favor of alternative strategies.

STATEMENTS RE IMPACT ON HEALTH OUTCOMES

The inability of MTA to challenge the medical model should be no
surprise in light of the mandate bestowed by decision makers and
shaped by the American value system. Despite the best intentions
and efforts of the assessors, it is virtually impossible to break out
of the confines created by society. Under conventional MTA the
process places the burden of proof on those persons or groups who
want to block new technologies and procedures, a virtually impossible task given the vagaries and complexities of medical science. Any
reasonable doubts are resolved in favor of going ahead with development and diffusion of the technology even when a full assessment
is carried out.

If we are serious about assuring that medical innovations (and
existing practices) are indeed safe, effective, and efficient in producing health for investment, the burden of proof for demonstration
must be shifted to the proponents. This would put medical procedures on more equal grounds with drugs and biologics. I agree with
Callahan that in weighing the consequences of technologies we
should assume the worst outcome and put the burden on the opti-
mists to prove the assumption wrong: "I believe we have reached a

point in medical progress where we can begin to assume that, unless proved otherwise, the consequences of medical advances are as likely to be harmful as beneficial - and that is precisely because we have made so much progress already, making future progress not less likely but more problematical in its beneficial outcome" (Callahan 1994:128).

To this end I argue we should institute the concept of health impact statements analogous to environmental impact statements. The purveyors of new medical technologies, and particularly new intervention areas such as neural grafting and pre-implantation genetics, would need *by law* to attain approval from a health out-comes board before they could claim status as a clinical procedure and receive health care dollars. Without approval, the intervention would remain on a pre-clinical or experimental status. More impor-tantly, the burden of proof not only for safety and efficacy but also as to its contribution to health would be rigorous, thus denying approval to intervention areas that were judged insufficient by these criteria. Although the health outcomes board could not prohibit use of techniques or procedures, reimbursement through the health care budget would not be possible until preliminary approval. Furthermore, any patients who undergo the intervention must be informed as to its current status regarding health outcomes. Had IVF been exposed to such a process early in its development, its history would likely have been considerably different.

While this proposal is bound to be attacked as unduly slowing medical progress and as unjustified interference with medical pre-rogative, it is not a revolutionary concept. As discussed in chapter 6, countries with global budgets in effect do this on a regular basis. Before new techniques or procedures are reimbursed proponents must demonstrate that the innovation will do the job better than existing methods and/or do it in a more cost-effective way.

Although execution of this approach is more difficult in the private insurance U.S. system, private insurers should embrace a process that protects them from paying for unproven and unapproved techniques. The health outcomes impact approach would go a step further, how-ever, in requiring evidence of a clear contribution to population health in proportion to the cost of the innovation thus addressing the concern of Lomas and Contandriopoulos (1994) that alternative, nonmedical pathways to health be considered on an equal basis when assessing medical technologies.

NEED FOR ANTICIPATORY POLICY

Whatever approach is taken, whether it be to intensify/broaden technology assessments or institute health impact statements, there is an urgent need for an anticipatory policy founded in solid goals as to where we want to be in ten years, twenty years, and beyond. What type of society do we want to leave our children and where does health fit into this? We have left an uncontrolled health care arena to flourish that has set unrealistic precedents that cannot be sustained—we cannot continue relying on ad hoc, reactive policymaking any longer. The question no longer is *whether* to set societal limits, the questions are *how* and *by whom?*

What agency can make anticipatory policy? Unlike other Western nations, to date the U.S. government has been hesitant to intervene directly to set limits, instead trying to encourage demand-side constraints for cost containment and assuming that providers, insurers, and the public will somehow work it all out. Without clear policy guidance, however, the medical profession has avoided sharing responsibility for the allocation of resources while the insured public is skeptical of reforms that might encroach on their preferences and benefits.

At the broadest level the debate in the United States has centered on a dichotomy between public and private regulation of medical care. Although the public has ultimate responsibility for the health of the population, the dominance of the medical model and the power of the private sector has meant that the predominant proportion of health care has remained the domain of nonpublic interests. In reality the range of regulatory options is more complicated than the public–private distinction suggests. Figure 7.1 illustrates the range of options available for control. Given the complexity of medicine and health it is likely that a workable approach will involve some combination of these mechanisms.

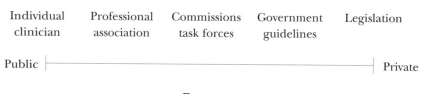

| Individual clinician | Professional association | Commissions task forces | Government guidelines | Legislation |

Public ├───┤ Private

FIGURE 7.1
Regulatory Mechanisms

Traditionally in the United States the practice of medicine, as distinguished from public health, was treated as a private matter between the health professional and the patient. Although professional ethics and standards of practice provided a guide to clinician discretion, overall the individual physician held considerable autonomy. The emergence of professional societies and the increased nationalization of standards shifted professional control from individual practitioners to state and national organizations, but was nevertheless acceptable to most clinicians for the protections it offered to those who adhered to the professional guidelines. It was also viewed as preventing more active government involvement. Therefore, "Presenting itself as a 'profession,' medicine has been able to deflect any external examination of this relationship, retaining in the hands of medical practitioners themselves responsibility for ensuring the linkage between medical care and health" (Lomas and Contandriopoulos 1994: 254).

Although the self-regulation approach has largely served the medical community and patients well, it has discouraged resource allocation questions and served to reinforce dominance of the medical model to the exclusion of societal-wide considerations. It has also obscured the limited impact of medical care on population health. What it has meant is that "decisions to use sophisticated and sometimes invasive [and expensive] medical technologies are being made almost solely by those who have been trained to use that technology" (Fuller 1994:29).

Despite factors that appear to justify a public role in regulating medical services, public choice in medical matters remains problematic. Bonnicksen, for instance, argues that public action is "unlikely, premature, and unwise in many areas of biomedicine" (1992:54). Rapidly changing technologies and social values raise prospects of instant obsolescence of any law no matter how carefully framed (Walters 1987). Legislation, then, risks freezing technology in place and is unlikely to offer the flexibility needed to adapt to new applications. Furthermore, the moral underpinning of the debate over medical technologies means that legislation is likely to be made on the basis of emotions rather than dispassionate, rational choice. There is no guarantee that government involvement will be objective nor helpful in resolving the problems discussed above especially in light of the public faith in the medical model.

Attempts to fit medical decision making into models used for other areas of public policy also fail to account for several unique features of medicine. First, as noted earlier, traditionally the conduct of medical decision making has been based on professional judgments made without governmental intervention and monitored primarily by medical standards of care. Government involvement in the 1970s largely reinforces this tradition by granting the medical community accountability through the establishment of institutional review boards and ethics committees.

A second special feature of medical decision making is its focus on the human body. As such it is protected by constitutionally based liberties and the common law principle of self-determination. Governmental intervention in the physician-patient relationship necessarily involves substantive decisions about medical care that can "threaten individual liberty and medical privacy" (Bonnicksen 1992:54). However, all governments have at their disposal a broad range of powers to intervene in matters of public health. Although courts in most democracies traditionally have been hesitant to intervene in medical decisions concerning individual patients, increasingly they are becoming embroiled in birth and death decisions.

In order to avoid the dangers inherent in applying public choice models to medical decision making, Bonnicksen argues that the focus of medical decisions should remain outside the public sector. Although there is a need for standard and systematic rule making in medicine, this is better served by a private policy model which "views regularized rules and procedures in the medical setting as the desired end of biomedical decision-making" (Bonnicksen 1992:54). To this end, figure 7.2 illustrates the progression of process that culminate in private policy or "rules developed in the private sector . . . regarded as obligatory by those who practice" (Bonnicksen 1992:61). Such policy, then, is manifested by professional society guidelines that somehow are binding on all practitioners in a given field. Unfortunately, Bonnicksen does not explain how this will be accomplished without some type of universal accreditation or licensing authority.

While the debate at the practical level turns on whether a public or a private regulatory model is the most effective and feasible approach, at the conceptual level debate centers on the role of the public in a democracy. Should there be a public role in decision making regarding the use of public funds or services. It is useful to briefly examine this controversy as a conflict between two democratic models, the technocratic elite model and the egalitarian model.

The technocratic elite model emphasizes the democratic ends rather than the means of making the decision. Technocracy is ruled by technically competent professionals and assumes that modern problems require a degree of knowledge beyond the technical capacity of both citizens and their elected representatives. Experts alone have the interest and knowledge necessary to make informed decisions on these complex and largely technical issues. Moreover, in medical areas the critical role of professionals trained to make clinical decisions makes public control unfeasible. In fact, according to this model, to expand public control is to invite trouble because resulting decisions are bound to be uninformed and simplistic.

In contrast, proponents of broadened public control emphasize the importance of the means of making democratic decisions. They argue that the public is as qualified as experts to make policy decisions on issues that are as much social and moral as they are technical. The extensive social and legal consequences of specific technological applications warrant close public scrutiny. Although there is a tendency for some supporters of public control to assume that the entire public ought to be involved in policymaking, it is more rea-

FIGURE 7.2
Progression of Processes in Private Policy
SOURCE: BONNICKSEN 1992:54.

sonable to define the effective public as composed of more or less specialized attentive publics and the elected representatives. Although public control does not exclude a role for experts, ultimately the decisions are made by the public through the government.

There is a need for conceptual clarification of the applicability of public control based on the distinction between making technical decisions requiring medical expertise and establishing broad social priorities as to the goals of medicine. While the first dimension depends on technical competence, the second depends on moral competence, which is not monopolized by experts. Figure 7.3 illustrates the interaction of this specialized-generalized continuum with the competing models of democracy.

The weakest case for egalitarian democracy is in quadrant 1. Continued low levels of scientific and technological literacy exhibited by the populace make it problematic that many citizens are either able or willing to develop a familiarity with the technical aspects of medical technology. Similarly, technocrats have no valid claim to monopolize decision making in quadrants 2 and 4, which

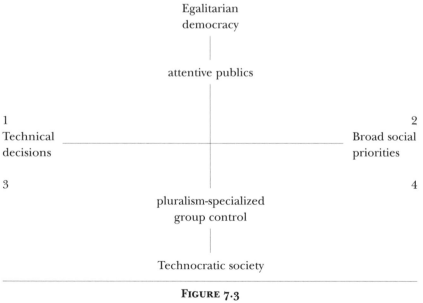

FIGURE 7.3
Public Role in Making Policy
SOURCE: BLANK 1990:198.

are dependent on moral, not technical, competence. Expertise in a technical area does not ensure, and in some cases might even obscure, attentiveness to the social implications of technology. The kind of specialized knowledge experts have is not adequate in itself to deal with the unique ethical value dimensions of these issues. Although technical experts must be included in the debate over social priorities, and, in fact, might take the lead in a public debate, extensive public involvement is most critical here—the closer we approach full participation, the better for democracy.

Because the most difficult issues surrounding medical care are inextricably linked to broader social goals, all but the most technical decisions should be open to public dialogue and public control. The major issues discussed here center on values concerning health and medicine as well as individual rights and the common good. How we resolve the technical decisions largely reflects how we perceive these broader issues.

There is, however, a paradox in arguing for more public involvement in health policy. Given the American value system and the strong belief of the public in the illusions of medicine, heightened public involvement might solidify support for the dominant medical model. If the value system as I have described it is accurate, it is unlikely that more attention to the public will do much to resolve the problems. In fact if the public really demanded the changes that I have argued are necessary, policy shifts in that direction would have already been forthcoming. What is needed then is not simply a broadened debate but an enlightened one led by courageous leaders who are willing to fight for the necessary conceptual and practical changes. Health care reform appears to be one area where the value system effectively works against change that is critical to the public's health both literally and figuratively.

It may very well be that the only way to make the hard decisions necessary to reform the health care system in the fragmented and incrementalist U.S. system would be to adopt the strategy offered by Light (1985). In his book on the Bipartisan Commission on Social Security, Light concludes that there are certain public issues that are best dealt with in secret negotiations outside of the public spotlight. Those issues that involve cutting benefits or raising taxes, rather than distributing the government largess, he terms "dedistributive." Health care issues appear to be a prime example of such issues that can never be resolved in the public forum because they elicit insurmountable opposition from powerful interests on many sides. According to Light: "With the public and interest groups firmly opposed to most of the major options in the dedistributive agenda, Congress and the President are well advised to build prenegotiated packages outside the constitutional system, returning to the normal process only at the last minute" (1985:6). Light argues that the opportunity for closed-door negotiation must therefore be returned to Congress.

Light advocates that bipartisan commissions act mainly as fronts for secret bargains made between the president and congressional leaders. This process circumvents the need to debate and defend the various alternatives in public. Just as the Commission on Social Security Reform provided the opportunity for a "gang of nine" to build a compromise, wrap it in a bipartisan flag, and ram it through Congress, so Congress might deal with the painful choices concerning health allocation and rationing.

In an earlier work (Blank 1988:185) I argued that although this approach was intuitively attractive, any such efforts to neutralize the public contribution to health policymaking would be counterproductive. Also, unlike Social Security, which was explicitly created as a national program, health care is a complex mix of private and public dimensions with extremely elusive jurisdictional boundaries. I then argued that medical allocation policy that establishes priorities about who lives and who dies should never be made in secret negotiations, no matter how efficient such a strategy might appear. Legitimizing deception by government leaders under the guise of bipartisanship would in the long run frustrate, rather than facilitate, progress toward lasting resolution of health care problems.

In light of events over the past decade, particularly the failure of the Health Security Act and other proposed reforms, and the continuing paralysis of traditional U.S. political institutions to make the necessary changes, I now believe that strategies of the type described by Light ought to be given serious consideration. The mandate given such a multipartisan body should focus on defining the broader goals of medicine and making suggestions as to how best to achieve these goals.

CHAPTER 8

LOOKING TO THE FUTURE

The task facing U.S. society in reordering the health system is herculean in scope and will require a reevaluation of basic values and beliefs of all Americans. It will also require a reassessment of the purpose of government and what type of society we want to be. As stated by Callahan:

> The ultimate problem behind the failure of cost containment and the quest for efficiency is an unwillingness to confront some disturbing implications of our highest ideas. We want to change the mechanics of the system rather than to examine the psychological, moral, and political assumptions that lie below it.
>
> *(1990:97)*

The crisis in the health system, like the emerging crisis in social security and the continuing crisis in welfare and in racial equality, go to the core of our view of what we are. By relying on incremental, nonplanned policy to guide us, we have given up the capacity to exert full control over the forces of technology. This failure to appreciate long-term implications of our policies is nowhere more evident than in our health priorities and our dependence on the medical model to provide health.

The aging population, the continued development and diffusion of new medical technologies, and the heightened public expectations will exacerbate the health crisis in the coming decades unless major changes are made. Since we can do little if anything to influence the aging population, our options are largely limited to altering the latter forces—medical technology diffusion and public demands and expectations. Society has to decide whether to continue to shift resources from other social areas and from future generations to satisfy our insatiable appetite for health care. For Beauchamp "the point is that we should decide collectively what level of growth we should undertake, rather than accepting the rate of growth that our present policy blindly levels on the republic" (1988:241). To take control of our destiny by constraining medical technology and our expectations for it, however, conflicts directly with the contemporary economic incentive structure, our individual-oriented value system, and our faith in the medical model.

Any moves in this direction must be accompanied by widespread public education on the limits of medicine and the need to set limits. Because the technological imperative is sustained as much by public demand as by corporate and professional control (Mechanic 1990:243), efforts must be made to reduce public demand for medical services. This can be accomplished only by placing more emphasis on individual responsibility for health and on disease prevention and environmental and occupational health. The pathetic record of funding for health education as a proportion of total health care expenditures must be remedied. More important is the need to instill in the public the value of collective self-restraint. At present neither patients nor providers are conditioned toward this end. The current structure of third-party reimbursement is a powerful bias for the allocation of more health care resources than would exist if patients bore a larger proportion of the costs for the benefits they accrued.

In other words, consumers of health care currently assess medical "needs" without considering the full price. Because "needs" largely define demand, there is an inherent bias in the system towards heightened allocation of resources. However, if "we allow individuals or groups to define their own needs we will be subject to the bottomless pit problem" (Chadwick 1994:89). Although a large proportion of the public agrees that cost containment in health care is essential, a substantially smaller proportion are willing to sacrifice benefits they presently hold in order to reduce overall costs to society. Moreover, few persons seem motivated to make drastic lifestyle changes out of a responsibility to reduce the overall cost of health care in the United States.

Although the themes discussed here have engendered substantial attention in the academic community and among some legislatures, in large part they have not played a central role in the recent national debate over health care reform. Instead of focusing on these more basic questions regarding the ends of health care and challenging the illusions we hold, the debate has focused on the means of providing health care—how medical care is to be funded, who will get the resources, and how to contain costs painlessly. The need to ration medical resources, the advantages to adopting an expanded model of health, and even the necessity of setting global limits remain largely the domain of the academic community. Most clearly absent is a dialogue on the broader questions as to what medical technologies can do for us and to us and how we can best assure the collective health of society.

RESPONSIBILITY TO FUTURE GENERATIONS

Generally obscured from the contemporary debate over health care reform is the impact of our actions on future generations. Although some observers such as Lamm (1992) and Callahan (1990) explicitly call for restraint by the current generation out of concern for our children, and others make reference to the future, by and large we treat the issue of health reform solely in terms of the needs of the now living.

We are, however, markedly affecting future generations, first by creating an imponderable national debt and second by setting unrealistic precedents and expectations that can be upheld only at great expense to a shrinking younger population. Although there is some danger of exaggerating the debt, it is clearly an illusion to believe we can continue to provide medicine without bounds. Already the younger generation is getting mixed signals. On the one hand they are encouraged to buy into the individualistic rights-oriented value system, but on the other they are beginning to realize

that their own standards of living, social security, and indeed health
care are unlikely to remain at current levels. It is crucial to ascertain
how much those in the cohorts below age 30 support continued
expansion of the supply state as they come to realize the burden they
and other succeeding generations will have to bear in maintaining it.

The shift in emphasis from individual health to collective health
in itself is not enough. Collective health of society must be broadened to take into account the impact of our goals and priorities on
those who follow. This challenges the very basis of liberal Western
ethics, which presupposes that the sphere of human action does not
reach beyond the present and immediate. As stated by Jonas: "All
enjoinders and maxims of traditional ethics, materially different as
they may be, show this confinement to the immediate setting of
action . . . . The ethical universe is composed of contemporaries and
its horizon to the future is confined by the foreseeable span of their
lives" (1984:5). Under these ethical frameworks, the timespan of
foresight, goal setting, and accountability is short, and proper conduct is defined by immediate or near consequences only.

In the wake of modern technology, however, all of this has drastically and irreparably changed. For Jonas (1984:6), "modern technology has introduced actions of such novel scale, objects, and consequences that the framework of former ethics can no longer contain
them." With the new-found powers we have to reshape nature, dis-
rupt the ecological balance, and alter the human condition comes
the corresponding ethical responsibility for the exercise of these
powers. Medical technology is at the center of this dramatic expansion of the range of human action and, thus, the new responsibility
toward future generations.

In response to modern technology, Jonas set forth a theory of
responsibility for both the private and public sphere. The axiom is
that "responsibility is a correlate of power and must be commensurate with the latter's scope and that of its exercise" (1984:x). Moreover, the discharge of this responsibility requires lengthened foresight, a "scientific futurology." The irreversible and cumulative char-
acter of technological intervention, unrecognized in traditional
ethics, mandates an extension of the relevant horizon of responsibility to the indefinite future where the impact of these interventions is
likely to be most felt.

Under the ethics of responsibility, unlike previous ethics, an agent's
concrete moral responsibility at the time of action extends far beyond

its proximate effects. How far it extends depends upon the nature of the object and on the extent of our power and prescience (Jonas 1984:107). As our capacity to intervene directly in the human condition expands and our power over future generations heightens, the time span of our responsibility widens appreciably. "In fact, the changed nature of human action changes the very nature of politics" (Jonas 1984:9).

The integration of a proper concern for the future into the policy-making process necessitates substantial alterations in the way we as a society make decisions. In fact, this new responsibility casts doubt on the capacity of representative government, as now practiced, to meet these demands. Under a pluralist system, only present interests make themselves heard and felt and require consideration by policymakers. Especially on issues as complex and emotionally charged as setting priorities for health care, single-issue interest groups become active, vocal, and influential. With few exceptions, their concern is with the near-term or immediate, not the distant, future. Also, because public officials are held accountable to their constituencies of the present, future-oriented policy gives way to placating those persons and groups whose demands are loudest. Because the interests of the day hold sway, the future is nowhere represented.

Moreover, the current election system, with its dependence on political action committee contributions, clearly exacerbates the inability and unwillingness to look beyond the next election. As long as policymakers are reelected on the basis for what they do for present-oriented interests, there remains a strong disincentive to become actively embroiled in controversial issues of the future. It is easier to avoid these "no-win" issues and ignore or obscure the long-term consequences of public inaction than recognize the ethics of responsibility to the future. Workable strategies to overcome this impasse and ensure proper consideration of these policy problems, then, require consideration of creative, even revolutionary, innovations in assessment mechanisms as discussed in chapter 7.

WHAT TO DO? NEEDED CHANGES

The resolution of the health care crisis will require making harder choices than the U.S. population and its representatives have to date been willing to consider. Although the debate initiated by President

Clinton at least raised health care to a national awareness, its general content has been disappointing in that it rarely has addressed the core issues discussed here. Unfortunately, the forces against a major change in orientation are powerful and the public remains complacent as to the disastrous consequences of continuation of the dominance of the medical model and individual-oriented health care. Although I do not presume to have the solution—since this must emerge from a national dialogue on societal goals—I believe that the following changes are essential if we are to meet the goal of collective health.

First, we must broaden the definition of health care to encompass social and economic factors and thus downplay the current emphasis on medical care. This in turn necessitates confronting the issue of whether continued investments in medical care represent the best use of societal resources for improvement in length and quality of life for the population. In an even broader sense we need to consider the question of what priority we should put on health as compared to other social goods. Then and only then can we determine how much and what kind of health we need in order to be a "humane and decent community of human beings" (Callahan 1990:11).

Second, we need to shift emphasis within health care from curative, episodic medicine to education, health promotion, and disease prevention, and to establish a core of primary services that should be available to all citizens. To this end, the imbalance between generalists and specialists must be resolved. I agree with the long-term goal suggested by the Robert Wood Foundation of a 50/50 split between generalists and specialists as compared to the 20/80 current distribution (CHER 1993:93).

Third, we must move toward an explicit rationing system for curative/rescue medical care. This will require inclusion of clear cost-benefit criteria and preclude the prevailing emphasis on unlimited and often inappropriate treatment regimes. While I favor setting categorical limits and a core services format to rationing services, there are any number of explicit nonprice, supply-side rationing strategies that should be considered. The main point, however, is to establish as fair and equitable approach as possible to setting limits . We must realize, however, that any rationing system will mean denial of potentially beneficial, and perhaps lifesaving, services to some patients.

Fourth, we need to clarify the relationship between social determinants of health and individual responsibility. Despite dangers of victim blaming, we have to assign individual responsibility for ill health that is clearly related to deleterious behavior. This shift in emphasis also requires intensified social responsibility for health education, counseling, and provision of treatment facilities to individuals at risk as well as heightened efforts to reduce social and economic inequalities that produce unhealthy behavior patterns. Although I argue that all persons should have access to primary care, because of the strong association between certain high-risk lifestyles and health care usage, those who refuse to adopt healthier lifestyles should risk surrendering claims for unlimited medical resources.

Fifth, we must institute a system of universal coverage for a set of basic services with co-payments based on income. This must be accompanied by global budgeting and a national fee structure to control the amount of resources devoted to medical care. Global budgeting of both public and private spending will also allow restructuring the incentive structure to aid in shifting priority from curative to primary health care. As noted by Mechanic (1994:236), managed competition without global budgeting offers little possibility of slowing dynamic forces that accelerate the costs and application of new technologies. Although I strongly favor a single payer system as the most effective means to global controls, I realize this is unlikely in the United States. As noted in chapter 6, however, there are other options for multipayer systems. In any case, setting limits to health needs and to medical progress will require that constraints be imposed from outside by political force (Callahan 1990:98). Self-regulation by definition will not work. Only government regulation has a chance of controlling medical technology.

Sixth, we must establish a continuing and vigorous dialogue on national goals and the future of the republic. The agenda should include a thorough reevaluation of the impact of unbounded individual rights on solidarity and collective good. It should also address the kinds of issues raised by the first five recommendations stated here. Although it is both unrealistic and unfeasible to expect that these basic policy shifts can be accomplished in the short run because they are so alien to American perceptions of health care, they must become part of the broader debate that to this point has obscured them. If some or all are rejected so be it but at least they should be deliberated.

The need to consider the limits of medical care, individual responsibility for health, and health goals of society is urgent and the debate overdue. Although these actions call for courageous political leadership, ultimately we cannot legislate new attitudes, beliefs, or values on these issues either within the medical profession or the public. Moreover, the illusions discussed here will not be easily shattered even with zealous leadership and animated dialogue. These illusions are reassuring because they lead us to believe that hard choices and rigid limits are avoidable and that no price can be set on human life. They are comfortable and attractive especially for the insured population and the medical industry. As a result, they are highly resistant to change in part because they serve powerful interests but also because they allow all of us to avoid a harsh reality that we have been led to believe applies only to other nations. The illusions reinforce our feelings of superiority, of being first.

Reality is that we are not first nor on many measures even a close second. Moreover, the reality of the future of our health care system, given the trends discussed earlier, is far from comforting, although in our illusions we can blithely treat health care as business-as-usual. Many experts and presumably some political leaders know we are on a sure path to disaster, but getting society to understand this will be most difficult because there are many forces working to perpetuate the illusions for their own interests or their own peace of mind. The key to resolving the health care crisis ultimately will turn on whether society as a whole can break free of these myths and face head on the price of life.

BIBLIOGRAPHY

Aaron, Henry J. 1991. *Serious and Unstable Condition: Financing America's Health Care.* Washington, D.C.: The Brookings Institution.

Aaron, Henry J. and William B. Schwartz. 1992. "Rationing Health Care: The Choice Before Us." In Robert H. Blank and Andrea L. Bonnicksen, eds., *Emerging Issues in Biomedical Policy,* vol 1, pp. 48–63. New York: Columbia University Press.

AARP. American Association of Retired Persons. 1994. *Coming Up Short: Increasing Out-of-Pocket Health Spending by Older Americans.* Washington, D.C.: AARP.

Abel-Smith, Brian. 1984. *Cost Containment in Health Care: The Experience of 12 European Countries, 1977–83.* Luxembourg: Commission of European Countries.

Abelson, Philip H. 1990. "The Asbestos Removal Fiasco." *Science* 247 (4946): 1017.

Achenbaum, W. Andrew. 1994. "Why U.S. Health Care Reform Is So Difficult." *Hastings Center Report* 24(5): 23–25.

Al-Anon. 1989. "Alcoholism: A Merry-Go-Round Named Denial." New York: Al-Anon Family Group Headquarters, Inc.

Anderson, Gerald F. and Earl P. Steinberg. 1984. "Hospital Readmissions in the Medical Population." *New England Journal of Medicine* 311(21): 1349–53.

Angell, Marcia. 1993. "Privilege and Health–What Is the Connection?" *New England Journal of Medicine* 329(2): 126–27.

Annas, George J. 1995. "Sex, Money, and Bioethics: Watching *ER* and *Chicago Hope.*" *Hastings Center Report* 25(5): 40–42.

Appleby, John. 1992. *Financing Health Care in the 1990s.* Buckingham: Open University Press.

Babcock, Lyndon and Anthony Belotti. 1994. "Defining and Measuring Health over Life." In George Tolley, Donald Kenkel, and Robert Fabian, eds., *Valuing Health for Policy: An Economic Approach.* Chicago: University of Chicago Press.

Baird, Patricia. 1993. *Proceed with Care: Final Report of the Royal Commission on New Reproductive Technologies.* Ottawa: Minister of Government Services Canada.

Baker, Dean B. and Philip J. Landrigan. 1993. "Occupational Exposures and Human Health." In Eric Chivian et al., eds., *Critical Condition: Human Health and the Environment.* Cambridge: MIT Press.

Baker, Robert. 1995. "Rationing, Rhetoric, and Rationality: A Review of the Health Care Rationing Debate in America and Europe." In James M. Humber and Robert F. Almeder, eds., *Allocating Health Care Resources*, pp. 55–84. Totowa, N.J.: Humana Press,

Bandow, Doug and Michael Tanner. 1995. "The Wrong and Right Ways to Reform Medicare." *Policy Analysis* No. 230. Washington, D.C.: The Cato Institute.

Banta, H. David and Stephen B. Thacker. 1990. "The Case for Reassessment of Health Care Technology." *Journal of the American Medical Association* 564(2): 235–49.

Barer, Morris L., Robert G. Evans, Matthew Holt, and J. Ian Morrison. 1994. "It Ain't Necessarily So: The Cost Implications of Health Care Reform." *Health Affairs* 13(4): 88–99.

Beauchamp, Dan E. 1988. *The Health of the Republic: Epidemics Medicine, and Moralism as Challenges to Democracy.* Philadelphia: Temple University Press.

Beauchamp, Tom L. and James F. Childress. 1994. *Principles of Biomedical Ethics*, 4th ed. New York: Oxford University Press.

Belloc, Nedra B. and Lester Breslow. 1972. "Relationship of Physical Health Status and Health Practices." *Preventive Medicine* 1:419.

Berk, Marc L. and Alan C. Monheit. 1992. "The Concentration of Health Expenditures: An Update." *Health Affairs* 11(5): 145–49.

Berkman, Lisa F. and Lester Breslow. 1983. *Health and Ways of Living: The Alameda County Study.* New York: Oxford University Press.

Bipartisan Commission on Entitlement and Tax Reform. 1995. *Final Report to the President.* Washington, D.C.: GPO.

Blank, Robert H. 1988. *Rationing Medicine.* New York: Columbia University Press.
—— 1992. "Regulatory Rationing: A Solution to Health Care Resource Allocation." *University of Pennsylvania Law Review* 140(5): 2550–74.

Blendon, Robert J. and John M. Benson. 1994. *Public Opinion Update on Health Care Reform.* Boston: Harvard Program on Public Opinion and Health Care.

Blendon, Robert J., Jennifer N. Edwards, and Andrew L. Hyams. 1992. "Making the Crucial Choices." *Journal of the American Medical Association* 267(18): 2509–20.

Blendon, Robert J., John Marttila, Matthew C. Shelter et al. 1994. "The Beliefs and Values Shaping Today's Health Reform Debate." *Health Affairs* 13(2): 274–84.

Blustein, Jan and Theodore R. Marmor. 1992. "Cutting Waste By Making Rules: Promises, Pitfalls, and Realistic Prospects." *University of Pennsylvania Law Review* 140(5): 1543–72.

Bonnicksen, Andrea L. 1989. *In Vitro Fertilization: Building Policies from Laboratories to Legislation.* New York: Columbia University Press.

—— 1992. "Human Embryos and Genetic Testing: A Private Policy Model." *Politics and the Life Sciences* 11(1): 53–62.

Borren, Pim and Alan Maynard. 1993. *Searching for the Holy Grail in the Antipodes: The Market Reform of the New Zealand Health Care System.* York, UK: Centre for Health Economics.

Brandon, Robert M., Michael Podhorzer, and Thomas H. Pollack. 1992. "Premiums Without Benefits: Waste and Inefficiency in the Commercial Health Insurance Industry." In Vincente Navarro, ed., *Why the United States Does Not Have a National Health Program.* Amityville, N.Y.: Baywood.

Brock, Dan W. 1994. "The President's Commission on the Right to Health Care." In Audrey R. Chapman, ed., *Health Care Reform: A Human Rights Approach.* Washington, D.C.: Georgetown University Press.

Brody, Baruch A. and Amir Halevy. 1995. "The Role of Futility in Health Care Reform." In Robert I. Misbin et al., eds., *Health Care Crisis: The Search For Answers*, pp. 31–40. Frederick, Md.: University Publishing Group.

Bronzino, Joseph D., Vincent H. Smith, and Maurice L. Wade. 1990. *Medical Technology and Society: An Interdisciplinary Perspective.* Cambridge: MIT Press.

Brook, Robert H., J. Ware, W. Rogers et al. 1984. *The Effect of Coinsurance on the Health of Adults.* Santa Monica. Calif.: Rand Corporation.

Bunker, John P., D. S. Gomby, and B. H. Kehrer. 1989. *Pathways to Health: The Role of Social Factors.* Menlo Park, Calif.: Henry J. Kaiser Family Foundation.

Bunker, John P., Howard S. Frazier, and Frederick Mosteller. 1994. "Improving Health: Measuring Effects of Medical Care." *The Milbank Quarterly* 72(2): 225–55.

Butler, Stuart M. and Edmund F. Haislmaier, eds. 1989. *A National Health System for America.* Washington, D.C.: The Heritage Foundation.

Butter, Irene H. 1993. "Premature Adoption and Routinization of Medical Technology: Illustrations from Childbirth Technology." *Journal of Social Issues* 49(2): 11–34.

Califano, Joseph A. Jr. 1992. "Rationing Health Care: The Unnecessary Solution." *University of Pennsylvania Law Review* 140(5): 1525–38.

Callahan, Daniel. 1987. *Setting Limits: Medical Goals in an Aging Society.* New York: Simon and Schuster.

—— 1990. *What Kind of Life: The Limits of Medical Progress.* New York: Simon and Schuster.

—— 1992. "Symbols, Rationality, and Justice: Rationing Health Care." *American Journal of Law and Medicine* 18(1&2): 1–3.

—— 1993. "Intolerable Necessity: Limiting Health Care for the Elderly." In Gerald R. Winslow and James W. Walters., eds., *Facing Limits: Ethics and Health Care for the Elderly.* Boulder: Westview Press.

—— 1994. "Manipulating Human Life: Is There No End to It?" In Robert H. Blank and Andrea L. Bonnicksen, eds., *Medicine Unbound: The Human Body and the Limits of Medical Intervention.* New York: Columbia University Press.

Callahan, Tamara L., Janet E. Hall, Susan L. Ettner et al. 1994. "The Economic Impact of Multiple-Gestation Pregnancies and the Contribution of Assisted-Reproduction Techniques to Their Incidence." *New England Journal of Medicine* 331 (4): 244–49.

Caplan, Arthur L. 1990. "Arguing with Success: In Vitro Fertilization Research or Therapy?" In Dianne M. Bartels et al. *Beyond Baby M.: Ethical Issues in New Reproductive Techniques.* Totowa N.J.: Human Press.

CDCP. Centers for Disease Control and Prevention. 1994. "Deaths Resulting from Firearms and Motor Vehicle Related Injuries—United States, 1968–1991. *Morbidity and Mortality Weekly Report* 43:37–42.

Chadwick, Ruth. 1993. "Justice in Priority Setting." *Rationing in Action*, pp. 85–95. London: BMJ Publishing Group.

Chambers, Christopher D., James J. Diamond, Robert L. Perkel, and Lori A. Lasch. 1994. "Relationship of Advance Directives to Hospital Charges in a Medicare Population." *Archives of Internal Medicine* 154:541–547.

Chapman, Audrey R. 1994a. "Assessing the Clinton Administration's Health Security Act." In Audrey R. Chapman, ed., *Health Care Reform: A Human Rights Approach.* Washington, D.C.: Georgetown University Press.

—— 1994b. "Policy Recommendations for Health Care Reform." In Audrey R. Chapman, ed., *Health Care Reform: A Human Rights Approach.* Washington, D.C.: Georgetown University Press.

CHER. Center for Health Economics Research. 1993. *Access to Health Care: Key Indicators for Policy.* Waltham, Mass.: Center for Health Economics Research.

Chivian, Eric. 1994. "The Ultimate Preventive Medicine." *Technology Review* (Nov/Dec): 34–40.

Christiani, David C. 1993. "Urban and Transboundary Air Pollution: Human Health Consequences." In Eric Chivian et al., eds., *Critical Condition: Human Health and the Environment.* Cambridge: MIT Press.

Churchill, Larry R. 1994. *Self-Interest and Universal Health Care: Why Well-Insured Americans Should Support Coverage for Everyone.* Cambridge: Harvard University Press.

Clinton, William. 1993. "U.S. Must Strengthen, and Fix Health Care System." President's Address on Health Care. September 22, Washington, D.C..

Coddington, Dean C., David J. Keen, Keith D. Moore, and Richard C. Clarke. 1991. *The Crisis in Health Care: Costs, Choices, and Strategies.* San Francisco: Jossey-Bass.

Collins, M. S. and J. A. Bleyl. 1990. "Seventy-One Quadruplet Pregnancies: Management and Outcome." *American Journal of Obstetrics and Gynecology* 162:1384–92.

Cross, Peter J. and Barry J. Gurland. 1987. "The Epidemiology of Dementing Disorders." Contract Report for Office of Technology Assessment. *Losing a Million Minds.* Springfield, Va.: National Technical Information Service.

Culyer, A. J. 1990. "Cost Containment in Europe." In *Health Systems in Transition: The Search for Efficiency*, pp. 29–40. Paris: OECD.

Culyer, A. J., J. E. Brazier, and O. O'Donnell. 1988. *Organising Health Service Provision: Drawing on Experience*. London: Institute of Health Services Management.

Cundiff, David and Mary Ellen McCarthy. 1994. *The Right Medicine: How to Make Health Care Reform Work Today*. Totowa, N.J.: Humana Press.

Danis, Marion, Leslie I. Southerland, Joanne M. Garrett et al. 1991. "A Prospective Study of Advance Directives for Life-Sustaining Care." *New England Journal of Medicine* 324(13): 882–88.

Danzon, Patricia M. 1992. "Hidden Overhead Costs: Is Canada's System Really Less Expensive?" *Health Affairs* 11(2): 21–43.

David, Ronald. 1993. "The Demand Side of the Health Care Crisis." *Harvard Magazine* (March/April): 30–32.

Davis, Karen. 1990. "Introduction." In *Health Systems in Transition: The Search for Efficiency*, pp. 112–15. Paris: OECD.

De Ferranti, David. 1985. *Paying for Health Services in Developing Countries: An Overview*. World Bank Staff Working Paper 721. Washington, D.C.

Donaldson, M. S. and Alexander M. Capron, eds. 1991. *Patient Outcomes Research Teams: Managing Conflict of Interest*. Washington, D.C.: National Academy Press.

Drake, David F. 1994. *Reforming the Health Care Market: An Interpretive Economic History*. Washington, D.C.: Georgetown University Press.

Drummond, Michael F. 1993. "Health Technology Policy and Health Services Research." In Michael F. Drummond and Alan Maynard, eds., *Purchasing and Providing Cost-Effective Health Care*. London: Churchill Livingstone.

Dunning Committee. 1992. *Choices in Health Care: A Report of the Government Committee on Choices in Health Care*. Netherlands: Ministry of Health, Welfare, and Cultural Affairs.

Durie, Mason. 1994. *Whaiora: Maori Health Development*. Auckland: Oxford University Press.

Eddy, David M. 1990. "What Do We Know About Costs?" *Journal of the American Medical Association*. 244: 1161–66.

—— 1991. "Screening for Cervical Cancer." In David M. Eddy, ed., *Common Screening Tests*. Philadelphia: American College of Physicians.

—— 1991a. "What Care Is 'Essential'? What Services Are 'Basic'?" *Journal of the American Medical Association* 265(6): 782–88.

Elhauge, Einer. 1994. "Allocating Health Care Morally." *California Law Review* 82(6): 1449–1544.

Emanuel, Ezekiel J. and Linda L. Emanuel. 1994. "The Economics of Dying: The Illusion of Cost Savings at the End of Life." *New England Journal of Medicine* 330(8): 540–44.

Emanuel, Linda L., Michael J. Barry, John D. Stoeckle et al. 1991. "Advance Directives for Medical Care: A Case for Greater Use." *New England Journal of Medicine* 324(13): 889–95.

Engelhardt, H. Tristram, Jr. 1984. "Allocating Scarce Medical Resources and the Viability of Organ Transplantation." *New England Journal of Medicine* 311(1): 66–71.

Enthoven, Alain C. 1990. "What Can Europeans Learn from Americans?" In *Health Care Systems in Transition: The Search for Efficiency*. Paris: OECD.

Evans, Robert G. and Morris L. Barer. 1990. "The American Predicament." In *Health Systems in Transition: The Search for Efficiency*. Paris: OECD.

Evans, Robert G. and Gregory L. Stoddart. 1990. "Producing Health, Consuming Health Care." *Social Science and Medicine* 31(12): 1347–63.

Evans, Robert G. 1994. "Introduction." In Robert G. Evans, Morris L. Barer, and Theodore R. Marmor, eds., *Why Are Some People Healthy and Others Not?* New York: Walter de Gruyter.

Fitzgerald, Faith T. 1994. "The Tyranny of Health." *New England Journal of Medicine* 331(3): 196–98.

Folland, Sherman, Allen C. Goodman, and Miron Stano. 1993. *The Economics of Health and Health Care*. New York: Macmillan.

Fox, Daniel M. 1993. *Power and Illness: The Failure and Future of American Health Policy*. Berkeley: University of California Press.

Fries, James F. 1988. "Aging, Illness, and Health Policy: Implications of the Compression of Morbidity." *Perspectives in Biology and Medicine* 31:408–32.

Fries, James F., C. Everett Koop, Carson E. Beadle et al. 1993. "Reducing Health Care Costs by Reducing the Need and Demand for Medical Services." *New England Journal of Medicine* 329(5): 321–25.

Frum, David. 1995. "What To Do About Health Care." *Commentary* June: 29–34.

Fuchs, Victor R. 1994. "The Clinton Plan: A Researcher Examines Reform." *Health Affairs* 13(2): 102–14.

—— 1993. *The Future of Health Policy*. Cambridge: Harvard University Press.

Fuchs, Victor R. and Alan M. Garber. 1990. "The New Technology Assessment." *New England Journal of Medicine* 323(10): 673–77.

Fuller, Benjamin F. 1994. *American Health Care: Rebirth or Suicide?* Springfield, Ill.: Thomas.

Galletti, Pierce M. 1988. "Artificial Organs: Learning to Live with Risk." *Technology Review* (November–December): 35–40.

Gelijns, Annetine and Nathan Rosenberg. 1994. "The Dynamics of Technological Change in Medicine." *Health Affairs* 13(3): 28–46.

Gertler, Paul and Jacques van der Gaag. 1990. *The Willingness to Pay for Medical Care: Evidence from Two Developing Countries*. Baltimore: Johns Hopkins University Press.

Gillick, Muriel R. 1994. *Choosing Medical Care in Old Age: What Kind, How Much, When to Stop*. Cambridge: Harvard University Press.

Ginsberg, Eli. 1990. "High-Tech Medicine and Rising Health Care Costs." *Journal of the American Medical Association* 263(13): 1820–22.

Godfrey, C. 1993. "Is Prevention Better than Cure." In Michael F. Drummond and Alan Maynard, eds., *Purchasing and Providing Cost-Effective Health Care*. Edinburgh: Churchill Livingstone.

Graig, Laurine A. 1993. *Health of Nations: An International Perspective on U.S. Health Care Reform.* 2d ed. Washington, D.C.: Congressional Quarterly Press.

Greer, D. S., V. Mor, J. N. Morris et al. 1986. "An Alternative in Terminal Care: Results of the National Hospice Study." *Journal of Chronic Diseases* 39:9–26.

Guralnik, J. M., K. C. Land, D. Blazer et al. 1993. "Educational Status and Active Life Expectancy Among Older Blacks and Whites." *New England Journal of Medicine* 329:110–16.

Haan, Ger. 1991. "Effects and Costs of In-Vitro Fertilization." *International Journal of Technology Assessment in Health Care* 7(4):585–93.

Haan, M. N. and G. A. Kaplan. 1985. "The Contribution of Socioeconomic Position to Minority Health." In Report of the Secretary's Task Force on Black and Minority Health. Washington, D.C.: Department of Health and Human Services.

Hadley, Jack. 1982. *More Medical Care, Better Health.* Washington, D.C.: Urban Institute Press.

Hadorn, David C. and Robert H. Brook. 1991. "The Health Care Resource Allocation Debate." *Journal of the American Medical Association* 266(23): 3328–31.

Haines, Andrew. 1993. "The Possible Effects of Climate Change on Health." In Eric Chivian et al., eds., *Critical Condition: Human Health and the Environment.* Cambridge: MIT Press.

Hanson, Mark J. 1995. "The Seductive Sirens of Medical Progress: The Case of Xenotransplantation." *Hastings Center Report* 25(5): 5–6.

Harrop, Martin. 1992. "Introduction." In Martin Harrop, ed., *Power and Policy in Liberal Democracies.* Cambridge: Cambridge University Press.

HCHP. Harvard Community Health Plan. 1992. "The LORAN Commission: A Report to the Community." In Robert H. Blank and Andrea L. Bonnicksen, eds., *Emerging Issues in Biomedical Policy,* vol. 1. New York: Columbia University Press.

HCTI. Health Care Technology Institute. 1994. *Cost-Effectiveness Analysis: Assessing the Value of Medical Technology.* Alexandria, Va.: Health Care Technology Institute.

Holden, Constance. 1991. "Probing the Complex Genetics of Alcoholism." *Science* 251:163–64.

Hu, Howard and Nancy K. Kim. 1993. "Drinking-Water Pollution and Human Health." In Eric Chivian et al., eds., *Critical Condition: Human Health and the Environment.* Cambridge: MIT Press.

Hurowitz, James C. 1993. "Toward a Social Policy for Health." *New England Journal of Medicine* 329(2): 130–33.

Hurst, Jeremy and Jean-Pierre Poullier. 1993. "Paths to Health Reform." *OECD Observer* 179:4–7.

Ikegami, Naoki. 1992. "Japan: Maintaining Equality Through Regulated Fees." *Journal of Health Politics, Policy and Law* 17(4): 689–713.

Illich, Ivan. 1976. *Limits to Medicine: Medical Nemesis: The Expropriation of Health.* London: Penguin Books.

Immergut, Ellen M. 1992. *Health Politics: Interests and Institutions in Western Europe.* Cambridge: Cambridge University Press.

Institute of Medicine. 1985. *Assessing Medical Technologies.* Washington, D.C.: National Academy Press.

—— 1993. *Access to Health Care in America.* Washington, D.C.: National Academy Press.

Jacobs, Lawrence R. 1993. *The Health of Nations: Public Opinion and the Making of American and British Health Policy.* Ithaca, N.Y.: Cornell University Press.

—— 1995. "Politics of America's Supply State: Health Reform and Technology." *Health Affairs* 14(2):143–157.

Jacobs, Lawrence R. and Robert Y. Shapiro. 1994. "Public Opinion's Tilt Against Private Enterprise." *Health Affairs* 13(2): 285–97.

Jacobs, Lawrence et al. 1993. "Poll Trends: Medical Care in the United States - An Update." *Public Opinion Quarterly* (Fall): 394–427.

Jayes, R. L., J. E. Zimmerman, D. P. Wagner et al. 1993. "Do-Not-Resuscitate Orders in Intensive Care Units: Current Practices and Recent Changes." *Journal of the American Medical Association* 270:2213–17.

Jennett, B. 1986. *High Technology Medicine: Benefits and Burdens.* London: Oxford University Press.

Jonas, Hans. 1984. *The Imperative of Responsibility: In Search of an Ethics for the Technological Age.* Chicago: University of Chicago Press.

Jonsson, Bengt. 1990. "What Can Americans Learn from Europeans?" In *Health Systems in Transition: The Search for Efficiency,* pp. 87–103. Paris: OECD.

Kahn, Jeffrey P. 1995. "Sin Taxes as a Mechanism for Health Care Finance." In James M. Humber and Robert F. Almeder, eds., *Allocating Health Care Resources,* pp. 177–202. Totowa, N.J.: Humana Press.

Kane, R. L., L. Bernstein, J. Wales et al. 1984. "A Randomised Controlled Trial of Hospice Care." *Lancet* (April 21): 890–94.

Kassler, Jeanne. 1994. *Bitter Medicine: Greed and Chaos in American Health Care.* New York: Birch Lane Press.

Keeney, Ralph L. 1994. "Decisions about Life-Threatening Risks." *New England Journal of Medicine* 331(3): 193–96.

Keil, J. E., S. E. Sutherland, R. G. Knapp et al. 1993. "Mortality Rates and Risk Factors for Coronary Disease in Black as Compared with White Men and Women." *New England Journal of Medicine* 329:73–78.

Kennedy, Ian. 1981. *The Unmasking of Medicine.* London: Penguin Books.

Kidder, D. 1992. "The Effects of Hospice Coverage on Medicare Expenditures." *Health Services Research* 27:195–217.

King, Guy. 1994. "Health Care Reform and the Medicare Program." *Health Affairs* 13(5): 39–43.

Kitzhaber, John. 1992. "A Healthier Approach to Health Care." In Robert H. Blank and Andrea L. Bonnicksen, eds., *Emerging Issues in Biomedical Policy,* vol. 1. New York: Columbia University Press.

Kizer, Kenneth W., Mary J. Vassar, Randi L. Harry, and Kathleen D. Layton. 1995. "Hospitalization Charges, Costs, and Income for Firearm-Related Injuries at a University Trauma Center." *Journal of the American Medical Association* 273(22): 1768–73.

Kosterlitz, Julie. 1992. "Wanted: GPs." *National Journal* 24 (September 5): 2011–15.

—— 1993. "Dangerous Diagnosis." *National Journal* 25 (January 16): 127–30.

Lagasse, R., P. C. Humblet, A. Lenaerts, I. Godin, and G. F. Moens. 1990. "Health and Social Inequalities in Belgium." *Social Science and Medicine* 31:237–48.

Lamm, Richard D. 1992. "Rationing Health Care: Inevitable and Desirable." *University of Pennsylvania Law Review* 140(5): 1511–24.

—— 1993. "Intergenerational Equity in an Age of Limits: Confessions of a Prodigal Parent." In Gerald R. Winslow and James W. Walters, eds., *Facing Limits: Ethics and Health Care for the Elderly.* Boulder: Westview Press.

Lantos, John D., Peter A. Singer, Robert M. Walker et al. 1989. "The Illusion of Futility in Clinical Practice." *American Journal of Medicine* 87:81–84.

Lawrence, Deane B. and Clifton R. Gaus. 1983. "Long-Term Care: Financing and Policy Issues." In David Mechanic, ed., *Handbook of Health, Health Care, and the Health Professions.* New York: Free Press.

Leaf, Alexander. 1993. "Loss of Stratospheric Ozone and Health Effects of Increased Ultraviolet Radiation." In Eric Chivian et al., eds., *Critical Condition: Human Health and the Environment.* Cambridge: MIT Press.

Leichter, Howard M. 1991. *Free To Be Foolish: Politics and Health Promotion in the United States and Great Britain.* Princeton: Princeton University Press.

Lemco, Jonathan. 1994. "Conclusion." In Jonathan Lemco, ed., *National Health Care: Lessons for the United States and Canada.* Ann Arbor: University of Michigan Press.

Leutwyler, Kristin. 1995. "The Price of Prevention." *Scientific American,* April: 124–29.

Light, Paul. 1985. *The Politics of Social Security Reform.* New York: Random House.

Littell, Candace L. 1994. "Innovation in Medical Technology: Reading the Indicators." *Health Affairs* 13(3): 226–35.

Lomas, J. and A.-P. Contandriopoulos. 1994. "Regulating Limits to Medicine: Towards Harmony in Public- and Self-Regulation." In Theodore R. Marmor, ed., *Understanding Health Care Reforms,* pp. 253–86. New Haven: Yale University Press.

Lonergan, Edmund T., ed. 1991. *Extending Life, Enhancing Life.* Washington, D.C.: National Academy Press.

Lubitz, James D. and Gerald F. Riley. 1993. "Trends in Medicare Payments in the Last Year of Life." *New England Journal of Medicine* 328(15): 1092–96.

Lubitz, James D., James Beebe, and Colin Baker. 1995. "Longevity and Medicare Expenditures." *New England Journal of Medicine* 332(15): 999–1003.

Luke, Barbara. 1994. "The Changing Patterns of Multiple Births in the United States: Maternal and Infant Characteristics, 1973 and 1990." *Obstetrics and Gynecology* 84(1): 101–16.

Lundberg, George D. 1992. "National Health Care Reform: The Aura of Inevitability Intensifies." *Journal of the American Medical Association* 267(18): 2521–24.

MacManus, Susan A. 1996. *Young v. Old: Generational Combat in the 21st Century.* Boulder: Westview Press.

Maksoud, A., D. W. Jahnigen, and C. I. Skibinski. 1993. "Do Not Resuscitate Orders and the Cost of Death." *Archives of Internal Medicine* 153: 1249–53.

Manning, Willard G., Emmett B. Keeler, Joseph P. Newhouse et al. 1991. *The Costs of Poor Health Habits.* Cambridge: Harvard University Press.

Marmor, Theodore R. 1994. "Japan—A Sobering Lesson." In Theodore R. Marmor, ed., *Understanding Health Care Reform.* New Haven: Yale University Press.

Marmor, Theodore R. and David Boyum. 1994. "American Medical Care Reform: Are We Doomed to Fail?" In Theodore R. Marmor, ed., *Understanding Health Care Reform.* New Haven: Yale University Press.

Maxwell, R. J. 1988. "Financing Health Care: Lessons from Abroad." *British Medical Journal* 296:1423–26.

Maynard, Alan. 1993. "The Significance of Cost-Effective Purchasing." In Michael F. Drummond and Alan Maynard, eds., *Purchasing and Providing Cost-Effective Health Care.* London: Churchill Livingstone.

—— 1994. "The Economics of Rationing Health Care." In Michael Tunbridge, ed., *Rationing of Health Care in Medicine.* London: Royal College of Physicians.

McGinnis, J. Michael and William H. Foege, 1993. "Actual Causes of Death in the United States." *Journal of the American Medical Association* 270:2207–2212.

McKeown, Thomas. 1979. *The Role of Medicine: Dream, Mirage, and Nemesis.* London: Nutfield Provincial Trust.

McLeer, S.V. and R. Anwar. 1989. "A Study of Battered Women in an Emergency Department." *American Journal of Public Health* 79: 65–66.

McPherson, Klim. 1990. "International Differences in Medical Care Practices." In *Health Systems in Transition: The Search for Efficiency,* pp. 17–24. Paris: OECD.

Mechanic, David. 1992. "Professional Judgment and the Rationing of Medical Care." *University of Pennsylvania Law Review* 140: 1713–54.

—— 1994. *Inescapable Decisions: The Imperatives of Health Care.* New Brunswick, N.J.: Transaction Publishers.

Mendelson, Daniel N., Richard G. Abramson, and Robert J. Rubin. 1995. "State Involvement in Medical Technology Assessment." *Health Affairs* 14(2): 83–98.

Menzel, Paul T. 1993. "Counting the Costs of Lifesaving Interventions for the Elderly." In Gerald R. Winslow and James W. Walters, eds., *Facing Limits: Ethics and Health Care for the Elderly.* Boulder: Westview Press.

Miller, C. Arden. 1984. "The Health of Children: A Crisis in Ethics." *Pediatrics* 73(4): 550–58.

Moreno, Jonathan D. and Ronald Bayer. 1985. "The Limits of the Ledger in Public Health Promotion." *Hastings Center Report* 15(16): 37–41.

Morgall, Janine Marie. 1993. *Technology Assessment: A Feminist Perspective.* Philadelphia: Temple University Press.

Mueller, Keith J. 1993. *Health Care Policy in the United States.* Lincoln: University of Nebraska Press.

Murphy, Donald J. 1993. "The Appropriateness of Life-Sustaining Care for Older People." In Gerald R. Winslow and James W. Walters, eds., *Facing Limits: Ethics and Health Care for the Elderly.* Boulder: Westview Press.

Murphy, Donald J., David Burrows, Sara Santilli et al. 1994. "The Influence of the Probability of Survival on Patients' Preferences Regarding Cardiopulmonary Resuscitation." *New England Journal of Medicine* 330(8): 545–49.

Navarro, Vincente. 1992. "Why Some Countries Have National Health Insurance, Others Have National Health Services, and the United States Has Neither." In Vincente Navarro, ed., *Why the United States Does Not Have a National Health Program.* Amityville, N.Y.: Baywood.

NCHS. National Center of Health Statistics. 1991. *Vital and Health Statistics: Educational Differences in Health Status and Health Care.* Hyattsville, Md.: U.S. Department of Health and Human Services.

Neumann, Peter J., Soheyla D. Gharib, and Milton C. Weinstein. 1994. "The Cost of a Successful Delivery with In Vitro Fertilization." *New England Journal of Medicine* 331(4): 239–43.

NHMRC. National Health and Medical Research Council. 1990. *Discussion Paper on Ethics and Resources Allocation in Health Care.* Canberra: Australian Government Publishing Service.

OECD. Organisation for Economic Cooperation and Development. 1987. *Financing and Delivering Health Care: A Comparative Analysis of OECD Countries.* Paris: OECD.

—— 1988. *Ageing Populations: The Social Policy Implications.* Paris: OECD.

—— 1992. *The Reform of Health Care Systems; A Comparative Analysis of Seven OECD Countries.* Paris: OECD.

Okolski, Marek. 1986. "Relationship Between Mortality and Morbidity Levels According to Age and Sex and Their Implications for Organizing Health Care Systems in Developed Countries." In *Consequences of Mortality Trends and Differentials.* New York: United Nations.

Olshansky, S. Jay, Bruce A. Carnes, and Christine Cassel. 1990. "In Search of Methuselah: Estimating the Upper Limits of Human Longevity." *Science* 250:634–40.

OTA. Office of Technology Assessment. 1988. *Infertility: Medical and Social Choices.* Washington, D.C.: GPO.

Palmer, George R. and Stephanie D. Short. 1989. *Health Care and Public Policy: An Australian Analysis.* Melbourne: Macmillan.

Pappas, Gregory, Susan Queen, Wilbur Hadden, and Gail Fisher. 1993. "The Increasing Disparity in Mortality Rates Between Socioeconomic Groups in the United States, 1960 and 1986." *New England Journal of Medicine* 329(2): 103–9.

Patrick, Donald L. and Pennifer Erickson. 1993. *Health Status and Health Policy: Allocating Resources to Health Care.* New York: Oxford University Press.

Perry, Seymour. 1989. "Medical Technology in a Cost Containment Environment." In *The Future of Health in America.* Hearings before the Joint Economic Committee, U.S. Congress, 100th Cong., 2d sess.,May 1988. Washington, D.C.: GPO.

PHS. Public Health Service. 1995. *For a Healthy Nation: Returns on Investment in Public Health.* Washington, D.C.: GPO.

Porter, Roy. 1994. "A Professional Malaise: How Medicine Became a Prisoner of Its Success." *TLS* (January 14): 3–4.

Powell, Margaret and Maxzahira Anesaki. 1990. *Health Care in Japan.* London: Routledge.

Price, R. Arlen. 1987. "Genetics of Human Obesity." *Annals of Behavioral Medicine* 9(1): 9–14.

Randall, Teri. 1993. "Demographers Ponder the Aging of the Aged and Await Unprecedented Looming Elder Boom." *Journal of the American Medical Association* 269(18): 2330–31.

Reinhardt, Uwe E. 1990. "Commentary." In *Health Care Systems in Transition: The Search for Efficiency.* Paris: OECD.

—— 1990a. "Health Care Spending Soon Out of Control?" *American Medical News,* January 12: 25–26.

—— 1992. "The United States: Breakthroughs and Waste." *Journal of Health Politics, Policy, and Law* 17(4): 637–67.

Reiser, Stanley J. 1984. "The Machine as Means and Ends: The Clinical Introduction of the Artificial Heart." In Margery W. Shaw, ed., *After Barney Clark: Reflections on the Utah Artificial Health Program.* Austin: University of Texas Press.

Renaud, M. 1994. "The Future: Hygeia verses Panakeia?" In Theodore R. Marmor, ed., *Understanding Health Care Reform.* New Haven: Yale University Press.

Rhodes, Robert P. 1992. *Health Care Politics, Policy, and Distributive Justice.* Albany: State University of New York Press.

Ricardo-Campbell, Rita. 1982. *The Economics and Politics of Health Care.* Chapel Hill: University of North Carolina Press.

Richmond, Julius B. and Rashi Fein. 1995. "The Health Care Mess: A Bit of History." *Journal of the American Medical Association* 273(1): 69–71.

Riegleman, Richard K. 1991. "Taming Modern Technology." In Jonathan D. Moreno, ed. *Paying the Doctor: Health Policy and Physician Reimbursement.* Westport, Conn.: Auburn House.

Rogers, R. G. 1992. "Living and Dying in the U.S.A.: Socioeconomic Determinants of Deaths Among Blacks and Whites." *Demography* 29:287–303.

Roos, Noralou P., Evelyn Shapiro, and Robert Tate. 1989. "Does a Small Minority of Elderly Account for a Majority of Health Care Expenditures?: A Sixteen-Year Perspective." *Milbank Quarterly* 67(3/4): 347–69.

Rosenthal, Elisabeth. 1989. "Crowding Causes Agonizing Crises in Intensive Care." *New York Times* (August 22): 17, 21.

RSG (Radical Statistics Group). 1976. *In Defence of the NHS.* London: RSG.

Rublee, Dale A. 1994. "Medical Technology in Canada, Germany and the United States." *Health Affairs* 13(4): 113–17.

Russell, Louise B. 1994. *Educated Guesses: Making Policy About Screening Tests.* Berkeley: University of California Press.

Schapira, David V., James Studnicki, Douglas D. Bradham, Peter Wolfe, and Anne Jarrett. 1993. "Intensive Care, Survival, and Expense of Treating Critically Ill Cancer Patients." *Journal of the American Medical Association* 269(6): 783–86.

Schenker, Joseph G. and Yossef Ezra. 1994. "Complications of Assisted Reproduction Techniques." *Fertility and Sterility* 61(3): 411–22.

Schieber, George J., Jean-Pierre Poullier, and Leslie M. Greenwald. 1992. "U.S. Health Expenditure Performance: An International Comparison and Data Update." *Health Care Financing Review* 13(Summer): 1–30.

—— 1994. "Health System Performance in OECD Countries, 1980–92." *Health Affairs* 13(4): 100–112.

Schneiderman, Lawrence J., Richard Kronick, Robert M. Kaplan et al. 1992. "Effects of Offering Advance Directives on Medical Treatments and Costs." *Annals of Internal Medicine* 117(7): 599–606.

Schwartz, William B. and Daniel N. Mendelson. 1994. "Eliminating Waste and Efficiency Can Do Little To Contain Costs." *Health Affairs* 13(2): 224–38.

Scitovsky, Anne A. 1984. "The High Cost of Dying: What Do the Data Show?" *Milbank Memorial Fund Quarterly* 62: 591–607.

—— 1988. "Medical Care in the Last Twelve Months of Life: The Relation Between Age, Functional Status, and Medical Care Expenditures." *Milbank Quarterly* 66: 640–60.

—— 1994. "'The High Cost of Dying' Revisited." *Milbank Quarterly* 72(4): 561–91.

Seedhouse, David. 1991. *Liberating Medicine*. Chichester: Wiley.

Sheldon, Trevor A. and Alan Maynard. 1993. "Is Rationing Inevitable?" In *Rationing in Action*. London: BMJ Publishing Group.

Singer, Peter A. and Frederick H. Lowy. 1992. "Rationing, Patient Preferences, and the Cost of Care at the End of Life." *Archives of Internal Medicine* 152:476–79.

Smedira, Nicholas G., Bradley H. Evans, Linda S. Grais et al. 1990. "Withholding and Withdrawal of Life Support from the Critically Ill." *New England Journal of Medicine* 322(5): 309–15.

Starzl, Thomas E., D. Van Thiel, A. G. Tzakis et al. 1988. "Orthotopic Liver Transplantation for Alcoholic Cirrhosis." *Journal of the American Medical Association* 260:2542–44.

Sullivan, Louis W. 1990. "Healthy People 2000." *New England Journal of Medicine* 323:1065–67.

Temkin-Greener, H., M. R. Meiners, E. A. Petty, and J. S. Szydlowski. 1992. "The Use and Cost of Health Services Prior to Death." *Milbank Quarterly* 70:679–701.

ten Have, Henk A. M. J. 1995. "Medical Technology Assessment and Ethics: Ambivalent Relations." *Hastings Center Report* 25(5): 13–19.

Thorpe, Kenneth E. 1992. "Health Care Cost Containment: Results and Lessons from the Past 20 Years." In Stephen M. Shortell and Uwe E. Reinhardt, eds., *Improving Health Policy and Management*, pp. 227–74. Ann Arbor: Health Administration Press,

Tolley, George, Donald Kenkel, Robert Fabian, and David Webster. 1994. "The Use of Health Values in Policy." In George Tolley, Donald Kenkel, and Robert Fabian, eds., *Valuing Health for Policy: An Economic Approach.* Chicago: University of Chicago Press.

Wagner, Marsden G. and Patricia A. St. Clair. 1989. "Are In-Vitro Fertilization and Embryo Transfer of Benefit to All?" *Lancet* 1989 (October 28): 1027–30.

Waldo, Daniel R. et al. 1989. "Health Expenditures by Age Group, 1977 and 1987." *Health Care Financing Review* 10:116–18.

Wallner, Manfred. "Introduction to Symposium: A View of Our Future." *Western State University Law Review* 21 (1) 1–10.

Weissman, A., N. Yoffee et al. 1991. "Management of Triplet Pregnancies in the Late 1980s: Are We Doing Better? *American Journal of Perinatology* 8:333–37.

White, Lawrence W. and Mary Ellen Waithe. 1995. "The Ethics of Health Care Rationing as a Strategy of Cost Containment." In James M. Humber and Robert F. Almeder, eds., *Allocating Health Care Resources*, pp. 21–54. Totowa, N.J.: Humana Press.

Wiener, Joshua M. 1992. "Rationing in America: Overt and Covert." In Martin A. Strosberg, Joshua M. Wiener, and Robert Baker, eds., *Rationing America's Medical Care: The Oregon Plan and Beyond.* Washington, D.C.: The Brookings Institution.

Wilkinson, R. G. 1992. "National Mortality Rates: The Impact of Inequality?" *American Journal of Public Health* 82:1082–84.

Winkleby, M. A., D. E. Jatulis, E. Frank, and S. P. Fortmann. 1992. "Socio-economic Status and Health: How Education, Income, and Occupation Contribute to Risk Factors for Cardiovascular Disease." *American Journal of Public Health* 82 (6): 816–21.

Wolfe, John R. 1993. *The Coming Health Crisis: Who Will Pay For Care For the Aged in the Twenty-First Century?* Chicago: University of Chicago Press.

Wright, J. D. and E. Weber. 1987. *Homelessness and Health.* Washington, D.C.: McGraw-Hill.

Young, I. D. 1993. "Diagnosing Fragile X Syndrome." *The Lancet* 342:1004–05.

Zook, Christopher J. and Francis D. Moore. 1980. "High Cost Users of Medical Care." *New England Journal of Medicine* 302 (18): 996–1002.

INDEX

ical technology, 24; of screening
tests, 88–89
——of health care, ix, 1–2, 4;
medical technology and,
26–27; prevention strategies
and, 87–91; public expecta-
tions and, 34; technology and,
30; uncontrolled, 2–3
Cost-sharing by consumers, 138–39
Council for Long Range Societal
Guidance, 98
Council on Health Care Technology,
163
CPR (cardiopulmonary resuscita-
tion), 77–78
Crisis of health care, public and,
42–43, 45
Critically ill patients, 76–77, 82
Criticisms of MTA, 166–68
Cross, Peter J., 14
Cultural iatrogenesis, 47, 49
Culture: and health, 47, 48, 51–52,
60; and individual responsibility,
110, 118
Culyer, A. J., 141, 142
Cundiff, David, 35, 38, 58, 65, 87,
103, 156; and ``sin taxes,'' 121
Curative medicine, 50, 125

Danzon, Patricia M. 87
David, Ronald, 22, 26, 58
Davis, Karen, 148
Deafness, noise-induced, 70
Death: causes of, 104; firearm-
related, 65; health and, 51; med-
icalization of society and, 49
Dedistributive issues, 177–78
Deductibles in health insurance,
138–39
Definitive medical technologies, 28
Degenerative chronic diseases, 103
Demand for health care, 33–37,
180–81; market created, 23
Demand-side cost containment, xi,
94, 138–39

Dementia, 14
Democracy, public role in, 174–77
Denmark, health care system, 148
Diagnosis-related groups (DRGs), 142
Diagnostic tests, 88–89
Diet: and health, 103, 105; social
class and, 60
Direct controls, cost containment,
140
Direct payment funding, 132
Disease: cultural context, 48–49, 51;
medicine and, 50; self-inflicted,
105
——prevention of, x, xi, 125, 180,
184; behavior alteration for, 24;
and health care costs, 87–91;
incentives for, 6; as investment,
118; and lifestyle choices, xii;
responsibility for, 102; technol-
ogy and, 30
Disincentives to unhealthful behavior,
118–19
Distribution of health care, 1–8;
aging population and, 8–12
Distributive-type policies, xiv
DNR (do not resuscitate) orders, 81
Doctors, deification of, 26
Donaldson, M. S. 164
Donelan, 42
Drake, David F., 24, 57, 129, 130
DRGs (diagnosis-related groups), 142
Driving, reckless, 112
Drug abuse, 105; homelessness and,
66; social class and, 60
Drummond, Michael F., 34, 51
Dunning Committee, 96
Durable powers of attorney, 75, 81,
83
Durie, Mason, 52, 53, 54
Dying, costs of, 73–83

Economic environment, and health, x
Ectopic pregnancies, 160
Eddy, David M., 34, 88, 96, 97,
145–46